AN EDUCATIONAL JOURNEY

Raphael Wilkins

First published in the UK in March 2021 by
Journey Books, an imprint of Bradt Travel Guides Ltd
31a High Street, Chesham, Buckinghamshire, HP5 1BW, England
www.bradtguides.com

Text copyright © 2021 Raphael Wilkins
Edited by Samantha Cook
Cover illustration/cover design by Neil Gower
Layout and typesetting by Ian Spick
Production managed by Sue Cooper, Bradt & Zenith Media

ISBN: 978 1 78477 832 3

British Library Cataloguing in Publication Data
A catalogue record for this book is available from the British Library
Digital conversion by www.dataworks.co.in
Printed in the UK by Zenith Media

To find out more about our Journey Books imprint, visit www.bradtguides.com/
journeybooks.

ABOUT THE AUTHOR

Raphael Wilkins was born in Eltham, south-east London. He chose education for his career, starting as a geography teacher in Bromley, then progressing to education officer posts in three other London boroughs. Next he worked in parliament, then for the Association of London Authorities, before returning to local government in senior education officer roles. In 2001 he switched to consultancy, working with a number of national organisations and universities on matters of education policy, leadership and development. In his professional field he published two books, and over 70 articles, book chapters and research reports. In 2007 his focus broadened to international consultancy, and the extensive global travel which that involved stimulated his desire to become a travel writer. *An Educational Journey* is his second volume of travel memoirs. He lives in Barnard Castle, County Durham.

ACKNOWLEDGEMENTS

I am grateful to the many individuals – they know who they are – who enabled me to undertake the journeys described in this book; to the colleagues who came with me; to my wife Mary and daughter Kathryn for tolerating my globetrotting lifestyle; and to the whole team at Journey Books, especially Samantha Cook, who improved the quality of my writing.

Contents

Introduction

This book is a travel memoir, concerning destinations in Asia and Latin America. It is a reflection on a period of intensive travel to contrasting countries; an exploration of identity and mobility; a story of a search for things which eluded me, but which instead yielded insights, self-knowledge and life-changing memories.

I learnt that travelling can take us out of ourselves while also helping us to find ourselves; and that some of our issues and concerns we can leave at home, while others stick to us like burs. I know now that positive perceptions of places are coloured by relationships and feelings, which make the sun brighter, the sea bluer and the food tastier. People can lead us to feel absorbed into one place and like a detached observer in another. Can we ever get away from our habit of perceiving places by comparing them to others?

Who am I to offer a view on these matters? At a late point in a life firmly rooted in one place, unexpected opportunities led me to make 49 international journeys spanning 20 countries and five continents. For the most intense few years of that activity, travel dominated my life, insofar as the planning and execution of those trips amounted to a full-time occupation. Of course, lots of people spend their lives travelling: there is nothing unique about that, but nor is it commonplace for someone as entrenched in a locality as I was to transform into a traveller in late middle age, and that is why I have a tale to tell.

I worked in education, initially as a geography teacher, and my whole career was based in London. International travel wasn't an element in my life. In childhood and teenaged years I benefited from a few cheap foreign holidays, then settled down to concentrate on making ends meet and building a career. For over 20 years I didn't leave the UK; my partner's lack of interest in doing so reinforced my own. I developed a mindset in which I saw travelling to distant, exotic places as being far too expensive for me to afford, far too complicated for me to arrange, and the point of a limited visit unclear. That is not the same as lacking desire: to the contrary, the thought of exotic travel had always been attractive to me, but in the same way that the thought of being famous, or a millionaire, is attractive. Desirable, but not a practical likelihood.

I overcame my mental block about travel. After a few missed opportunities which I chickened out of, at the age of 47 I forced myself (yes, it did feel like that) to attend a conference in Canada. Over the next few years I went to similar conferences in Europe and America. The spell was broken: if there was a point to doing so, I could get myself on to a plane in the same way that everyone else seemed to find so easy.

Meanwhile, the route taken by my career had broadened my perspective. I started off teaching in a school before progressing into what was then called local education authority administration. It seemed like a massive broadening of horizons, and after doing that in several different London boroughs I felt quite proud of the breadth of my knowledge. I then moved to the national scene, working for Parliament and other national organisations, which led me to realise how parochial I had been: like a child moving from primary to secondary school. Suddenly vast new vistas of issues, ideas and policies opened up for me to get my head around.

In 2006, at the age of 55, I started a job in an organisation which had global reach. My work concerned education in London, but the following spring I was invited to go to India: a totally unexpected and amazing experience. This was followed, within a few months, by similar short visits to Saudi Arabia and Singapore. I had never anticipated being able to travel, as part of my work, to faraway places with different cultures and climates. The opportunity to do so removed all three of the barriers I had previously perceived: the costs were covered, the purpose was clear, and there was support with practical arrangements.

In 2008 I was able in a similar way to visit Bangkok and Beijing. Then in 2009 I made three visits to Yemen, and another to China. In 2010 a pattern had set in, and the trips became more frequent. Between January and July I made three visits to Saudi Arabia, two to China, and one to Kenya and South Sudan, and I also attended short conferences in Kuala Lumpur and Denver.

The fact that these trips were enabled through my work, rather than being holidays or private expeditions, was much less of a distinction than might be imagined. When I am on holiday, I do not sunbathe or go in the sea, or engage in vigorous physical activity, or dance or attend wild parties. Being shy, nor do I make new friends.

When my daughter was young, we holidayed in self-catering accommodation at Hunston Mill near Chichester, often going several times a year. When she was older and my means improved, we would revisit the same hotels: notably, the Royal County in Durham, the Feversham Arms or Black Swan in Helmsley, and the Lodge in Old Hunstanton. We made the half-serious observation that rather as the Queen spends time at Balmoral or Sandringham when not working in London, so we found relaxation in the familiarity of these homes-from-home.

Sometimes I would take academic books to read on holiday, or think about an article I was writing; once I spent most of a break working on a book proposal. Similarly, of the international trips I've mentioned above, while some were dominated by work, others included much free time and opportunities for sightseeing. And in Chapter Four I describe finalising my first academic book while on a self-funded conference visit to Cyprus. My point is that for me, given my interests and lifestyle, travel is travel, with a blurred distinction between 'work' and 'holiday'.

The big difference is that we choose where to go on holiday, whereas work-related travel is determined by opportunities. People have their favourite places, and strategies for exploration; they research destinations and look at their budget and make a decision. Whatever the criteria for selection, the choice will reflect the identity, tastes and interests of the person choosing.

By contrast, my work-related travelling involved responding to opportunities wherever they arose, including in places where tourists either do not or cannot go; including some that I had long regarded as desirable to visit and others that would have been among the last places on Earth I would have chosen. Distance and costs were not significant considerations. Being, as it were, taken by the hand of chance and led on such a random walk made an enormous contribution to what I learnt from the experience.

Journalist Tom Feiling, in his book *Short Walks from Bogotá*, identified several travelling patterns after observing young backpackers in a remote and scenic part of Colombia. He saw Victorian travellers as toughening up their minds and bodies by journeying to distant lands and encountering foreign cultures; in some ways those voyages were similar to a military exercise. In the 1960s, Western travellers went to the same places but to seek spiritual renewal: to soften up. Feiling defined holidaymakers, by contrast, as generally wanting rest and sensory pleasures during their brief time off work. The backpackers he encountered seemed to represent another pattern: in a remote location, but firmly connected to their moorings through laptops and social media. With their information and schedules, they were 'doing' Colombia with the same serious application they might bring to a university assignment.

Echoes of all those patterns applied to my own kind of travelling. 'Toughening up' was certainly a factor in coping with my middle-aged introduction to the process. Eventually, mercifully, I reached the stage where I could get off a flight without a throbbing head, and where I could limit the violent disruption of my digestive system. I learnt to travel lighter, more confidently, less stressfully. And 'softening up' followed the traditional adage that 'travel broadens the mind': I learnt in practice what I knew in theory, that what is appropriate depends on context. Also, I am sure that some of the ways of thinking, and approaches to life, that I encountered in different cultures rubbed off on me long-term. Some of my experiences were pure tourism, but like the backpackers, I was never severed from my moorings: I was travelling as an agent of my organisation.

Throughout the greater part of my business travel experience, it never entered my head that I might one day want to write about the travelling itself. Not until the last year of my career, beyond the period covered in this book, did I reach the stage of consciously gathering notes as I went along in order to create a memoir. In *Travels with Epicurus* Daniel Klein explores how to enjoy old age and, in the course of that reflection, discusses how some old people are drawn to autobiographical writing. He points out the inevitably subjective and cherry-picking nature of that endeavour. The writer wants to find patterns which will give form and coherence to life's journey, and selects material to reinforce those patterns. When a person writes their own history, they may succumb to the temptation to gild their image.

So I want to explain at the outset – I don't think this spoils the narrative – that my business travelling did not lead to any significant success. In the early journeys in particular, I thought it was just a matter of time before the contacts made and relationships started would lead to major new projects. Later, I began to understand better the obstacles inherent in the local situations, and the shortcomings in the range and price of the services we had to offer. Had it been otherwise, professional success would have been its own story, told through a longer and steeper career trajectory, and through higher-profile academic writings.

One of Klein's arguments drawn from Epicurus is that to enjoy retirement, 'We must free ourselves from the prison of everyday affairs and politics'. When I first read that it annoyed me, because I hadn't fully made that transition. Now, with the perspective of hindsight, I get the point, and see the things in myself which got in the way of me making more of my work opportunities. Too late, I recognise with horrible clarity those shortcomings which would have been apparent to others at the time. So yes, there are patterns in the accounts which follow, but they did not need any contriving and I am not proud of them.

I described the first 17 international trips that were enabled through my work (between the summers of 2007 and 2010) in my book *Accidental Traveller*. The changes they represented for me were profound: from being a stuck-in-a-rut person to a globetrotter. My life was suddenly colourised: great splodges of vivid pigments landing on a palette previously covered in greys. To people used to global travel, some of my experiences would not in themselves be worth sharing – except that it is my own story I am telling. Other experiences would, I think, count as notable by any standards: meeting a crown prince in Riyadh; the sunset call to prayer on a rooftop in old Jeddah; working with scary political leaders in Yemen; going upcountry in a light plane in war-torn South Sudan.

Opportunities for travel continued. This book concerns 18 journeys I undertook between the autumn of 2010 and the summer of 2012 (two educational years), covering places new to me, including Pakistan and Latin America. There was a watershed between these first and second phases of travel, which has become more significant in hindsight, and has called for a different approach to reporting and reflection. Of course, the extreme novelty of global travel wore off when I was doing it quite often. Amazing, life-transforming wonderment gradually became blended with a more complex and discerning mixture of reactions. After I came back from Guangzhou in July 2010, I was ready to stop being flabbergasted and to start a more reflective phase of learning.

Graham Greene's *The Lawless Roads,* his memoir of travelling in Mexico, published in 1939, includes the following comments on border-crossing (which, in the style of his day, assumed that only men travel):

> Over there everything is going to be different; life is never
> going to be quite the same again... The man seeking scenery
> imagines strange woods and unheard-of mountains; the romantic
> believes the women over the border will be more beautiful and
> complaisant than those at home; the unhappy man imagines at
> least a different hell; the suicidal traveller expects the death he
> never finds.

Greene was interested in religion and compared the atmosphere at the border with 'a good confession: poised for a few happy moments between sin and sin'. His comments convey somewhat bleakly the 'grass is greener' wistfulness of wanderlust. In fact it is only rarely greener, but the quest may be lubricated by the pleasure of accumulation: metal badges screwed on to walking sticks.

I am, these days, neither suicidal nor religious, although I have spent time in both of those places, but can otherwise relate to Greene's sentiments about crossing borders into new territories. My own experience also brought in the issue of scale. Through my working life my focus progressed from institutional, to local, national and then international. At a certain point – how many visits to how many countries does it take? – a very patchy global perspective starts to emerge. The modern world is partially globalised and heavily networked, while retaining immense local variation. Seeing patterns of similarity and contrast between different places, and seeing different patterns of connectedness to global and regional perspectives, formed an important part of my travel experience.

Then, there was also the fact that my work travels led me to revisit places to the point where I gained some slight familiarity with them. This is nothing like the deep knowledge people gain when they live in another country for an extended period. For example, in his memoir *Shanghai Stirfry*, Peter Duffett shares his jottings about a four-year expatriate stint in Shanghai. It is a distinctive stance, viewing a country and culture over time, but from within a settled domestic set-up, a work organisation and an expat community. My organisation had no overseas annexes and, with one notable exception, I never developed anything that could count as a 'mooring' in the places I visited.

In chapters Four and Five I recount the experience, vivid and educative for me, of eight days in Mexico, including the scenic journey from Guadalajara to Tepic. But that brief trip was put into perspective when recently I read Robin Bayley's book *The Mango Orchard*, recounting his travels in the same region while pursuing a family history project. It took him many months; he learnt fluent Spanish, stayed in the houses of complete strangers, and spent weeks living with new-found relatives getting enmeshed in the local culture and history.

This book ends with an illuminating five-day trip to Chile. Compare that to *Chile: Travels in a Thin Country*, Sara Wheeler's account of travelling from one end of Chile to the other: a young woman on her own, hitching rides from truckers, meeting up with total strangers and going off into the desert to camp with them – experiences as far beyond my capabilities as pole-vaulting.

Anna Hart subtitles her book *Departures* 'A guide to letting go, one adventure at a time'. It is a sparkling account of events and learnings from a much-travelled young life. Interestingly, her reported developmental gains did not in any way correlate with the scale of the adventure: a 'micro-adventure' visiting castles in Scotland in good company counts for as much as seriously extreme mountaineering among strangers in the tropics. Like works of art, travel writing spans monumental sculptures and exquisite miniatures. Sara Wheeler spent months journeying the length of Chile; in *To the River*, Olivia Laing spent a week walking the length of the River Ouse in Sussex. Both produced a book's worth of enjoyable observation, research and reflection.

Those examples put my own travelling in perspective: much of it the equivalent of taster experiences, like being a chef for a day or having a flying lesson. The novelist Andrés Neuman described a whistle-stop tour of South America which had been organised for him after winning a literary prize. There was no time to look properly at the places he visited. His book *How to Travel without Seeing* is a collection of the jottings he made during the tour. There were elements of that in some of my own trips, when I was escorted straight from the airport to the venue.

And yet, by the time I finished this sequence of travels I had visited Pakistan 12 times: enough to feel more than a transient familiarity. My relationship with the country could never be the same as with familiar UK holiday haunts such as Helmsley and Durham, but it was not insignificant. I started to associate the place with a sense of relaxation and bonhomie, engendered by the people, the ambience and the activities, which once or twice caused me to catch myself saying, 'when I am back from holiday...' before setting off for a work assignment in Pakistan: an example of how little I distinguished between travelling for business and pleasure.

That said, I do describe my work in these accounts, sufficiently to explain the journeys, to maintain a line of narrative, and to convey the tensions and frustrations that troubled me. I write about how I spent my time, and the people I met, but I have tried to do that in a journalistic rather than technical voice, in the hope of retaining the interest of the general reader. To share my perceptions frankly while respecting the privacy of those I worked with, I have been deliberately vague about many of the individuals and organisations which feature in the story. In my professional persona I theorised about my experiences, in articles and in my book *Education in the Balance*. But not here: this is not an academic book about education in other countries, and my choice of title refers mainly to my learning and development at a personal level.

So I take up my story in Ad Dammam, a Saudi Arabian coastal city on the Persian Gulf, just north of Bahrain. It was my fifth visit to Saudi Arabia and my first to Dammam. My previous experiences of the country had woven a somewhat mixed tapestry of joy and frustration. Overall my fascination for the exotic distinctiveness of Arabian culture meant that I was happy to be there. I noted earlier that I had been plunged into that otherness in my second ever international consultancy assignment, when I went to Riyadh, in all my naivety, as my organisation's ambassador to liaise with potential partners for a project which might or might not happen. I was feted, shown off and entertained with Middle Eastern hospitality. Of course that was enjoyable, but the project never developed.

My second trip to the country had some similar features. With the support of a Saudi woman, Fatima, who was of very high social status, my organisation set up a business development trip and asked me to be part of the delegation. We went to Jeddah, an attractive coastal city, and stayed in the opulent comfort of the Jeddah Hilton. We were given a memorable tour of the old town: a truly spiritual experience. I gave lectures and led seminars and was received as an honoured guest. Despite all the pleasantries and contacts established, nothing actually came of it. From Jeddah we flew to Riyadh for a similar round of activity, but there it was a much more humdrum, workaday experience. Nothing came of that, either.

Then we got involved in an actual project, with an income stream, requiring my team to make a set of course materials and to carry out teaching activities on four occasions over a two-year period. That upside was almost outbalanced by extremely complex and unsatisfactory structures for the contracting and project management of the work. I went with the first working delegation to Riyadh, and on the basis of that experience decided the team didn't need me for the second trip, to Jeddah. My fourth trip to Saudi Arabia was of a different nature: I was invited to visit the construction site of the King Abdullah Economic City being created to the north of Jeddah, and to make proposals for an education project that was to be based there. Nothing came of the proposals. The visit to Dammam which opens this book, my fifth to the country, was for the next phase of teaching on what I refer to above as the 'actual project'. Apart from fitting a natural chronological order, it makes a good starting point for the 'journey' this book is about. This trip marked the beginning of a distinctive phase in my professional work and thinking, which took on the nature of a quest. It also illustrates the frustrations I repeatedly encountered, in one form or another, along the path.

Chapter One

Workaday Challenges in Dammam and Delhi

On Sunday morning, Fran marched into the foyer of the hotel in Dammam, disturbing my anxious lesson-planning reflections. Her black abaya flapped unfastened, her short spiky-tufted hair was uncovered, and she clutched a packet of Imodium. That was my first meeting with her. Some project managers must get their training at a business school fixated on performance indicators and the bottom line. Others seem to have been formed in an elite military academy specialising in attacking hard targets and interrogating prisoners. Fran might well have graduated from both. She was short and petite, that stature belying the strength of her personality. In her tour of the foyer she checked that all the arrangements were to her liking and that everyone knew what she expected of them.

For this assignment, the organisation I worked for had been contracted in by a project management company, which acted as the intermediary between us and the client for the project, the Saudi Ministry of Education. Fran was the ringleader of that company's local team. Leaving aside their project management personae, each of them was capable, pleasant and supportive. Incidentally, being personally familiar with the use of Imodium while on international assignments, and knowing the time interval required between dosages, I wondered about Fran's use of the packet as a stage prop. Perhaps she had just acquired it and hadn't taken any yet, which would explain her briskness.

This was in October 2010, and my team and I had come to work with the second cohort of participants on a programme we had started in February 2010, in the previous educational year. The programme involved principals and middle managers in a specially selected group of elite Saudi schools, and the participants were split into four groups: by organisational level and by gender. This meant that we were required to take a minimum of four staff, two men and two women, but Jolene would be leaving the organisation at Christmas, so I had also brought Sveta as a supernumerary to work alongside and subsequently replace her. '*How* many staff are you taking to Arabia?', my head of department had asked, counting on her fingers in the manner of an infant school teacher: 'One, two, three, four, five!' Normally I would have preferred to remain supernumerary myself, but it would have been excessive to add a sixth person to our delegation, so I had picked for myself the hard task of taking responsibility for the group of male principals.

The middle management groups, of both sexes, were easy and pleasant to work with. The men were not Saudis, and had come from all over the Middle East and beyond to work in these schools; the women's group included more Saudis in the mix. All were entirely keen and engaged. Reliable stalwarts Margaret and Gordon would work with these groups. The group of female principals was made up of Saudi women at the top of one of the few professions open to them: they were highly educated and keen, and would be a pleasure for Jolene and Sveta. By contrast, the male principals were also Saudis, but unlike the women, most of them expected to hold a senior office without exerting or inconveniencing themselves in any way.

The women's groups had to hold their programmes in windowless rooms in order to make certain that nobody could look at them. I went to meet the male principals, and found a large noisy group in an airy room the size of an assembly hall.

All of the hotel's facilities were good. We had left London on Friday 15th, and arrived on Saturday, with the remainder of that day being free for meetings and preparation. I had found a pleasant business lounge on the top floor which had views of the sea in both directions, suggesting the hotel was on a peninsula. I could see what looked like a spit with a lighthouse on the end of it, which made me think of Spurn Point, the southernmost tip of the Yorkshire coast. That was a place significant to me not only for its geographical distinctiveness, but also because it was near our second home: the house my partner grew up in and later inherited. Looking out of the hotel window, it was hard to get a sense of scale and distance. I assumed that what I could see were the indentations of the local coastline, and that Bahrain would be out of my line of vision somewhere to the south-east. Near enough, however, for the causeway linking it to the mainland to be a temptation for Saudis wanting access to alcohol. On our flight home at the end of the trip, I saw from the plane that the spit was a small manmade structure.

The others went off keenly in a taxi to explore the town. I chose not to go with them; not to leave the hotel at all. I had seen enough of Dammam on the ride from the airport to judge its attractions limited: a lower-league version of Jeddah, which I had toured extensively and pleasurably earlier in the year. From what I saw of it, Dammam reflected what the Saudis believed a seaside resort should look like – designed mainly for their own benefit, because any Western visitors would be there almost entirely for business. Saudi Arabia issued visas for business and pilgrimage, and only exceptionally for tourism. And Western tourists enjoying the comforts of the Gulf States would not have much interest in an excursion to Dammam.

It seemed to be a town of newish concrete rectangular buildings, mainly laid out in a grid pattern, punctuated by shop fronts with Arabic signs. Numerous mosques provided the main examples of traditional building styles. There were wide, breezy open spaces with palm trees, many dramatic abstract sculptures, and children's playgrounds with helter-skelters. Beyond, the pale sand, the turquoise sea dotted with various vessels, and the artificially constructed coastline of promenades and jetties did their best to proclaim the place to be a seaside resort. But self-consciously, as if saying to the world, 'Look, we're not all business and strict religion: we have made this imitation holiday resort!' A resort where the facilities for relaxation seemed to be largely deserted.

The hotel had three restaurants, and the local project managers had kindly arranged for lunch to be provided in a different one for each of the three days of the programme (Sunday to Tuesday). The main restaurant, which was my preferred choice for evening meals, was nominally Lebanese, a description that was really shorthand for a broad range of Middle Eastern dishes. The style and variety suited my tastes and appetite: when I e-mailed home to say I was being moderate, I meant relatively – not overeating to the point of paralysis. Glowing charcoal stood ready for fish and meat kebabs cooked to order. There were good courgettes stuffed with rice and minced lamb, vegetables, salads, flatbreads, dips, beans, spicy stews and sweet sticky desserts. I deemed it only polite to show my enthusiastic appreciation of these good things.

Perhaps a quarter or one third of the hotel guests were international: all there on business. The restaurant had refectory-style tables, and although it was not a rule for internationals, men and women generally adhered to the local custom by choosing to sit separately. A couple of times I sat opposite an American. He was white, with red hair and an untrimmed beard, and wore white robes and cap that advertised he was both a convert to Islam and thoroughly absorbed into the regional culture. He worked on this project and that, and was an interesting dinner companion. He had a working knowledge of Arabic and Hebrew, and I was partly involved in a conversation he was having with another man about the similarities between the spoken forms of these languages. This was something that I had noticed with interest when I had started trying to learn Arabic, following a similarly abortive attempt, many years previously, to grapple with the biblical languages.

One of the team mentioned having an upset stomach. I offered to bring down my bottle of J Collis Browne, and upon receiving a blank look explained that it was a mixture including morphine, whereupon Margaret told me to keep my voice down because it was illegal for me to have brought it into Saudi Arabia. I hadn't known this, although it seemed obvious once I was told.

I soldiered on with the male principals. The first day revealed the extent of the problem. Some of the group knew about the programme and had read the briefing materials. Others had not, and a sub-set of that group had no enthusiasm for it either, as the decision to take the school into the programme had been made by the proprietor rather than the principal. A rule of the programme, imposed by the Saudi Ministry of Education, was that the training courses (including the briefing materials) should be in English only. Some of the group did not have the necessary level of English, which added to their disengagement. There was a competitive atmosphere, in the sense that those who knew what they were doing were impatient with, and scornful towards, those who did not. Their body language reflected this, exemplified by one man sitting in a low chair at the front, who would throw himself back in the chair, folding his arms, his dishdasha disarrayed, crossing his legs and flashing dark hairy thighs.

On the evening of the first day I went through the predictably disappointing feedback forms with Fran, and she agreed to provide an interpreter henceforth. The second day went better, and the group's motivation improved when they understood that if they completed the assignments, they would receive a certificate at the end of the programme. On the third day, the group were eager to finish early, at 2pm, so that the participants from Riyadh and Jeddah could catch their flights, and I 'reluctantly' agreed. That left us a few hours of free time. Gordon had, with impressive diligence, brought with him a rucksack full of marking; I always felt tired at the end of assignments and preferred to relax.

Jolene's grip on her personal finances had not improved since our last trip together. She expressed concern about whether and how much we would need to pay when checking out of the hotel. She had no credit card, and only a small current account balance. 'I did have a spa treatment, but that was only...', she said, naming a sum in riyals which made me wonder whether she knew how much a riyal was worth. I decided not to get too close at check-out time, but as it happened, the project management company had very kindly settled the main bill.

I had plenty of reflections to fill the dead time before and after check-out. This had been my first international assignment in the current academic year, since getting back from Guangzhou in July. Assignments tended to fall into place at short notice, so of course I was pondering the prospects for the upcoming year, and whether there would be any improvements on the last.

Any measures of this would involve a blend of business, academic and personal objectives. On the business side, I needed to win contracts for work at rates which would at least cover costs, and carry them out successfully. 'Success' meant either raising possibilities for future additional custom from that client, or if not, then at least being able to establish a respectable track record which we could cite when promoting ourselves. When I had started working internationally, in 2007, trips like this one had been a wonderful unexpected bonus tacked on to my main job: a kind of working holiday. Since then, as their number had increased, they merged into my role, with the weight of expectation that brought to perform and deliver benefits to the organisation.

Academically, I was keen to learn not just about other education systems, but also to understand more about the synergy (intended, potential, actual) between UK-based so-called experts and the systems in other countries. I was clear in my rejection of any colonial-style assumption that the people we worked with should sit at our feet and absorb our superior wisdom. The ideal always would be to establish partnership relations of mutual respect. Unfortunately the ways in which projects were initiated, contracted and paid for tended to get in the way of that ideal. The dominant model of change was top-down, initiated by governments or international agencies, with all key decisions taken in advance and unilaterally. Even so, I was interested in exploring, at least in theory, how to work globally within cultural contexts, in order to generate ideas for my own academic writing on the subject.

On a personal level, I was still excited by the relatively new experience of being able to travel to exotic locations as part of my work. I suppose that included a tourist's interest in new places and people, but went well beyond. I hoped that every new assignment might turn out to be a new beginning, opening up new possibilities and avenues for development. I found the education scene in England somewhat bruising, with its competitive hierarchy, its unforgiving harsh judgements about success and failure, and its tribal politics. Away from all that, I hoped for chances to reinvent myself. To make fresh starts in different contexts, to win regard, to find friendship and human warmth: all of those vague yearnings drove me to keep travelling.

I couldn't see much prospect of any such benefits from the Dammam assignment, which formed part of a contract that had involved difficult interfaces and unfavourable terms from the outset. Getting through it without reputational damage seemed the most realistic aim.

The return flight involved a transfer at Doha, in Qatar, which seemed a strangely short hop for a full-sized plane, covering more distance circling around to gain height and then come down again than the 200 kilometres between the two airports. Doha is a massive transit point with lavish facilities, including a shopping area comparable to several floors of Selfridges. I don't feel any need or desire to shop at airports, but I do like to wander around, have tea, attend to comforts, and be a free agent. The three women in our group had different priorities. When we arrived at the seating area near the shops, Jolene said, 'We want to look at the shops – you don't want to shop, do you?', with a strong implication that the correct answer was 'No'. On hearing that answer, she responded, 'Oh good, so you won't mind keeping an eye on our luggage for a few minutes while we have a quick look round?' Gordon was already well absorbed in a book at his end of the bench, as a great pile of bags got dumped all around us. I opened a book and did not mind being so employed for the proposed 'few minutes'.

Half an hour later I felt peeved. Gordon was dozing peacefully, Jolene, Margaret and Sveta were nowhere to be seen, and I was marooned with an embarrassing pile of stuff that looked like the contents of a teenager's bedroom deposited from a dumper truck. I wanted to add a notice saying, 'This isn't mine: I'm just stuck with it'. After an hour or so, the women returned, obviously having had a lovely time and carrying more bags. I was both pleased to see them and cross at having been ill-used, especially when Jolene blatantly declared her ruse. 'Yes, it's a good system: get the men settled down with their books, then off we go!' She also, in the same breath, accused me of flirting with Sveta, which I considered to be not really true – not enough to merit the comment.

*****

Despite very little satisfactory sleep during the night flight, when I arrived in London on Wednesday morning I had things to do, including making a trip to the visa agency. I needed to obtain a visa to visit India, and had to turn that process around in time to receive the visa before my flight the following Tuesday. Some delays in finalising the arrangements had meant that I had not been able to obtain it before setting off for Dammam.

For some months, my colleague Hilary had been leading negotiations with a contact in the British Council in Delhi regarding a two-day course which she and I would jointly design and conduct. That liaison had been protracted, involving changes of dates and various modifications to our proposals. One of the effects of the date changing was that this course now fell in the middle of a business development trip to India, in which Hilary was also involved with some other colleagues, making the arrangements complex.

The particular bit of business they hoped to develop concerned teacher training, and the specialists involved were Stella and Jane, both of whom had senior responsibilities in that field. Hilary was also a teacher trainer by background and was an integral part of the sales team. The other colleague involved was Lalita, an academic who was part of an important Indian family. She spent some of her time helping our organisation by networking with her highly placed contacts in India. She was there now, ahead of the rest of the delegation.

After many adjustments, the schedule finally adopted was for the three teacher trainers to catch the night flight from London on Monday 25th October, link up with Lalita, and start their series of business meetings on Tuesday evening to continue throughout Wednesday. I took the 8.45pm flight on Tuesday which arrived in Delhi at 9.45am on Wednesday, whereupon I would in due course join the others in their meeting.

These arrangements for the start of the trip required me to be braver and more self-reliant than my normal preference. I was joining colleagues whom I knew only slightly and who had already started their work. To make matters more complicated, on the day of my arrival, immediately after checking into the hotel I would need to go and find them at a venue somewhere in Delhi, to join in with a meeting that would already be in full swing.

Check-in at the Crowne Plaza proceeded smoothly. Of the numerous Crowne Plaza hotels in Delhi, this particular one was at Okhla, an industrial park somewhat to the south of the city. I didn't know that at the time, not having had an opportunity to research the matter; I just knew I was somewhere in Delhi. Nor had I looked up the place where the meeting was being held. To me, the brief address

I handed to the taxi driver – the names of a building and a street with some kind of postcode – was meaningless.

We set off in the ancient taxi and I began to enjoy the street scene, remembered from my introductory visit to India three years previously. Remembered in the sense of general ambience rather than specific recognition: I hadn't got a clue where I was, nor where I was trying to go, so had to rely totally on the taxi driver. At a much later date I looked again at where I had been. The venue was in Barakhamba Road, one of the many spokes of the spider's web centred on Connaught Circus. Approaching from the south, we probably passed by, or at least near, India Gate. I should have had a better sense of orientation – but then I had just come off a night flight.

The distinctive elements of the street scene included the sheer variety of vehicles: a mix of old and modern, global and local styles. The latter included crowded old buses and swarms of mechanised rickshaws. Among these were pedal-powered rickshaws – mainly used to transport goods – hand carts and donkey carts. Between and around them, large numbers of light motorbikes each carrying two or three people whizzed about. Not surprisingly, with that mixture of different speeds and sizes of conveyances, lane discipline was haphazard. In all but the most major through-routes, there was also a distinctive zone between the carriageway and the building line, filled with a varying combination of street enterprises, parked cars and carts, cows and people.

Towards the end of the journey, the taxi driver stopped, saying, 'It is near here'. He got out; I followed, assuming my ride was finished. The driver asked directions of a policeman, who was grey-whiskered, very smart, and of the old school: he gave me a sort of half-salute. Back in the taxi, we creaked along a bit further, then stopped again. The driver led me on quite a walk back from the street frontage, down a paved alley, and pointed to a building at the back of the block. I would never have found it on my own, and contrasted this kind diligence with the 'It's somewhere here, mate!' I would have got from a taxi driver in the UK.

I entered the building and climbed the stairs with a sense of unreality. Was I really, this Wednesday morning, exploring the staircase in a strange building in Delhi? On the fourth floor, I wandered along a corridor and found my colleagues in a kitchen, finishing a lunch break between meetings. They were with Nick, an agent who arranged things, and who kept a small suite of offices in this building. After briefly introducing myself to him, I grabbed a modest portion of snack items from the fragments left over, and we moved to a meeting room. There we met the principal of a prestigious school in the north of India. The conversation was amiable enough, and after many later stages of negotiation which did not involve me, an ongoing working relationship did eventually develop.

We went back to the hotel in a couple of taxis. I was free to amuse myself while the others had a dinner engagement, after which Lalita, Stella and Jane set off on an overnight train ride to Jodhpur. I was very happy enjoying the facilities of the hotel. The restaurant at the Crowne Plaza offered an extensive and wonderful Indian buffet that gave me great pleasure, as well as the heaviness of overeating, which increased as the days passed. The buffet varied every day, so it was important to try things when they were offered, otherwise the opportunity would be lost. I remember wonderful biryanis and numerous forms of dhal, and fresh pineapple steeped in star anise. There was an open view from the dining area through to the kitchen – always a reassuring sign. On one occasion, a cook was adjusting the heat of a dish by shaking an ordinary bottle of Tabasco over a frying pan.

I formed the view that poppadums as served up in international hotels in India are different from, and more enjoyable than, those available in the UK. In this particular hotel they came in a variety of textures and incorporating different whole spices. I particularly liked those with holes and a bubbly texture, which as well as a pleasant crunchiness had a moreish bitter flavour. At the time I simply enjoyed these delights; more recently I have wondered whether the variations reflect differences in what raising agent is used, how much of it and for how long. On the teaching days, a plentiful lunch buffet was provided for participants and staff, in addition to mid-morning and mid-afternoon snacks with tea. The appetising aroma of these milestones in the day meant that the conditioning process into overeating was well paced and thoroughly reinforced.

The educational programme that provided my reason for being there occupied the days on Thursday and Friday. We had a group of 55 principals and vice principals, and to cater for that number Hilary and I had planned to take it in turns to give a lecture to the whole group at the start and end of each day. For the rest of the day, we split the group into two, taking one group each for the first day and the other on the second. Some participants found this confusing, being sure that they must be missing some sessions, but it provided a reasonable level of interaction. The participants had plenty to contribute. Just under half of the total group were men, and during the tea and lunch breaks it was the men especially who had a lot they wanted to say to me.

As usual, some had specific business to raise beyond this programme. One woman, responsible for staff development, was keen to explore the possibilities of an accreditation scheme which I managed. I also met Pankaj Das. He was the principal of a school in Assam – the participants came from all over India – and after an initial few words we arranged a proper sit-down discussion outside the working day, using the white leather chairs and smoky glass table of one of the lounge areas. He was keen to bring a party of his staff to London for a short course and wanted to talk through the practicalities and what might meet their interests.

On Thursday evening I had to watch a film. This was part of the official schedule, set up as part of the detailed planning between Nick and my organisation's management. We were to go to Nick's house to watch *Three Idiots*, an Indian, Hindi-language coming-of-age comedy, because it was considered that this would help us to understand some of the issues in the higher education scene in India.

Stella, Jane and Lalita had flown back from Jodhpur during the afternoon. At the hotel, Hilary and I met up with them and we looked for the pair of taxis which had been requested. After some conversations it became apparent that only one taxi was available. The women devised a scheme to avoid my having close proximity with any of them: that seemed more important than their comfort. Stella, Jane and Hilary were big mature women. They decided that they would sit on the back seat, and that Lalita, who was petite, would sit across their legs. I was to sit in the front with the driver, thereby observing the standards of propriety I associated more with Arabia than India. I could see that Lalita's couch would be well upholstered, but she was a high-born Indian and I was surprised she was prepared to sacrifice her dignity in that way. In the event the arrangement was effected with jollity, and I enjoyed my massively spacious front seat.

The driver coaxed the taxi into life and nursed it along jerkily. Every half kilometre or so the engine would splutter and die, then be gently resurrected. We arrived in a quiet residential street. Nick greeted us and led us to the first floor of his house where we were to be entertained.

The floor was open-plan, an oblong running between windows at the front and the back. The front portion was furnished with a table on which was set a pleasant array of home-cooked cold dishes; we were invited to help ourselves. Nick opened and distributed a bottle of Indian champagne, which I found sweeter and softer textured than I would have preferred, but pleasantly drinkable.

The back half of the room was largely unfurnished, with an empty central space that looked as though it might double up as a gymnasium. In fact it doubled up as a private cinema. There were settees along one wall, and low tables supporting a laptop computer and projector. The opposite wall was painted white and served as a projection screen. The windows looked out on to trees and were slightly ajar for ventilation. Nick explained that monkeys could be a nuisance, coming in to steal food.

We got settled, with more wine; the lights dimmed, and the film started. The image covered the whole of the wall, so it felt the same as being in a cinema. So far as I could recall, I had not previously watched a Bollywood film right through, although I had seen long silent sections of them over people's shoulders on aeroplanes, including a lot of lively dancing at weddings and on top of trains.

The storyline in the film did indeed offer quite a comment on aspects of higher education in India, but while duly noting that theme I quickly became fully immersed in the film as entertainment. I loved the sloppy sentimental bits, and was blown away with the music, song and use of colour and pattern to convey the romantic elements. In the sad bits I was glad the room was dark. As so often, I thought that I was lucky to earn my living in such interesting ways.

We returned with the same driver. The women were visibly socially relaxed, but would not vary the seating arrangements, despite my pointing out that Lalita could fit into the front seat with a hand-width between us. So they formed their pile, and the car groaned, coughed, spluttered and kept conking out, but did complete the journey. At the time this achievement seemed almost like a miracle, but probably the car had been like that for years and would carry on a good few more.

The second day of the programme was broadly similar to the first, except that both parties engaged in a different way with the programme and with each other. The polite reserve of the first morning had melted. The participants settled back into their preferred roles, whether as raconteur, networker, self-publicist or studious scholar. They were more ready to form their view of the usefulness of the course to them personally, and to select their style of engagement accordingly. I was more active in exploring their willingness to see some 'usefulness' in the process of discussion and reflection rather than in answers offered on a plate. The latter was never going to fill a teaspoon in a general two-day course delivered cold: what could we usefully tell these senior and experienced people without first understanding something of the issues in their working lives?

I shared some of those thoughts in the final review meeting with British Council colleagues, which confirmed what I already knew. Self-contained short courses with visiting experts are a popular market niche. It would make them too expensive to set up pre-course liaison with the participants. Getting enough bums on seats meant drawing in a group whose interests would be broad and diverse, reducing the relevance of much of the course material for quite a number of them. It also became clearer that this course was almost certainly a one-off, not leading to a process of further course provision, development and partnership building. So all that liaison and preparation had been for two days' work. But the customer is always right, I reflected on

Saturday's return flight, planning in my mind how over the next week or so Hilary and I would craft our report, using the broadly positive feedback from the participants, but building in our recommendations for how things might be done better.

Chapter Two
Karachi: the Clifton Scene

The Commander was short and dapper, impeccable in a blazer with metal buttons, white shirt and tie. It was difficult to estimate his age, but he had been retired from the Pakistan Navy for a while, engaging in successful business ventures, and involving himself at some senior organisational level in Pakistani cricketing affairs. He also had educational interests, which was why I found myself in a meeting with him in our Bloomsbury headquarters. The meeting had been convened by the senior manager who headed the international side of our work: an astute and much-travelled individual. Right now he was appraising the Commander with penetrating shrewdness. The Commander wanted to benefit education in Pakistan by enabling our organisation to conduct professional development there.

At least once a week someone came knocking at the door, either literally or through e-mail, peddling a bright idea for how they could set up in partnership with our organisation to develop income-generating activities. Generally, these 'partnership' suggestions meant finding a way to attach our organisation's reputable global brand to some substandard local provision, and dividing the spoils disproportionately in favour of the local entrepreneur. These chancers got short shrift, because their ideas brought nothing to the table except the prospect of risk and hassle, and broke our quality assurance rules. Among the clouds of such chaff, wheat did occasionally fall to the floor. Over the course of the last century, sufficient grains had sprouted to amount to a global array of genuine and useful partnership projects.

On our side of the table, we looked at each other and saw that we shared the impression that there was something real about the Commander and his approach. Very quickly some principles were established, some lines for strategic development set. About 20 minutes after the initial handshake, the Commander warmly expressed his pleasure at this progress. 'Well, I don't know what more to say!', he concluded economically, tripping off to his next engagement somewhere in the club-land of St James's.

The correspondence leading up to the meeting had been initiated by Taymur, who was the founder, proprietor and principal of a school in Karachi. He had taken a higher degree by distance learning at our organisation. The Commander had helped Taymur to raise the finance for his school, and was the chair of its trustees.

The Commander, with his business acumen, had correctly predicted what our objections would be to the usual sort of partnership proposal, and had designed them out. He wanted to set up a new charitable trust, with the sole purpose of promoting our organisation's engagement in Pakistan, with all key teaching inputs being made by our own personnel, on a cost-recovery but non-profit-making basis. He would tap local philanthropists to help make the provision affordable. Our office would begin to draft a memorandum of understanding, and I would make a familiarisation visit. Our willingness to go ahead with this visit was seen as a significant and symbolic step by both parties. Certainly for my part I was keen. I had been to India and to the Arabian Peninsula, and reckoned that Karachi would be an interesting midway location between the two. Geographically and culturally, that was actually a pretty fair assessment.

That first meeting, which took place during the summer vacation, led me to take more of an interest in Pakistani affairs. My visit was scheduled for late November, to allow time for the elaborate process of getting a visa. While I was in Dammam, news had broken of trouble in Karachi. I hadn't known whether the English press had covered this, but as my family had raised their eyebrows a bit in response to my interest in working in Pakistan, I had e-mailed to tell them that if the trouble wasn't sorted soon I would delay my visit.

The rules about this sort of thing seemed very simple to me and I was entirely happy to work within them. The Foreign Office issued guidance for travellers which was regularly updated. It set out a country-by-country three-fold classification: avoid all travel; avoid all but essential travel; and travel taking normal sensible precautions. According to the fashion of the times, these gradings developed into a red, amber and green traffic-light coding. Ordinary UK citizens travelling on business for their employer could not go into 'red' areas. That privilege was limited to special categories such as diplomatic, military, media or aid agency personnel. For ordinary people travelling on business, it had nothing to do with the bravery or foolhardiness of the individual, and very much to do with the legal implications of how insurance underwriting operated. Corporations had no option but to pull their personnel out of 'red' areas, regardless of the actual details of their own local risk assessment, and regardless of whether or not the individuals on the ground would prefer to stay.

If people based in 'red' areas wanted to access our knowledge or advice, they came to London for that purpose. London-based programmes for international delegations formed another significant sector of my work. The 'amber' category was the one that caused discussion from time to time. In my professional role I took the view that travel to 'amber' areas could be treated as 'essential' if contractual and travel arrangements had already been made, and course delivery had already been organised with participants. In these cases, I would discuss with the local partner whether any additional security would be advisable, and would make it clear to my colleagues or team members that they were free to make their own judgement about whether or not to go ahead with their participation in the assignment.

In reality, the need for such judgements arose less often than I would have expected. I had been surprised that Yemen and South Sudan had remained 'green' in the periods I was working in them. The rational part of my mind told me that the Foreign Office classifications would always be based on completely objective risk assessment. In more cynical moments I wondered whether diplomatic and political judgements ever moderated these assessments. I noticed Bahrain remaining 'green' throughout some pretty nasty domestic unrest.

The Foreign Office guidance helpfully divided up the more troublesome countries internally, distinguishing the urban centres where Westerners do business from the mayhem in more remote areas. The latter tends to be most newsworthy and colours opinions about countries as a whole. In the long relationship I developed with Pakistan, the cities where I did my work were always 'green'. On average, Karachi's homicide rate didn't seem to be in such a different ballpark from London's. Getting ready for that first visit, I did, however, pore over maps carefully, because my hosts had kindly offered to take me to a flood relief camp, which was a fair drive out from Karachi and I needed to check that it was within the 'green' zone. It was, just.

I felt privileged and excited by this promised excursion. The Indus Valley was prone to flooding, in most years on a minor scale, but every so often very seriously. The monsoon season of that year, 2010, had seen exceptionally heavy flooding that had caused widespread destruction and human misery. The waters had substantially subsided by the time of my visit, but even so it was unusual for a Western civilian not attached to an aid agency to be allowed into the flood zone.

On Saturday 27th November 2010, I left London at 9.25pm on an Oman Air flight to Muscat, where it landed at 8.40am the next morning. The plane was not very full – the seat next to me was empty – but I couldn't sleep much. Part of the problem was that there were only two cabin crew, who managed to spin out for three hours the rigmarole of dumping down a small tray of dinner and eventually picking it up. A few hours later another whole hour was spent doing the same again for breakfast. As this was a relationship-building familiarisation trip, I was not worried about the work, and spent time on the flight reading *A Streetcar Named Desire.*

The descent into Muscat afforded views of rugged hills glowing orange in the morning light. My connecting flight left at 10am: a mercifully limited stay in a dreary terminal. It had none of the class and comfort of the more major nodal airports of the Middle East. In particular, when I was waiting in the departure room (it certainly didn't merit being called a 'lounge') it reminded me of Yemen – which was, after all, the country next door to Oman – being hot, stuffy and crowded with travellers who were probably mainly migrant workers. I was the only Westerner. There seemed to be a lot of activity by military planes, and a lot of people just waiting with refugee-like sufferance and hopelessness. The view through the dirty glass walls was of dusty desert with emaciated wild birds, including sparrows and hooded crows. There were no information screens. Eventually, staff shouted and everyone was herded on to buses, where, clinging to a pole, I was squashed rather too intimately among my fellow travellers, trying to breathe as little as possible.

The flight to Karachi took most of two hours, but crossing another time zone meant it was scheduled to land at 12.45pm. A meal was served, of local style. It was hot and oily. I ate something round and dark which I thought might be a baby aubergine. It exploded in my mouth into a mass of seeds so fiery that it set me hiccupping and gasping for breath. I spent the next few minutes sweating while my diaphragm juddered and stomach heaved, wondering what kind of taste buds would find such heat pleasurable.

The sky was clear, the sea was blue, and the view from the plane window was marred only by a slight haze. The sea was scored with the wakes of ships bound for Karachi. Land began to appear: the outlying fringes of the Indus Delta. I saw low-lying islands of brown mud dotted with scrub, fringed on their seaward side with pale sand and on their landward side by patches of dark green vegetation. Their outlines were much indented with channels. These general characteristics continued on to the delta itself, which was massive in extent, and densely penetrated by braided channels showing extreme meandering. After a vastly extensive area of delta, the hard ground of the coastal region came into view as a low plateau of uniform yellow ochre, dissected by winding valleys.

Tired, confused and excited, I endured stoically the mixture of chaos and military regimentation at Karachi airport, eventually finding the 'foreigners' queue, clutching my passport with its precious visa. It had taken some getting, and had made entering Saudi Arabia seem simple by comparison. Later, someone told me that the demands imposed were partly in retaliation for the way that Pakistanis seeking to enter the UK were treated.

The requirements went beyond the form, photos, letter of invitation and employer's letter that many countries required. Although I was travelling on business, and fully supported by my employer, I had to produce my personal bank statements from the last three months in order to prove my solvency, which I resented. Of course, the normal monthly issue of the statements does not necessarily coincide with the date of the visa application: in my case the most recent two or three weeks were unaccounted for. The visa agent told me to request an exceptional statement or to find out how to get it online. I refused, and was warned that this might lead to my application being refused. I also had to prove my home address by providing utility bills: more irritating intrusion. Even when I became a frequent visitor to Pakistan, all of this was required for each new visa.

Then there was the form: typically South Asian, with fussy layout, tiny print, and boxes bearing no relation to the amount of information intended to go in them. The form sought details of – with minutely itemised dates, addresses and names of supervisors – every employment ever held, which I could not have provided, so I described my previous career in a summary sentence. It had two whole pages asking about military service, including details of deployment way beyond the 'name, rank and number' convention. The form also required information about the applicant's parents, which I regarded with an irrational intensity as irrelevant. I am not a child! I never knew my father, and had been socially distant from my birth family for about 40 years, so I invented the entries required.

These negative thoughts about the process were lingering in my mind as I edged forward. After the stamping of my passport, effected with parade-ground flourish, I found my way through some further formalities and into the baggage hall, where several different types of officials, agents, licensed helpers and possibly unofficial helpers wanted to take charge of the search for my suitcase. As an Englishman in a business suit I attracted attention, and generated attentiveness. Some was probably economically motivated, but some reflected a complex blend of sentiments towards Britain as the former colonial power, of which I became more aware during the visit.

I didn't know who would be meeting me. Outside, all seemed confusing. Tired and blinking in dazzling sunshine, I looked for a name board. A man beckoned me: he was the driver from the Avari Towers Hotel. He was talking with another man, in Western casual dress, who was with a little girl. The second man introduced himself as Taymur, the school principal who had set up the visit. It became apparent that I had a choice to make. 'We've both come to meet you', Taymur said. 'So you can take your pick.' I came close to making a terrible social blunder. I was in that dazed 'Just want to get to my hotel' state of mind, which inclined me to want to keep to the planned schedule for work encounters, rather than plunging in straight away. Seeing my hesitation, Taymur prompted me: 'I am the *headmaster* who will be working with you'. I accepted his kind offer to take me to the hotel and we settled into his workaday Mercedes saloon. While his daughter sat politely in the rear seat, he made reassuring small talk on the drive into town.

The traffic was a typical South Asian mix, including many motorbikes with side-saddle pillion riders. We passed decorated lorries, both on the road and parked at drunken angles on uneven patches of earth. I mean seriously, heavily decorated, like Christmas trees worked on by someone determined to use up every ornament in the box. Intricate painting, baubles and festoons covered every available surface from mudguards to cabin-tops. Those surfaces being deemed insufficient, many lorries had extra bits added to their structure to create additional surfaces for ornamentation: bumper extensions, pelmets, canopies, gables, all smothered in a tinkling, swaying mass of exuberant attention seeking – 'Here am I, this is my personality, look at me!' Taymur explained that lorries were manufactured in standard factory finish, and that their owners took them to firms specialising in elaborate beautification. I read recently that some drivers like to think of their lorry as being dressed as their bride.

We arrived at the hotel. The entrance was one of the exits from a roundabout. Taymur drove through an open gateway in a high, secure wall to a security checkpoint, which included a retractable ground barrier, a liftable windscreen-height barrier, and a kiosk with armed guards who checked inside the bonnet and boot: the standard entry to an international hotel in Pakistan. In the cool, spacious foyer, which smelled of cinnamon, Taymur supervised my check-in. The papers the receptionist produced were marked 'Gratis: guest of Mr Avari'. This was part of the local philanthropic support which had been arranged to keep down the costs of my trip, so that the activities developed could be offered at prices the participants could afford. The proprietor of the hotel chain waived accommodation charges for me, and my colleagues, for the duration of the project.

So there I was, my body weary and senses pounded, looking from my bedroom window in the Avari Towers Hotel at dozens of large raptors – I think red kites – sailing around among a similar number of medium-sized crows. Karachi was a vast, sprawling mass of urban development that looked at that moment to be without form or bearings. I had no idea where I was in relation to the coast, or the airport, or anywhere.

Of course being the proprietor's guest caused the staff to be even more deferential than normal. I was fussed over, escorted to the room and shown round it in great detail. This was actually a little wearing because I was eager to relax in privacy: to use the bathroom, make tea, get organised and take a siesta would have been most welcome. But no, just as I was starting to get settled, there was a knock on the door and an attentive gentleman told me I needed to move to a better room in a nicer position, which had a better bed. When that had been achieved, and all the features of the new room explained, he poked about in the wardrobe and came brandishing the towelling slippers, offering to put them on my feet, downcast at my refusal. When I finally got organised and was starting to doze, he was back again delivering a bowl of fruit. Shortly after, some building work started nearby which involved prolonged hammering. So instead of attempting to sleep, I wrote an e-mail home, noting that the internet here was better than in Old Hunstanton, one of our frequent holiday haunts – a boast spoilt a little by a short power cut which took place as I typed.

Taymur came to collect me a bit after 7pm to take me to the Commander's house for what was described on the programme as a welcome reception dinner in my honour. He parked outside a substantial house in a desirable residential district. It was dark, and the garden seemed full of people. Our host found us quickly; I remembered him from our meeting in London. After a word of welcome, he asked, 'What can I get you to drink? Wine or spirits?' This threw me somewhat, because Pakistan is a 'dry' country, and I like to respect the cultures of the places I visit. I was also tired and disorientated from travelling and being in a new situation, and really would have preferred a soft drink. 'Do you have something softer?', I asked. 'Yes, there is beer.' I accepted that as the softest option available, learning something about the Commander's ways.

He introduced me to some of the people standing in small groups, glasses in hand. He had drawn the cream of Karachi society to his garden. There were members of the old land-owning aristocracy, including the grandson of a rajah: a big, light-skinned man with a broad smiling face and enormous curled moustache, like a character from an illustration in a fairy-tale. There were diplomats, senior educationists, members of the armed forces, philanthropists and entrepreneurs. Most of the names passed in a blur, but I was introduced a bit more carefully to Captain Sajid of the Pakistan Navy. I came to learn that these groups represented the people who, between them and in collaboration, kept the wheels turning in Pakistan. Camera flashes regularly punctuated my brief conversations with each group. Two pages of pictures subsequently appeared in the regional social gossip magazine: dreadful photos of me, black suited, white faced, stooping attentively, looking serious.

The Commander steered me to an extensive barbecue picnic. A row of substantial metal frames like high iron bedsteads held beds of glowing coals, attended by staff traditionally clad in tall, elaborate headdresses. Tables held an array of additional dishes. The Commander caringly took charge of my choices, as if I was a young sub-lieutenant: 'You can have this one, best not have that on your first visit, nor that, this is good…'

Some people were eating at tables; he guided me to a vacant seat next to an incredibly beautiful young Saudi woman. Her smiling eyes met mine as she gestured her own invitation to me to occupy the vacant chair. She was eager to entertain the 'guest of honour', and did so most charmingly. I checked with her that she was indeed Saudi, which in the case of women is not quite so obvious from their dress as it is with men, and told her of my numerous visits to her country, which delighted her. I never thought to ask what she did or why she was in Karachi: the fact of her existence and proximity was sufficient.

Tiredness and tension drained away. The Commander had shown astute insight in this matter also.

Relaxed and unguarded, I found myself chattering on about my admiration of the (then) king's policy of educating women as a strategy for long-term social change. I talked about my visit to the women's university in Jeddah, and my contacts with Saudi women given scholarships to study in London. This was just flowing out: my actual opinion, with no thought to politics or diplomacy. My magically wonderful companion eagerly agreed, lapping up these views like cream; I think she was surprised and pleased both by my knowledge and attitude. It was only at the end of the meal that I became properly aware of a Saudi man sitting among a group on the other side of the table, in front of a large glass of red wine. He was her father, and he was the consul.

People were leaving, the Commander's wife taking her share of the gracious farewells. She was a person of social and business standing in her own right: I think art dealing might have been among her interests. The Commander introduced me to two male members of staff, putting an arm around the shoulder of each. 'These are my permanent sources of support' – I didn't catch either of their names – 'helps me with domestic affairs, and… helps me with business affairs'. I gathered that he had brought in a team of outside caterers from the Sindh Club, to which he belonged: they had been the ones with elaborate uniforms.

Breakfast on Monday was in Asia Live, the hotel's main eating area, near the foyer. Glass walls offered views over the garden and outdoor swimming pool. The restaurant had a central, square, walk-around buffet, and a further selection of offerings along the side opposite the garden. The table mats were covered with effusive exhortations to try all the options: 'The best breakfast in Karachi, Pakistan, the World (think big!)', including 'our local speciality, lamb brains, go on, try it!'

Which I didn't, on that first trip, aiming instead for the nearest approximation to the kind of breakfast I had at home. Some poached eggs were arranged neatly on squares of crumbly white bread; there were chicken sausages and steamed vegetables including carrots much redder than those in Europe. I had a dollop of a sweet mixture made out of squash; a waiter brought black tea.

Having seen the gardens from the breakfast area, I looked again from my bedroom window for any clue as to orientation, but the journey from reception involved too many turns for me to be sure which way I was facing, and the sun was too weak to use as a compass. I looked down on to the top of a flat roof and saw the usual clutter of ventilation outlets and communications dishes. Beyond, a road ran dead straight, devoid of traffic; peachy-coloured tower blocks rose among a plentiful scattering of dark green trees. Further away there was a half-finished tower block, to its left denser high-rise urban development, and to its right a vista of scattered low-rise buildings including houses.

Taymur met me in the cinnamon-fragranced lounge and drove me southwards to his school. Both of its campuses were in the Clifton area: a peninsula of respectability. We began at the primary campus, which Taymur had started six years previously, partly to enable children to be better prepared for their entry to the secondary school. In addition to offering the British national curriculum and 'A' levels, he followed the International Baccalaureate curriculum and teaching methods. It was helpful for children to experience that approach while young, and to improve their English-language skills.

I met the primary headteacher. She had 13 staff and outlined how these were organised, and – the focus of my visit – her approaches to professional development. My part was to show keen interest, to listen and learn, while privately concerning myself with two big questions: what elements in the local social and cultural context did I need to be aware of; and how might my organisation be able to offer relevant, credible and affordable support?

Then we took the short drive to the secondary campus, which was larger, older, and in a district of high-grade mature residences. Taymur parked in the wide tree-lined street opposite a gate. An elderly employee of military bearing crossed the road, saluted, and took possession of briefcases.

Inside, as we climbed a staircase among the bustle of students moving between lessons, I was reminded again of the basic similarities among schools worldwide. In Taymur's office, he introduced me to Colin, an elderly Englishman who was joining the day's briefing discussions and was the principal of Karachi Grammar School; also to Samia, middle school co-ordinator, and Fazana, who was responsible for 'A'-level courses.

As we were getting settled, Taymur passed on a bit of news from the Commander, concerning a project to open a boarding school on a six-hectare plot on the border of Sindh. The foundation that had initiated the project had run into trouble, the site now being deemed to be too near a chemical plant to house a boarding school: a day school might be acceptable if the site was reconfigured. The foundation was casting around for new partners to step in, but Taymur identified several major challenges.

This brief conversation about a project which in fact was nothing to do with any of us illustrated both a general sense in the air among the people I was dealing with of willingness to appraise entrepreneurial opportunities, and the existence of networks for such conversations.

Later in the same meeting, Taymur mentioned that his school might be able to acquire an additional 1.5-hectare site, on which he would create space to accommodate teacher training activity.

They told me there was no national framework for teaching qualifications: there were regulations for government schools which were not enforced, and the content and usefulness of the B.Ed. degree were very variable. In Taymur's school teachers needed to develop the skills to deal with certain forms of special needs, and to acquire the motivation to read books and articles for their own independent professional learning.

Colin mentioned that in the wider school system teachers needed strategies to deal with large classes; that in summer the noise made by fans was a problem, with many teachers having to use microphones; and that in some schools it was acceptable for teachers to outsource marking, using funds from their own private tutoring outside school hours.

I watched Aysha's humanities lesson, which was comparable in every respect to a lesson in an elite school in the UK, although I privately noted some ways in which her method of engaging the class by asking questions could be improved. Then we went back to Avari Towers for mid-morning refreshments and to begin a series of group discussions.

These were held in a room on the floor below the lobby, leading out to the garden. The first was with headteachers, followed by a buffet lunch in Asia Live. While trying to eat, I was interviewed by a reporter from the local edition of the *Herald Tribune*, who had unfortunately lost her voice, which made understanding her questions a laboured process. Next there were three further discussion sessions: with teachers; educational leaders and trainers; and with parents. In fact roles and interests overlapped among the groups, and the issues identified were consistent.

I was interested to note the existence and significance of a Roman Catholic education sector. Taymur later explained that the white band edging the Pakistani flag was to represent minorities. The Ismaili sect also had a prominent role to play in education, the city's Aga Khan University being a major provider of initial (pre-service) and in-service teacher education.

I learnt more about the prevalent tuition culture. Many parents paid for their teenaged children to have tuition after school. The tuition was generally provided by teachers working in school during the day, as a means of supplementing their wages. They would tell classes preparing for examinations, 'If you want to pass, you had better come to my tuition'. The worse the education they provided at school, the more the demand for tuition. This practice attracted great criticism, especially from school management, but they could not really ban it. Even if there was a sure way to do so, they would lose their staff. The system, schools and parents alike, was obsessed with grades, and anything that improved the pass rate was welcomed by schools. Parents saw tuition as a safe and affordable means of getting their children out of the house. The young people themselves welcomed it because it enabled them to meet and interact with members of the opposite sex. So a practice that seemed wholly undesirable in fact brought benefits to all the parties involved.

That afternoon I met Kiran. She stood out among group participants because of her quick-witted, fluent contributions, her energy and self-confidence. She was tall, slim and athletic-looking, with short black hair and big glittery eyes.

Colin had listened to the discussions but had not taken part. Of course he was already familiar with the system and its issues. He supported our intended project and gave his time generously to it, and on that first day I interpreted his manner not as negative but as reserving judgement. Whereas Taymur was the enthusiastic visionary, Colin seemed to cast himself as the cynical realist.

We went to the Commander's house to report progress, over refreshing drinks, and for me to pose with him for photographs of us signing the memorandum of understanding between our organisations. Among the diplomatic pleasantries, the Commander and Taymur both made a big thing of my not having been put off by an incident on Saturday night, while I was in a plane somewhere over Arabia. A bomb had exploded in the town; Captain Sajid had had some direct personal involvement in dealing with the aftermath. Probably he had just finished with those adventures when I met him at the party on Sunday evening. 'But you still came!', they enthused, taking it as a sign of commitment. In fact the truth was more prosaic: I had been in transit and knew nothing about the incident; I hoped my organisation wouldn't get to hear about it either.

Our review of the day's discussions was beginning to identify what professional development my organisation should initially offer. The major unknown factor was whether schools would be willing to pay for it. The problem wasn't just the expense, which would seem high in comparison to local prices, but also the lack of any established tradition of schools investing significantly in the development of their staff.

Then Taymur took me off to a meeting somewhere nearer the city centre, at the headquarters of a significant philanthropic organisation. This reinforced the impression I had gained at the Commander's party of just how important philanthropy was to keeping various aspects of civil society functioning, and how willing some younger entrepreneurs were to support it generously. We had a long discussion, trying to find a point of connection between what we wanted to do and the organisation's current priorities. It was positive but also inconclusive. It would be easier to make an attractive case after we had actually started to achieve something we could point to.

Everything was still blurred with unfamiliarity: I didn't take in names or locations, and that applied to the restaurant where I was entertained to dinner by Taymur, his wife and Colin. It had pleasant eating areas outside and in, and the cuisine was Italian: I enjoyed my choice of grilled fish.

Chapter Three
Contrasts in Sindh

The programme arranged for me on Tuesday morning showed the other side of education in Pakistan. We were to visit two schools run by The Citizens Foundation (TCF), the first being a primary school serving the population of an illegal shanty-town slum which had grown up on an area of mudflats. One of the local TCF managers acted as our guide: I rode in Taymur's car, and he followed the guide's car; Colin was with us. I was keen to learn about TCF at first hand. I knew from my reading that it had something of a global reputation as a really effective charity, running schools mainly in Pakistan in places where the state system just wasn't working.

We were on a stretch of major road, with quite heavy traffic, in a rough-looking area, when the guide indicated we were to stop at the roadside. Taymur broke out in a minor explosion as the guide got out of his car. 'No! He surely can't be expecting me to leave my car here!' The guide made reassuring gestures as we got out, and explained that the cars would be valet parked in the secure compound of the second school we were due to visit, while we would travel in a different vehicle into the shanty. Valet parking was common: I noticed when we went into the city that people seemed quite happy to entrust their cars to complete strangers.

A few seconds later, a very small minibus parked behind us; two men got out to take over the cars, and we stooped and squashed ourselves into its miniature confines. I learnt that TCF operated a fleet of these minibuses. The driver turned off the road into a nondescript wasteland of rubble and debris, towards a great settlement of very crude simple shelters. Moving slowly, he followed one of numerous narrow, rutted muddy tracks cutting through this extraordinary village: a larger vehicle would have had problems. As well as the tracks, the settlement was also cut through by open sewers full of rubbish.

I decided straight away that photography was out of the question, as crassly insulting, so I strained to memorise as much as possible of the experience. My geography teacher's mind whirled with half-comparisons: a medieval village, a pioneer frontier community, a refugee camp… these had their different kinds of organised official framework. The shanty – unplanned, spontaneous, organic – must also have had some internal authority structures and conventions of behaviour.

The guide explained that the shanty housed about 7000 people, including 2000 children; most were Bengalis from Bangladesh. The total population of illegal Bengali immigrants in the surrounding area was now about 700000; they had been arriving by boat since the Bangladesh Liberation War in 1971. The minibus turned tight corners in the maze of narrow tracks, while faces stared in at us. It swayed and lurched its way to a secure-looking wall with gates: we had arrived at the TCF primary school.

It was the start of the school day and children were arriving, well presented in a simple uniform. They had been trained to organise themselves: they sang songs and did a physical exercise routine while forming themselves into rows in the yard. A teacher appeared, the national anthem was sung, she registered each group and sent them into the building.

Getting to that point – present and ready to learn – in itself seemed a minor miracle. 'They live in the conditions of animals', the guide said. Their shelters had no sanitation, nor any clocks. The school kept the same time all the year round: it was not practical to follow the national daylight-saving clock changes. The school had an earth latrine, and a lorry delivered water each day so the children could wash. Illegal power cables trailed around the shanty; TCF had obtained a lien for its school to be on encroached land and had formalised an electrical supply.

The building was two-storey, basic and functional. When children enrolled, their first lesson was to sit on chairs, of which they had no previous experience. Many of the learning resources in the classrooms were made out of recycled rubbish. The school day was organised into two shifts: 8am to 12.30pm, and 12.30 to 5pm. The teachers – all female – were bussed in for their shifts. They were paid less than half as much as teachers in government schools. The principal worked a long day covering both shifts and liaising with the community. Some of the parents wanted their children to stay for both shifts so that they could spend the day in a clean environment.

The shanty economy was based on catching and peeling shrimps. Half of the men were involved in shrimp fishing; the other half lived off family earnings and what the guide described simply as 'illegal activity'. The shrimp peeling (the guide called it 'cleaning' but I can't use that term in relation to such an environment) was wholly the work of women and children – especially children, because their small hands were considered an advantage. The arrival of a shrimp catch could happen at any time of day or night. It would be announced from the mosque loudspeaker and the women and children would come to collect a load to take back to their insanitary shelters for peeling, where the accumulated shrimp waste added to the stench. I made a mental note to be more wary regarding the sourcing of shrimps.

From this income, an impressive proportion of parents were prepared to invest in their children's education, although the sums involved seemed impossibly small. The monthly cost per child to TCF for providing the primary school was 900 rupees: roughly £6.30. The principal authorised scholarships so that parents paid between a minimum of 10 rupees (7p) and a maximum of 200 rupees (£1.40) per month. The upper end of this range equated with the fees charged at the bottom end of the private school sector.

The private school sector was stratified into many layers according to parental budgets. Those at the top were world class. At the bottom was a patchwork of small schools meeting in makeshift premises, including 'front-room schools', kept going by charitable ventures, under-qualified volunteers and small-time entrepreneurs. I wondered why there was such a demand, when the law required the government to provide free education for all children.

As we left the primary school, Colin said, 'What you have seen is several levels above the average government school'. That made me wonder why they were so poor. 'No-one cares. Some of the government schools are ghost schools, where the staff stay on the payroll but none of them bother to turn up for work.'

After seeing the primary school, we squeezed back into the minibus to go to the secondary school. Near the edge of the shanty our way was blocked for a few minutes, which gave me the chance to look a bit longer without staring. I saw more signs of a simple economy in operation: donkeys, and a board with a few provisions on it set up as a shop. A smartly plumaged cock strutted proudly across the goods.

The secondary school campus was a short drive away, the other side of the main road, and connected by a footbridge to the shanty settlement. It was well constructed and reasonably spacious, currently serving 1200 students, and equipped to a basic level. The principal explained that gang warfare was a major issue in the area, which impacted on school attendance. Baluchi was the students' mother tongue (Baluchistan is the province to the west of Sindh, bordered by Iran and Afghanistan): in school, Urdu or English were allowed, and all examinations were taken in Urdu. There were 36 students in each class; their examination results were well above the national average.

We went back into the city for lunch at the TCF headquarters with its chairman. That this had been arranged was proof of how seriously our project was being taken by people in senior positions. Yet during the car ride I reflected on the morning's experiences. Fantastic for my own learning – I felt truly privileged – but what could I or my organisation offer? The barriers of language, culture and social context looked insurmountable. When I weighed what my organisation needed to charge for each day of a consultant's time against what other things that money might buy locally, I couldn't see a way forward.

That morning, the *Herald Tribune* had given our project generous column inches based on the interview I had given the previous day. I had kept emphasising to my voiceless interlocutor, as strongly as I could between mouthfuls of curry and rice, that the project was about partnership, developing the skills and confidence of local people to lead change. Predictably, none of that flavour came through: the news story followed the colonial line, about 'experts' who were going to be flown in to tell people what to do.

Mushtaq, the TCF chairman, welcomed us and introduced his head of human resources. I learnt that TCF was recruiting between 1200 and 1500 teachers each year; turnover was high. There was an annual cycle of professional development, in which a key element was the preparation of 250 master trainers. TCF provided each new entrant with at least 100 hours of pre-service training between March and August; serving teachers were expected to attend 70 to 80 hours of development during June and July; schools conducted staff development days; and there was a one-week Principals' Academy covering school improvement planning, leadership, counselling and community outreach. We discussed how our project might add value to all this activity, in particular exploring possibilities for certification. TCF left the door open for us to come up with proposals.

The meeting and the school visits brought alive for me what I had previously read about the quality of TCF's work. The complexity and sophistication of their operation, which they managed to achieve on a shoestring, contrasted with the inadequacies of the government school sector. Yet I saw the philanthropists' dilemma, and wondered how others saw it. A need arises because the government isn't implementing its own laws and is beset with ineptitude. TCF steps in to fill the gap, as a moral and humanitarian response, but by so doing lets the government off the hook. I could imagine situations where the success of TCF acted as a disincentive to government officials to improve their own sector. Was there any means by which some of that energy and know-how could get the government schools working properly?

After lunch, and for a further contrast, we went to a school run by the Pakistan Navy. Pakistan's armed forces run a lot of schools (and some universities): those led by the army are centrally managed, while the navy schools have local autonomy. The gate guard would have phoned through our arrival: the principal stood outside ready to receive us, and saluted as the car stopped. He was immaculate in a white uniform – dazzling in the sunlight – with shorts, and I recognised Captain Sajid to whom I had been introduced at the Commander's garden party. Was that only two days ago?

Sajid was grey-moustached, near to retirement, and exuded a combination of the wisdom of experience with the physical fitness of his profession. He summed up his approach: 'Whatever you are doing, concentrate on doing your duty within that remit, and do it right; don't criticise others'.

We talked about the professional development needs of the school staff, and Sajid focused straight away on pedagogy. 'Teachers are mainly experts in their subjects: less so in the practical skills of teaching, meeting the needs of individual children, helping young people develop as citizens.'

Most of the campus seemed to be made of gleaming icing sugar. After a general talk in his office, Sajid showed us the Cambridge Wing, named after the UK examination board most popular in Pakistan. All teaching and examinations throughout the school were in English. We saw students in groups of 16 taking 'O'- and 'A'-level courses. Equipment was of a good standard, and the teaching was quite formal and traditional, but with a good level of student interaction: overall, exactly what one might see in an elite English school.

Next we were taken to the Primary Wing, housed in older buildings that had formerly been a barracks. Children were around – it must have been a break time – and as we walked a number of them spoke to Sajid; from his responses it was clear he had a good and kindly relationship with them. A distinctive feature was the large extent of the primary provision: 30 classrooms and 900 pupils.

Another drive took us to the last site on our day of educational tourism. This was the school campus of the Defence Housing Association, where we met the principal and proprietor of the early years and primary school. It was partly a courtesy visit, because the principal was on the board of trustees of Colin's school, but that did not detract from its interest. The principal was talkative.

'In the UK I did private tutoring while becoming a chartered accountant, then in Pakistan I was involved in developing a grammar school over three premises and 2500 students. I had American friends who were starting charter schools and we wanted to bring that to Pakistan. They said we should tie up with government; we chose the army. Then after 9/11 the Americans vanished: the American school is nearly empty.

'My wife's family is in education, and my sister runs a string of schools. My sister-in-law runs an NGO in Punjab concerned with educating 125000 girls. They go into villages, get premises and teach girls up to class six. The level of illiteracy is appalling: they have 100 support staff who can't sign their name and can't count. The government hasn't prioritised education; the government schools failed because the staff don't attend.'

He explained that he took children from age 2 up to 8, then they went next door to the main school. He started with 38 children; now he had 400. It was open admission but he interviewed parents to check whether the child had any special needs. He followed the British curriculum.

'In the lower classes we have eight children in a group, that increases to an average class size of ten: so currently we have 45 teachers. The biggest problem is finding good teachers. We hire girls with "A" levels, deploy them as teaching aides attached to a senior teacher for a year, and then they become teachers. We rotate all the staff through classes and age groups. We also run an internship programme to offer girls a taste of teaching.'

The principal emphasised the need for teacher training, offered at a reasonable price. All the while he was walking us through the premises, which were empty because classes had finished for the day. The floor was very shiny – I was conscious of taking care not to slip – and the style of building slightly unusual. 'Purpose-built schools can be very expensive; it's better to adapt empty spaces. We've done that here', he explained.

Taymur took me to a shopping mall, in case I wanted to buy things to take home. I didn't, which I sensed put him out a little, because this had been his plan for filling in time before we reported back to the Commander. On my first few business trips abroad in 2007, when it was all a major, surprising adventure, I had bought souvenirs. It was a deeply ingrained 'holiday' behaviour, and showed that I thought of people at home while I was away. Pretty soon I got the message that this useless tat was unwelcome. That was probably just as well: this was my twentieth such trip, and shelves and cupboards would have been getting a bit crowded if I hadn't broken the habit. Now I hoped to spend as little as possible. Superficially this mall could have been anywhere, with its car park and modern building; actually, as Taymur was keen to point out, I could see that the range of goods was wide and prices low by Western standards. The mall was full of shoppers going about their business in groups and families, carrying bags. We stuck out a bit in our suits, and set off again soon.

The meeting with the Commander was to take stock of how we had got on in our liaisons and to plan the next steps. Taymur does not touch alcohol, but I accepted some welcome refreshment. We agreed we needed to start in a small way to establish our presence and to test the market. We planned to offer two short courses at the end of the spring term – one in school leadership, and one in pedagogy and assessment – and to repeat this offering in the three major cities of Pakistan. After this business planning was concluded, some of the other trustees of the charity set up for our project arrived and joined us in less formal conversation.

Taymur had arranged dinner at another restaurant he wanted me to see, again with his wife and Colin. We drove into town amid a bustle of people and swaying vehicles. Near the restaurant a parking valet took over the car; I was led to a modern building, past an open-sided kitchen where charcoal blazed on open grills, up several flights of stairs and out on to the rooftop. As we sat in the dark at a wooden table, my hosts explained that this was a barbecue restaurant set up by a couple of Afghan brothers. Taymur pronounced 'Afghan' and 'Afghanistan' differently from me – I don't think I could transliterate it. After a few failed attempts to understand, during which he must have thought I wasn't much of a geography teacher, he said, 'That's the country next to us', and I finally twigged. He admired them. 'They came here with just the shirts on their backs.' Normally lamb would be the popular choice, but the waiter explained there were no lambs left because of the feasting for Eid al-Adha the previous week. We had chicken kebabs instead, with flatbreads.

On Wednesday 1st December, Taymur collected me from Avari Towers at 9am and led me to our transport for the day: a Pakistan Navy minibus. There I met a youngish, pleasant and deceptively gentle captain who held a senior position in the special forces, and three of his men, who were going to look after us on our visit to Thatta. Colin was in the minibus also, as well as a great box of ice cubes with bottles of Coke and lemonade poking out of it. The fact that I don't like either was not an issue, as I was worried about how many hours I would be spending without access to a toilet. Taymur and Colin were casually dressed and in holiday mood. I had given thought to what clothes to pack for this excursion. A Pakistani colleague in my office in London (speaking before the floods had subsided) had suggested Wellingtons, but I had chosen a comfortable cream linen suit, the weight and texture of pyjamas. It was the right choice: the previous evening Taymur, as a caring host, had warned about dust and dirt, and I had reassured him that it was already grubby with the red earth of South Sudan.

On the outskirts of town, we passed haulage yards where great lorries were parked in front of crude sheds filled with piles of rocks and stacks of poles. The lorries were highly decorated but old and battered. Then the view settled into a straight tarmac road, edged with sandy dust, brown grass, low scrubby bushes and distant white buildings of one or two storeys. We passed through small settlements which had a scatter of open-fronted shops, and in one case a more developed centre with properly built shops and mature trees under whose shade people and donkey carts milled about. A row of market stalls made out of lashed poles seemed to be trading busily.

I noticed that we always had clear passage through: one look at our vehicle and its occupants seemed enough to incline other road users to get out of the way. About 27 kilometres out of Karachi, the driver turned left on to a dirt track which led to the Chaukundi Tombs. I hadn't been expecting any visits to ancient monuments to feature in this trip, and passed the next 40 minutes in a state of awe and wonder. We got out of the minibus into searing sunlight, on ground slightly higher than the surrounding plain: a terrain of sand and rocks, covered in ruins at different stages of dilapidation. Some were reduced to remains of walls nearly at ground level, while at the other extreme some seemed from 100 metres away to be pretty much intact.

There must have been a time when ancient monuments in England were just as accessible and unstaffed. I remember being taken to Stonehenge as a small boy and being free to poke about at will. At the Chaukundi Tombs I was disorientated by the lack of staff, turnstile, entry fee, board with a map showing 'you are here', guidebook and shop. The captain led the way to the most intact and interesting ruins: a seemingly never-ending collection of mausolea of the rich and powerful of the 16th and 17th centuries.

One of the most impressive buildings was helpfully labelled as the tomb of Meerza Isa Khan Tarkhan, 1644 AD. It was a massive, rectangular two-storey temple-like structure, with walls of intricately carved stone arches, topped with a large metal-covered hemisphere. Nearby, another of the better-preserved buildings was attached to an enormous walled courtyard. There were also several octagonal structures with inner and outer walls, the inner part topped by a round dome made cleverly of bricks that rose to a point. The external surfaces of all the buildings were now largely weathered, stone or brick, but here and there clung patches of vivid fluorescent turquoise, and tiles surfaced with intricate blue and white patterns. When these buildings were in their original, complete state, they must have been mind-blowing.

Inside one of these structures I saw a row of stone tombs with deep-relief carved surfaces, and more extensive remnants of lapis lazuli-glazed tiles on walls and floor. Outside, large ants seemed to be enjoying the warmth of the paving stones, and our escorts hung around waiting for us to finish.

Back in the minibus, the terrain changed as we got nearer to Thatta: more vegetation and more water. Conversation turned to the severity of the recent floods. Often the captain pointed to a feature several metres off the ground, saying that it had been underwater a few weeks ago. This area was in the lower reaches of the Indus, somewhat upstream of its vast delta, but the channel was already much braided and spread itself across a great expanse of floodplain. Roads and major tracks were built on embankments, where lines of crude shelters gave a small indication of the conditions that prevailed before the flood subsided. The lower ground between the embankments was still extensively flooded but not to great depth; fields looked like lakes and reservoirs.

Thatta sits at a junction in the highway, where the major branch heads north-east to Hyderabad. Some kilometres short of the town, the driver turned on to a track to a patch of higher ground where the navy – which had a base nearby – had set up its flood relief camp. The UK news coverage of the floods had included quite a few references to chaos and suffering in some of the camps set up by the aid agencies. The navy personnel who showed us round were keen to emphasise the contrasting orderliness of their own operation, and I was deeply impressed and inspired by the experience.

Rows of khaki tents were pitched in immaculate lines, and each 'street' had been given a name board and each tent a number, so that their occupants had the dignity of an address. A basic post office had been set up. The guide pointed out clinics, then said, 'You will want to see the school'. We were taken into a tent where about 40 children were sitting on carpets spread on the floor. Volunteers with rudimentary resources were entertaining them with the nearest equivalent they could make to the experience of a village primary school. The children were actively engaged, smiling, and delighted to receive visitors.

The camp was a vivid illustration of how places – physical sites and locations – are turned into spaces that have meanings and purposes for those who use them, as well as conveying positive or negative connotations. It is deeply embedded in human culture to create different kinds of spaces for living, for social eating and entertaining, for trading, for religious contemplation and for learning. Each kind of space – home, restaurant, shop, mosque, schoolhouse – conveys its own rules of behaviour, so people know what to do in order to co-operate effectively as a community. I had seen one version of this process at work in the shanty town on the Karachi mudflats. Here in the camp was a contrasting version.

From the camp we were driven to a field nearby, where the minibus parked and the captain led us to a couple of rows of partially completed huts. He explained that these were being built by navy personnel to provide transitional residences for the occupants of the tents, as a step towards normality. We walked up to them; I saw several dozen at different stages of completion. About the size of large beach huts, they were being made from rough coppice poles covered with sheets of what looked like woven reeds. Basic accommodation, but a step up from a tent, which I imagined would have a positive psychological impact on the people displaced by the flood. A great swarm of hornets was taking an interest in the construction. I couldn't remember having seen them in the wild before. These were enormous, the colour of milk chocolate and turmeric.

Next we were driven to the navy's local headquarters base so that we could have lunch and use the facilities. It was a single-storey building, with a central mess area bordered by smaller rooms. The buffet lunch offered meat curry, curds, white rice and doughy flatbreads, and while it was welcome I was anxious about the effects of this fare, devoid of vegetables or fibre. It was very pleasant to benefit from the navy's hospitality: the officer in charge was courteous and welcoming. I was aware, however, that we were a bit of a nuisance he could have done without: he seemed to be both frenetically busy and dog-tired. A senior officer was coming the next day to preside over an event and to review the progress of various projects; many matters of detail had to be organised and polished. The flood relief work had come on top of the ongoing business of fighting terrorists. The officer had his feet up on a settee while he refined document after document on his laptop; I saw micro-sleeps happening between keystrokes. I commented on how busy he was and apologised for the timing of our visit. I was mortified when I realised he had misunderstood me: he thought at first I was chastising him for being a poor host and I had to reassure him. It was a relief to get back into the minibus.

We went on a short way further to visit Thatta before starting the return journey. I retain only the most hazy impressions of that visit. This was right at the end of an assignment which, despite its intrinsic interest and the kindness of my hosts, I had found stressful and exhausting: I must have been half-asleep at that stage. It was only a token visit, not taking in the historic tourist attractions that I read about subsequently. They wanted to show me how high the waters had risen. We parked near a bridge over the road, and walked back to look at painted markings on its side that recorded the height of the recent, and earlier, floods. The newly added mark was about level with the top of the arch through which the traffic flowed. Seeing that brought home to me the astonishing amount of water the district had had to cope with. Near where the minibus was parked was a kiosk selling cold drinks. Taymur, Colin and the drivers excitedly went to replenish their stock of fizzy bottles: they seemed surprised that I didn't want any. I didn't explain why.

When I first heard about the possibility of this trip, Thatta for me had been an unremarkable dot on a small-scale atlas map. Now, on location, I saw just the patchy glimpses I have described. Later I learnt that Thatta had been the medieval capital of Sindh, and the ruling base of three successive dynasties. The city itself has several ancient mosques which are popular tourist attractions, and the surrounding wetlands are significant for wildlife tourism. A short way outside the city is the Makli Necropolis: one of the largest burial sites in the world, containing up to a million graves, including many of 16th-century architectural interest. Although I didn't go there, I visualise it as a larger version of the Chaukundi Tombs we had visited.

The schedule, which the navy driver kept to the minute, got me back to Avari at 3pm for 12 hours of free time. Transport to the airport was arranged for 3am on Thursday; my flight via Oman landed at Heathrow at 5.40pm. There was plenty to think about, quite apart from the immediate worry of how to have a nap without sleeping through the time I needed to check out. The trip had been a very full and deeply enriching familiarisation – a massive learning experience. I was delighted to have established links with people who were pleasant to work with, and who were committed to a long-term partnership project. The limitations were also clear: the kind of support my organisation could provide was culturally irrelevant and financially inaccessible to all but a small, elite segment of the Pakistani education system, so any plans would need to include ways for benefits to permeate more widely. I wasn't sure the people in my own organisation who made rules and managed money would show the patience and flexibility that the project would need.

There was another positive that outweighed those concerns and gave me a sense of optimism and well-being. There were no third parties controlling what was done and how. No box-ticking, bullying project management company, no commissioning agency with its own predetermined agenda. My colleagues and I could co-operate with Taymur and his associates as professional educators, experimenting creatively to solve problems and work towards something worthwhile. Ownership is energising.

Chapter Four
Mexico via Cyprus: a Prospect and a Mooring

The morning after I returned from Karachi, Friday 3rd December 2010, I had a meeting with Malcolm to talk about a project in Mexico. He was a great bear of a man: heavy, big-featured and hot-tempered, full of pent-up energy and always about to explode. Ages before – at least eight months previously – I had been told by my then head of department to meet and deal with a delegation of Mexicans who wanted to set up a school leadership centre. That was as far as the briefing went. When I met them I found that the group was of about eight men, most of whom had limited English. Malcolm was in charge and acted as interpreter. He spoke English with an accent and intonation which led me to assume, in that first meeting, that he also was Mexican.

I was excited about what they wanted to do and keen to get involved. Potentially this was a partnership project extending over a period, starting with our organisation advising and then leading into a supportive relationship. This was exactly what the department, and I personally, needed to add to our track records: the truth of the matter was that this would be a new step. I bluffed my sales pitch with a confident and authoritative tone, hoping no-one would think to ask, 'Give us an example of how you have worked in this way before'. No-one did. The deal was agreed in principle, with the schedule for delivery left a bit uncertain; then silence fell for many months, as so often happened.

Quite a while after that first meeting, I learnt that another department in my organisation had been working on a curriculum-development and standard-setting project for the national government of Mexico, which Malcolm had brokered, and which had made good progress. I didn't see any particular need to liaise with that team – departments were different worlds and Malcolm cast himself firmly in the role of gatekeeper. Later, he linked us into some of the publications that had arisen from that work.

'Our' project was a separate venture, which Malcolm had brokered with the state of Nayarit and a university, and he kept those dealings to himself. Later still, I think when we were in Mexico, I realised Malcolm was not Mexican: he merely lived there. He was European – I didn't get any clearer than that because he became absorbed in describing his formative years and early career in France. Then, months after that, it finally dawned on me that he was a colleague, on the payroll of the organisation I worked for. He must have thought some elements in my original sales pitch pretty strange, perhaps putting that down to the differences between departments.

On that December morning he apologised for the delay, referring vaguely to difficulties in getting various parties lined up in agreement, and asked whether my original proposal was still valid, which of course it was. 'Phew!', he exclaimed with dramatic relief. We agreed to aim for the fieldwork to happen in February, and he set out a structure for briefing and preparation which was impressively business-like.

My interpretation of the project was that its first phase would involve management consultancy, of the form I styled somewhat loosely as a 'gateway consultancy'. The purpose of this would be to appraise the starting position, establish how to move forward, and clarify the first set of practical actions that needed to be taken by our organisation and the client to bring partnership working into operation. After that, there would be a second phase lasting 18 months, which I called a 'critical friendship support package'. We would advise, assist and mentor our partners as they set up the new venture, and our help would taper off as they found their feet.

I judged that the work would be done best by a team of two people, so needed to decide which of my colleagues to involve. If the project took off, we would be advising on strands of activity for the client that would involve substantial financial risk. Questions could be raised at any stage regarding the competence of the consultants. I decided it would be wise for both team members to have an MBA degree among their credentials, and a track record of practical as well as academic accomplishments. So I offered the second position to Liz, as the only other member of the department I could think of who met those criteria. I had met her about ten years previously at a university in the East Midlands where I had completed doctoral studies, and where I subsequently worked on a project in which Liz was a colleague. She had moved south and joined our organisation a few years ago.

I met Malcolm again on Monday, and then again with Liz on Wednesday 8th December. Malcolm brought his assistant, Felix – who had been with the group I had met originally – and started a process of serious and thorough briefing about the project. It is no wonder that I was confused about who Malcolm really was. He introduced himself as the director of an organisation called the Institute for Education Research and Development, based in the state of Nayarit and serving Mexico's western region. This institute, he explained, was the outcome of co-operation between the federal government, state government, state university and two state ministries of education: one covering the 5 to 15 age group ('basic education'), and the other responsible for upper secondary education (15 to 18).

The Centre for Education Leadership that we were to help to establish would be part of his institute. Malcolm mentioned his other projects: the one I had already heard about, setting educational standards in primary and secondary schools for the federal government; and another to propose to the state of Nayarit a generic curriculum for the upper secondary phase. Dates were finalised: our trip would be from the 12th to the 20th of February.

Liz and I read the background papers that Malcolm had provided, and shared initial thoughts about how we would do the work and how we would best complement each other's contributions. That was not as simple or obvious as might be supposed, because of the creative problem-solving element of the work, and the application of personal insight and judgement. Like having two cooks in the kitchen, or two artists working on the same canvas, producing a coherent end product of which we could both feel ownership required a lot of communication. That took us up to the Christmas break, after which I went to Cyprus to attend a conference.

*****

This particular conference was held annually in early January by the International Congress for School Effectiveness and Improvement (ICSEI), which aimed to bring together academics, policy advisers and practitioners. So it was not stuffily theoretical: I never had any problem getting papers accepted. Many of the participants attended once every few years, and some every year, so the event had developed a bit of a family feel.

My first attendance had been at a significant point for me. In December 2000, after 20 years in local government, I had to walk away from a position as director of education into an uncertain, alien, impoverished phase of home-based freelancing while I reinvented myself. I was not exactly in disgrace, but doors that I had hoped might open remained firmly shut. Some professional acquaintances were kind and helpful. One, James, ran a school leadership centre attached to a university. I had been working with him in my director role, and it had been arranged that I would give a paper in a symposium session he was running at the ICSEI in Toronto in January 2001. That arrangement stood, and James introduced me as a 'consultant', although at that moment I did not know where my next earned crust would be coming from. It had been a harsh winter even by Toronto standards – an oddly chosen mid-winter venue – but the warmth and positivity of the people I was with provided a boost I desperately needed at that moment.

James's organisation became one of my sources of consultancy work, and as a member of its delegation I presented papers at ICSEI 2002 in Copenhagen and in Rotterdam in 2004. Then, after a break, I attended the Kuala Lumpur meeting in 2010, and now in Cyprus in 2011. I was reflectively conscious of my life's journey over the preceding ten years, which put this trip at the very borderline between business and personal. ICSEI was one of my moorings: a home port to return to from time to time, and an element of my identity. In addition to that, and the fact that I had not previously visited Cyprus, I had two specific motivations for wanting to attend the conference this year. I was completing work on a book – my first book, which mattered tremendously to me – and my conference paper was a draft of the final chapter, offering an opportunity to get some feedback and to advertise the work. The second attraction was the opportunity to meet up with an acquaintance called Christiana.

I set off from Heathrow at 9.45am on Monday 3rd January for the flight to Larnaca, wearing a three-piece suit in green tweed, with an outer shooting coat and cap in matching fabric. That choice combined practicality and comfort with my chosen level of formality, and conveyed archetypal Britishness. When I came out of the terminal at Larnaca I was surprised to be greeted by heavy showers. I shouldn't have been: I remembered instantly a Welsh geography teacher who used to chant rote-learning snippets in a staccato, sing-song voice. 'Hot dry summers, warm wet winters' was his summary of the Mediterranean climate.

The conference venue was a hotel complex at Limassol, a 75-kilometre taxi ride along the south coast. When I checked in, I was astonished to find (having only paid the standard inclusive conference fee) that I had been allocated an enormous suite overlooking the sea. Apparently this was simply the result of having booked early. It was the kind of suite that might have been saved for a VIP keynote speaker. I kept getting lost in it: it took a while to get my bearings.

A lot of delegates at conferences go as part of a friendship group or work team, or are so well known and networked that they never lack company and conversation. Then there is the scatter of loners, who sit apart earnestly studying their papers. I lack easy sociability – that's putting it mildly – and have never been able to enter a roomful of people already engrossed in their own groups and conversations and force my way in, unless they include people I know well. So on this occasion I was resigned to being one of the loners for most of the time.

On the other hand, I wasn't a stranger and a number of people were happy to greet me. A guy from Cambridge told me I was looking very smart. 'Raphael always looks smart!', riposted his colleague John, a distinguished person who had been kind to me in my wilderness phase, generously inviting me to co-author a pamphlet with him. My previous head of department, who had returned to her native

New Zealand, was there, and keen to catch up briefly. Some months previously my colleague Gordon, with whom I had worked recently in Dammam, had edited a book and had asked me to write one of its chapters. The author of one of the other chapters was at the conference; I introduced myself. He enthused about the book and about Gordon: that was the extent of his interest. A woman of Cypriot appearance, and wearing an outfit that looked like a uniform, was handing cups to people. I asked if I might have a black tea; amused, she informed me she was a delegate.

The sun had come out and I strolled on my own on the beach. On a small wooden jetty a young man was looking at the glittering waves; he turned and asked me in accented English if I was attending the conference. He told me it was his first time; he was on his own; he was looking forward to learning a lot from the sessions. I spoke encouragingly about the friendliness of the organisation and the range of benefits he could hope to gain, which seemed to reassure him. For some minutes after that conversation I felt a glow of satisfaction at having had the opportunity, in a small way, to pass on a favour.

In the times between the sessions I had planned to attend, I worked on the draft of my book. Titled *Research Engagement for School Development*, it was based on my work with school principals who use research, and encourage their teachers to use research, as a way to promote a culture of learning and reflection in their schools. The academic publishers handling it were rigorous, and had sent drafts to several expert readers for critical comments, in response to which I needed to make numerous small adjustments and clarifications. Which of course I did, being anxious to see the book in print and on shelves, but not always with enthusiasm, because I did not want to lose the personal voice and story the book incorporated. I felt that for quite a while, the interactions with the publisher had by many small nudges made the book more formal, conventional and undistinctive. Now, if I did everything these external critics seemed to want, then I would be writing the book they would write rather than my own.

My presentation went well. It is always pot luck how papers are grouped at conferences. On this occasion, mine was grouped with others sufficiently related to bring together a bunch of people able to have a proper debate about the subject. One of the other presenters subsequently wrote a supportive jacket blurb for my book.

I had arranged to meet up with Christiana at the hotel: she would come in the morning, we would talk and then have lunch together. I had met her about five years previously; she was not employed by my organisation, but by a small professional body of which I was a trustee. She came from Cyprus to take up a middle management position, under slightly difficult top management. My role occasioned us to interact quite a bit. I was impressed by her capabilities and also found her attractive in every way. For her part, I am wary of ascribing emotions, but I believe the core of her regard was professional respect for me (way beyond what I merited); she wanted very much to impress me with her intellect and skills, and to pick my brains. Our working interactions were always productive; beyond that we danced around each other with some ups and downs.

After a couple of years she became frustrated with changes her manager had introduced and she left without a job to go to. On her last day, she let me buy her lunch at Pescatori, an Italian restaurant on London's Charlotte Street. Subsequently, she briefly held a job in a college (as I discovered by seeing an article she had written in that capacity); later I heard that she had returned to her family home in Cyprus. Then, perhaps a year later, she appeared at my office door.

She had taken pains to keep the visit a surprise, getting one of her former colleagues to check that I was around. She wanted to explore the possibilities for developing some business in Cyprus for my team. Over a modest lunch in the senior common room I outlined what that would involve and gave the same briefing as I would to any potential international associate. We agreed to keep in touch by e-mail and I sent some further information. Some months passed with no news; when I followed up she wrote saying she had been ill and was awaiting surgery for cancer. After I had already enrolled for the conference, and wary of giving any impression of stalking, I wrote saying I was visiting, and the meeting was arranged.

She arrived at a time when all of the social areas were crowded and noisy, so I suggested it would be most practical if we talked in my suite. She did not hesitate, which I took as an indication of trust established. There was nothing remotely creepy about the ambience: the sitting room in my suite was just like a hotel lounge. We sat at opposite ends of a large sofa turned towards each other. The dark scar of Christiana's recent surgery ran from the base of her neck, across the collarbone and onwards, disappearing out of sight. She updated me on stuff going on in her life: issues and indecisions about future career direction. After an hour or so we agreed that it was time for lunch. We stood and she permitted me to hug her gently for the first time, which as we both knew, was also the last time. I didn't rush the process, enjoying the feel of her shoulder bones and her responding pressure on mine.

We had chosen to go down to the restaurant early, before it got busy: it was virtually empty. After placing our orders, Christiana wanted water. There were bottles of still and sparkling in an ice bucket but no staff around, so I performed the service, copying the flourish, mannerisms and napkin manoeuvres that a waiter would use. That brought a member of staff pretty quickly, saying, 'That's our job'. 'But you do it very well', she acknowledged, and implying that I might want to join her team, she added, 'So we start at six in the morning!'

Over lunch we talked about Cyprus. I wanted to get the local view on the breakaway northern part of the country. 'We call it the occupied territory', she said. I couldn't get my mind around how an illegal invasion could be left as it was for 35 years without the international community being bothered to do anything about it, beyond peacekeeping along the ceasefire line. Christiana raised again the possibility of her undertaking some local agency for my organisation, but I sensed her heart wasn't in it any more: she had some other direction in mind. I pointed out that I would be turning 60 that summer, and that no-one else in my organisation would lift a finger to help her. After lunch I escorted her down to the car park: she had borrowed her father's car, in which she drove out of my life but not out of my thoughts.

*****

Back in London, I refocused my attention on the Mexican project. On 1st February Malcolm came to see Liz and me to start a final series of briefings before we set off for Mexico. He met us again on the 2nd, and again on the 9th. As always he was accompanied by his assistant, Felix. I never quite understood Felix's exact role or status. He was petit, with elfin features and an unassuming manner. For the most part he did not join our meeting but sat at the conference table outside. If I said anything to him, such as, 'Are you OK there?', he would reply only with a beatific smile: I wondered if perhaps he knew little English.

While talking informally, Malcolm conveyed his solidarity with Mexico. Around that time, the BBC's *Top Gear* programme had got into trouble (a frequent occurrence) for making offensive remarks about Mexicans and Mexico. I can't remember how and by whom the matter was raised, but Malcolm boiled with indignation. Once triggered, it grew, like a poked wasps' nest or an active volcano. He said that they were racists, among other things, as he flushed and emoted.

Malcolm's professional briefing was structured and thorough. He gave out a programme covering several sheets, itemising everything that was going to happen: who we would be meeting, when and where, with exact timings. It was impressive, or, to be more accurate, I was impressionable: I believed all this was going to happen just as it was set out. Malcolm advised on temperatures and what to wear for the weather, and informed us that because appetite and digestion were affected by altitude and the thinness of the air, lunch was the main meal of the day. He made a point of explaining that when we changed flights at Houston, we should walk straight through and not collect our baggage, which would be transferred automatically. He told us to use US dollars to buy our pesos when we arrived at Guadalajara. To get clearance to travel I needed the precise address of the hotel we would be using in Tepic: Felix wrote it in my pad in tiny, beautifully neat letters.

Malcolm also told us more about the local culture, the local educational conditions and the severity of the problems which would need to be overcome. I was interested and keen, not least because this would be my first trip to a Latin American country, and my first consultancy assignment in the Americas. I had been to conferences in the USA and Canada, but this was a massive leap forward.

Liz and I shared a clear enough vision of what we wanted to achieve. She had been a founding team member of a leadership centre at the university where we met. I had been one of a team helping James to build up his leadership centre in Kent. Our current workplace was also a large and globally prestigious example of the same sort of thing: of course we had thorough knowledge of how it worked. So we knew what we were doing, and we had both worked in countries with a range of different cultures. Confident as well as excited, perhaps I should have been more worried by some of the things Malcolm was telling us.

Malcolm's passion for setting up a leadership centre reflected his perception of need. 'Leadership and development and a co-operative spirit are absent in Mexico', he said, 'It is individualised participation and reward. Teachers have no professional integrity, because teaching posts are bought and sold through the union. There are no permanent structures: everything depends on individuals'. The union's top officials were enmeshed into government: no-one would stand up to them.

He explained that the problems in the basic education phase were greater than in upper secondary (for ages 15 to 18), and that upper secondary was a mess because several different agencies – including some universities – were involved in running schools. There was no culture of co-operation among these different sectors. The leadership centre we were helping to establish would officially start off as a support for the upper secondary schools, but it was part of Malcolm's plans that the centre should bring about much wider change. His plans covered improvements in all phases and sectors, not only to schools but in how schools could support the rural economy. He was working with OECD (the UN's Organisation for Economic Co-operation and Development) and national government officials, and all his projects depended on better leadership development. He gave the impression that the agencies he liaised with were committed to this vision.

Yet, as it transpired, there was a randomness to how things happened. The money for the new centre could have been held either by the State Ministry of Education, or by Nayarit State University. Malcolm related that, at a particular meeting, it so happened that the minister had been absent but the rector of the university had been present, so the funds went to the university. It also became a given that the university would physically host the centre even though it could easily have been established in independent premises.

Malcolm said that he would not be continuing as director of the Institute for Education Research and Development. He would step back to give arm's-length advice and would base himself in the national Ministry of Education in Mexico City. His place would be taken by a new director, who had already been chosen. His replacement, Pablo, currently worked for the university, being responsible for the upper secondary schools that the university managed. It seemed strange to me that, in one fell swoop, the university had been allowed to take control of the proposed centre's funding, premises and management, but Malcolm didn't invite my opinion on the matter. It was also starting to become clearer that Malcolm's institute, of which the leadership centre was to form a part, was still pretty much just at conceptual stage rather than a functioning reality.

Malcolm explained that both formal and informal processes were important in Mexican culture, so, for example, our programme had to include a press conference. 'You must be nice to people, and nice about people', he advised. 'Pablo and I will guide you as to who you can trust.' He told a story about how someone had come to him and made criticisms about the university rector, who was recently appointed and lacked relevant experience, encouraging Malcolm to voice his agreement. Malcolm had avoided the trap, saying, 'Give him time', and had discovered that this person was the rector's friend, sent to test him out.

The day before our flight, Friday 11th February 2011, I was reading the *Times Educational Supplement* as I did every week. It carried an article (p. 19) about Mexico headed, 'Why won't these teachers apply for pay rises?' The article, drawing on material published by the Mexican Ministry of Education, reported that in Mexico seven out of ten teachers were refusing the chance to be evaluated for pay rises ranging from 20% to 150%. The evaluations, which had been recommended by OECD, assessed each teacher's training history, courses attended, classroom performance and student outcomes. Out of a possible score of 20, some teachers holding doctorate or masters degrees scored only between one and four. On the other hand, among those who opted to be evaluated were nearly 4000 uncertified teachers (with only primary or secondary schooling) who scored well enough to receive salary increases.

The article noted the problem of the teachers' union controlling and selling appointments, so that able entrants had to pay to get a job. That reminded me of Graham Greene's comment in *The Lawless Roads* on the difficulties of establishing schools in Mexico: 'The teachers when appointed usually formed a union, and controlled the school without reference to the owner'.

Finally, the article reported that neither the government nor state administrators knew how many teachers were on the payroll, and some checks had unearthed thousands of people being paid as teachers who in fact never turned up for work. This reminded me of the 'ghost schools' I had heard about in Karachi. The author of the article thought that this might explain why so few wanted to draw attention to themselves by applying for the pay rises. So, this was the context in which we were to advise on establishing an education leadership centre.

Liz and I set off for Mexico on Saturday 12th February 2011. The first leg, the flight to Houston, passed with the expected level of tedium. I had with me Malcolm's extremely detailed written instructions for the transfer. He had stressed that baggage should be checked straight through, and had given directions that showed just how accustomed he was to the journey. 'Once you have cleared immigration and gone through customs in Houston, you go out of the doors just beyond the little podium manned by customs officials and turn sharp right and go up the escalator at the end of the building. Do not put your hand luggage on the conveyor belt before proceeding to the escalator. Upstairs is another security check, and once through, turn left if the on-going flight is from Terminal E...'

Predictably, in the dazed disorientation that descends when coming off a flight, none of that careful guidance signified. Staff told us firmly that we would have to collect our baggage for the transfer. After a long and confusing diversion through the baggage hall, another member of staff told us our luggage would be transferred automatically. Now, very short of time, we found and joined the queue for the immigration formalities. Our flight was called and passengers told to hurry up or get left behind, but the official seemed determined to become even slower and more thorough. Finally, while I exuded the maximum possible air of impatience, eventually and with apparent reluctance he let us through. We walked briskly, trotted and finally ran to the sound of 'The gate is now closing', gasping and panting on board just before the door was slammed.

After landing, we went to the foreign exchange service and, as advised, used dollars to buy pesos. In my case, $50 bought 493 of them.

The transaction time was recorded as 8.55pm, so we must have landed ahead of the scheduled time which was 9.05pm. The currency was really 'just in case' money: I hoped that our client and host would pay for all the basics we needed to do our job. That was my normal experience: it made life easier, especially regarding accounting transactions back at the office.

That general principle was highlighted when we checked into the hotel. When the subject of money arose, I said that whoever had made the booking would settle the account. That wasn't what the receptionist was expecting, but fortunately she agreed that it could be sorted out in the morning when Malcolm came to collect us.

I had developed a strong view that neither I nor members of my team should have to use our personal credit cards to settle significant hotel bills when travelling on business. Normally the client covered these costs and used local knowledge to select the accommodation, so it was much simpler for them to pay the hotel directly and to maintain that local commercial relationship, rather than for the cost to be added to our invoice, which would mean adding a standard percentage of administrative on-costs. On the rare occasions when that didn't apply, our office could pay for the accommodation at the same time as buying the flights. So I felt it was sloppy, and I felt ill-used, to have to spend my personal credit and go through the lengthy and uncertain procedure of claiming it back, which only ever covered the original spend, not the interest paid on it while waiting. Apart from being worried about all the things which could go wrong when entrusting a card to a foreign system, I had once actually sustained a loss which, despite all due effort, I could not recover when a hotel in Yemen double-charged me. I was not financially comfortable in those days: staying solvent was a monthly balancing act, and I resented having to act as banker to the organisation I worked for.

It was difficult to tell the age of the hotel. It appeared to be a fairly modern concrete tower block, but incorporated older styling, including ceilings of vaulted bricks, left in their natural colour. Courtyard areas were filled with subtropical vegetation. My room was enormous, but had a tired, slightly stale feel to it. There were no tea-making facilities: always the first thing I look for. Being an airport hotel, breakfast service started early; Liz and I agreed an early time in order to collect our thoughts before Malcolm appeared. He came a little after 10am, and settled the hotel bill. He looked a bit surprised about that, but it established a pattern, and as events turned out I had reason to be glad that I had stuck to that position. Then he took us out to a minibus, with driver, for our scenic ride to Tepic.

Guadalajara's international airport is to the south of the city, which we would need to pass through on our route north-westwards. Guadalajara is the capital of the state of Jalisco, and according to my guidebook it had, until about 40 years earlier, been a quiet provincial town. Then a rapid phase of industrialisation had occurred, through which it had grown to become Mexico's second city.

Leaving the airport we joined an expressway which seemed at first to have at least eight lanes heading north, before it resolved itself into a four-lane carriageway. The views and environment were not particularly photogenic or distinctive, and could have belonged to the motorway approach to an airport in any number of countries. But this was my arrival in Mexico, so I stared eagerly at everything and snapped a collection of blurred, badly composed photos, wanting to remember these first impressions.

Those impressions included movement, of course: the pace seemed pretty brisk after a long period of sitting in aeroplanes and in the hotel. Then bright sun: high and casting short shadows despite it only being mid-morning. The traffic included enormous lorries of American design, with complicated cabs the size of double-decker buses. There were many trees and bushes despite the parched state of the ground, and a muddle of building development. Among a patchwork of industrial and commercial buildings were many sites where buildings were either under construction or being demolished: it was hard to tell the difference. There was also a distinctive pattern of street furniture which seemed to combine a forest of vertical poles, supporting cables, signs and lights, with horizontal metal gantries. The latter included, at frequent intervals, enormous metal footbridges spanning the carriageway, approached by long zig-zag ramps.

Between all that street furniture, vistas began to open up, of scrubby vegetation: tall yellow ochre grass and scattered small trees and shrubs, with townscapes beyond. From a distance, their pink and white patterns gave a pleasant impression: picturesque clusters of buildings with European-style tiled roofs. Nearer to, the reality was somewhat grimmer. The buildings were all single-storey with flat roofs, ranging in size from garden shed to small garage, crammed together and falling to pieces. The pink was the colour of the blocks of local building material. We passed what was probably a schoolyard: a rectangle of sand, a wonky goal net, a dozen children playing. Where these residential developments came close to the road I could see that the roofs were made of corrugated iron, and that some of the walls had been painted over with lime or with roughly crafted murals.

On our four-lane carriageway, a gantry of signs allocated lanes to destinations: we were heading to Guadalajara Centro. Straight away more substantial and more industrialised urban development came into view, still densely packed, with an unmistakable McDonald's logo poking up from its midst. Nearer the city centre we drove along a tree-lined boulevard, which had cycle tracks. Great clusters of cyclists waited in bright sunshine for the lights to change, of all ages but all wearing baseball caps and T-shirts. Our route through the city centre involved manoeuvring under a raised carriageway, which, with the heat and congestion, reminded me of Bangkok. This district had a smart modern look. One commercial complex, surrounded by palm trees, had thatched roofs: not the neatly trimmed straw of England, but rather as if straggly seaweed had been roughly strewn and left to dry.

The north-western fringe of the city was largely a repeat of the south-eastern approach. As growing cities do, Guadalajara had spread to engulf nearby small towns. Passing through one such, I saw a long line of single-storey shops, some with open frontages, just a few metres from the major road. The sense of muddle, congestion and enterprise that they conveyed led me to compare what I saw with some of the urban scenes I had experienced in developing countries. The differences were that here there was a kerb and sidewalk rather than an earthy no-man's-land between shops and traffic, and that here all the conveyances were motor vehicles.

Out in the countryside, the highway switchbacked over humps and troughs, curving around volcanic peaks. We were on high ground – roughly 1500 metres – with the valley of the Río Grande de Santiago falling away to the right. To the left, craggy mountains rose. Where bare rock was exposed near the road, its volcanic character was obvious in its twisted skeins of lava and sharp edges. The area was dotted with volcanoes: Tequila Volcano rose to nearly 3000 metres on our left. Malcolm said that following a period of dormancy, the volcanoes in the area had recently started to become active again. The skyline included some classically conical peaks, but also some asymmetrical knobs and bulbous protrusions. At road level, jagged hummocks were covered in rough yellow grass and small bushes. This was my first experience of the Western Cordillera: the previous May I had been in Denver and had glimpsed some peaks of the Rockies on the skyline, but here I was immersed in a proper close-up scenic tour. I drank in the experience self-indulgently, savouring its addition to my collection: speaking purely metaphorically, definitely a badge worth adding to my walking stick.

We pulled in at a viewing point where we could look across at Tequila. There was a car park, a shelter and a noticeboard. We got out of the minibus into blazing sun. I was pretty hot: I was wearing a Donegal tweed suit, and my concession to the climate was that it was lightweight, as tweeds go, and only a two-piece. The viewing point was on high ground, which fell away down a hummocky slope to the valley in which Tequila was sited. The upper part of the slope was covered with some kind of deciduous trees, their leaves parched and curled; the view was enjoyed by peeping through the gaps between them rather than as an uninterrupted vista. The lower part of the slope was covered with long yellow grass and scrub. A railway line followed the valley floor, beyond which the town sat in the middle of a ring of agave fields. The town was compact, and at that distance presented as a three-coloured, mottled patch: pink and white buildings and dark green trees.

We were not alone: a young couple of Mexican appearance were also enjoying the scene from the shelter. The shelter housed a bright yellow picnic table and benches, under a pantiled roof supported by four white columns. At the edge of the car park on the side facing the valley was a protective wall a metre or so high, and the shelter was between that wall and a lower one. Both walls were painted in startling black and white, in what I supposed was to imitate rough masonry, but in fact looked like the skin of a giraffe. As well as the car park, the viewing area included a maintained patch of park, and an explanatory sign, in Spanish and English, in a beautifully tiled surround.

The sign explained that the area had been enrolled as a UNESCO World Heritage site in July 2006:

'The landscape surrounding the villages of Amatitán and Tequila is unique in the world. Its singularity lies in the unique blue-green variety of agave plants, Agave Tequila Weber, that cover the region in millions…'

'The agave landscape represents the continuous link between the old Mesoamerican cultures and the present. Since the time the first intensive plantations were established in the 17th century there has been a continuous process of expanding and improving the cultivation of agave. The landscape made up by agave fields, distilleries, haciendas and villages is an exceptional example of a specialised cultural development in harmony with the land.'

Driving on from the viewpoint, we soon got close-up views of agave fields right beside the road. The comparison that came to me immediately was with lavender fields: just the initial impression, not in detail. The agaves were like pineapple tops of different sizes according to the maturity of the plants. They were grown in meticulously neat rows, sometimes straight but often curving – I couldn't understand why, as the curves were not following contour lines – and the red soil between the rows was kept impressively clear. Malcolm pointed out that the clocks changed as we crossed the provincial border from Jalisco to Nayarit.

Chapter Five
Tepic: a Mismatch of Visions

Soon we entered more rugged terrain, where the ground rose steeply either side of the road, rough with jagged protrusions and indentations, and covered with scrub. In one location I was delighted to see cacti growing among the trees: tall, straight green fingers poking up in clusters higher than the bushes, and looking like a bigger version of the cactus which grew in a pot by our French windows at home. The landscape opened suddenly to provide a vista to the east which included an old caldera: a perfectly conical volcano which had blown its top off. The sides of the frustum were covered in the same dark scrub as the surrounding area, while the dead-flat top was cultivated with a blue-green crop, probably agave. Our road was higher than the caldera, presenting a geography teacher's dream photo opportunity.

We passed a village built on a low hill. The buildings were mostly small, single-storey and flat-roofed, and dotted among trees. Some roads or tracks were cut into the hill like terraces, but most of the buildings did not seem to have roads going to them. That absence of roads reminded me of a village I had visited on a hillside in Yemen, and I guessed that here, like there, closer inspection would have revealed a network of footpaths. Further on, at another village or small town, Malcolm decided that we would stop for lunch. On the outskirts it seemed that people grew rows of agave in their back gardens. Then we were in a settlement of tranquil, sleepy squares filled with trees. Scorching sunlight on the exposed roads contrasted with inky shadows under the trees, whose trunks were all neatly painted with a thick coat of lime to protect them from pests. This lime coating was of uniform height and neatly finished, so had a decorative quality. Men in white fedoras lounged in the shade, their bicycles propped on kerbs or against trees. A refreshment kiosk was not doing any business.

We drove down a residential street, which was cobbled and tree lined, with raised pavements beyond the trees. The buildings were small and huddled, of one or two storeys, covered with painted plaster. There were quite a few parked cars, and the street scene was completed by numerous tall wooden poles and cables: street lights appeared to dangle from some of them. We parked near the town centre. The restaurant which Malcolm had planned to take us to was closed, so he guided us to another which I guessed was more workaday: I was hungry, I like food, I wasn't bothered about how posh it was. In a new country, where everything was strange to me, I had no criteria against which to make such a judgement. It was great to go inside, to get in the shade and sit at a table.

Bottles of mineral water and salad came, followed by a hot dish. Notwithstanding my previous comment about liking food, I have a bit of an issue avoiding headaches. I get one kind of headache if I am hungry, especially if it is a long while since my last proper meal. Some foods, especially citrus fruit (which is often hidden in cooking) and coffee (easily avoided) act pretty quickly as migraine triggers; other foods including cheese have a slower and more cumulative effect. Sticky stodge affects my intestines, which also leads to headaches, as does going too long without black tea. These susceptibilities are all exacerbated by new contexts and stress. So I had stoically accepted that I was unlikely to feel my best after a few days in Mexico. That morning in the hotel, to avoid cheese, I had asked for a plain omelette:

when it came, it was devoid of all the other fillings (which would have been fine), but smothered in cheese. The dish in front of me now was square, covered in a creamy, cheesy gunge, under which I found rolls of sticky starch filled with a different kind of gunge. From my later research I guess it was enchiladas suizas; at the time as I poked into it, hunger battled with caution, and hunger won.

Back on the road, we passed through densely wooded uplands, then came to an unusual feature: a lava field, where molten rock had solidified into weird shapes. Sufficient time had passed since the eruption that produced it for it to have become colonised by low scrub vegetation. Some sections of the field looked like sticky scree which had set solid.

We entered Tepic. A broad road, surfaced with large rectangles of asphalt with wide gaps between them, was lined with a hotchpotch of two- and three-storey buildings. Many telegraph poles, some not quite vertical, carried a cobweb of cables; horizontal bars of traffic lights dangled from them. Small trees and bushes were plentiful. A dark green mountain rose in the distance, and a nearer hilltop carried the imposing yellow frontage of a large church or cathedral. The hotel where Liz and I were to lodge was on a main street; its facilities were entirely adequate and it was a relief to be able to relax for the remainder of the day.

On Monday morning before breakfast I took a look outside, where the street was already bustling. It seemed to me that a high proportion of the women looked attractive. After a few minutes I realised that this was no truer here than elsewhere, but the bright fabrics, sunshine, smiles, and most particularly gait, movement and mannerisms, combined to give that impression. It also happened to be St Valentine's Day, about which more fuss was made than is normal in

England. Cars were festooned with paper decorations. People told me that parties and street events were common, which I saw for myself as the day wore on, adding to an air of jollity.

The schedule started with a breakfast business meeting at 9am. Malcolm was going to bring some people to the hotel restaurant; this was how business was done. A little after 9am, Liz and I decided to start eating so that we could be more polite and attentive when the others came. From an array of dishes I made the bulk of my meal from two that seemed the safest options. One was a sticky mixture of crushed beans (I know now that they are called 'refried', even though they are not fried, but it was all new to me at the time). The other was a wet gloopy mixture of bits of tortilla, chicken and tomato. There was also a good selection of fruit.

In due course we were joined by Malcolm and three men he had brought with him. He introduced them as Joel, from the Ministry of Education, who was the regional head of research councils; Pablo, who worked for the university and was designated as head of the proposed leadership centre; and Ruben, who was in charge of research and postgraduate studies at the university. Ruben's own subject field was agricultural sciences, and Malcolm enthused about the importance of this to developing the rural economy. We talked until 11am: the whole of the extensive restaurant area was full of such meetings, and press photographers loitered around having a good look at everyone, hoping for a scoop. Malcolm explained that after this meeting we would be going to look at the Knowledge City, currently under construction, where the leadership centre was to be housed. At a suitable moment I took the opportunity to ask Malcolm the name of the town or village where we had lunched the previous day, because I find it disorientating not to know where I am, or where I have been, although that is often the case on my business trips. He said it was Jala, which my map showed me was a village about 75 kilometres south-east of Tepic.

The Knowledge City was being constructed on a building site, somewhere on the industrial fringe of town, where enterprises were scattered sparsely among scrub and parched earth. There was something that looked like a chemical works, but overall perhaps 'enterprise' is not the right descriptor given the lack of visible activity. Nearby, a fat Mexican in an enormous sombrero ambled in front of a row of dilapidated sheds. One was filled with worn-out tyres. The sun burnt down out of a cobalt blue sky, over the distant blue peaks of the Western Cordillera.

I had seen many educational facilities under construction over the years in the UK and internationally. The previous summer I had a guided tour of the 'Education City' in the King Abdullah Economic City which was under construction to the north of Jeddah. Back in my days as a director of education I had led the creation of a campus acclaimed as 'Britain's most innovative school'. In the light of my informed experience, what was going on here was, on the face of it, reassuringly impressive.

The construction was of reinforced concrete. Parts were at the stage where steel rods poked out of the ground, others had steel frames, and some had walls and enough of an outer shell to show what the building would be like. It would be three storeys high, and a proportion of the floor area would undoubtedly be taken up by tall atria spanning the building's full height. We were issued hard hats and shown around. Groups of builders, not wearing hard hats, stood chatting, apparently doing nothing, as builders often seem to be the world over. A plan showed a quadrant of a circle as the core of the design. All of this indicated serious investment and awareness of current international standards and styles. The building would be a locus for various forward-looking activities, including Ruben's new developments in agricultural sciences, and would house the proposed school leadership centre. In reality, 'housing' the leadership centre would not amount to much commitment of space: an office, and access to communal facilities, but I allowed the experience of this site visit to lull me into believing there was real momentum behind the project.

Joel, the man from the ministry, had a nice place at the seaside, and offered to take us there. The coast was only about an hour's drive to the west of Tepic, and I would have loved to have my first sight of the Pacific Ocean, but by the time people had stopped talking and were ready it was too late to do the trip, which was vaguely rescheduled to Friday. So, the seaside being off the agenda for the day, Malcolm decided to take us to the ranch where he lived.

The group now comprised, as well as Liz and myself, Malcolm, Pablo and Felix, who had turned up as if out of the air. We drove, the shadows in my photographs suggest westward, along a straight, dusty road, towards a mountain, past parked lorries, an empty billboard frame, and buildings covered in bright paint announcing in large letters 'hotel' and 'restaurant'. Then the scene changed to an expanse of rough pasture with a distant line of buildings, against a range of peach- and mauve-coloured hills; in the foreground the roadside was strewn with litter and discarded tyres.

The road climbed through a rock cutting to a hilly, tree-scattered area. A sign indicated where to turn off for Mazatlán. Further on, the road was dead straight and the landscape flat; we seemed to be passing a miscellany of ribbon development as if on the outskirts of a town. A signboard with supposedly Greek-style lettering announced

Cesares Nightclub, with a picture of a woman dancing in a floaty bit of chiffon. The club itself was a shack with the addition of a crude imitation of a classical portico; it was crammed up against some kind of dump or lorry-breaking yard. Later, a smart sign showed a woman's face with a finger held to her lips, with the rubric 'Libramiento, Show Table Dance'. It was interesting that in a Spanish-speaking country these particular facilities advertised themselves in English.

We came to the place where Malcolm had planned for us to have lunch, but the restaurant was closed because the staff had all disappeared for the day, so he took us instead to a simple café nearby. It was set on an expanse of yellow earth with thin, parched grass and scattered bushes; one nearby was covered both with violet flowers and with brilliant red berries. A woman served our food in a homely fashion, from big pans in an open kitchen. We took our heaped plates to a table with a blue-and-white checked tablecloth set with tortillas, avocados, wedges of citrus fruit, radishes and chillies. Referring to the woman who had served us, who was the proprietor, Malcolm said, 'She has a PhD. She is a widow, and this business gives her the best income available here'.

The meal was excellent, and most welcome because it was a long time since breakfast. I had a stew of sun-dried pork, with rice and mashed beans, and cooked cacti, which was a new experience: similar to okra but with a nicer texture. Needing to avoid citrus fruit, I had a tumbler of hibiscus flower juice. Lunch was relaxed and jolly. Towards the end, Pablo drew our attention to the selection of sliced chillies, and explained that one kind was particularly hot. He offered Liz and me each a tiny sliver, telling us to be careful; it was similar to scotch bonnet. After this tasting he cautioned us not to touch our eyes, and insisted on squeezing lemon juice over our fingers. I needed to use the toilet and was directed to a shed at the back, where there was a hole in the floor. On the way I met a small flock of fowl. I was glad that the plan for lunch had been changed. In addition to eating well, I felt I had seen more of Mexico here than I would have done in a restaurant.

Then Malcolm took us to the ranch. I thought of a 'ranch' as a building surrounded by extensive livestock farming. Instead of that we turned off the road on to a gravelly drive leading through a thickly vegetated area, which resolved itself into beautiful gardens: mature with borders, trees and shrubs, and reasonably well tended. We were told that the main cash crop was bird of paradise flowers. The house was long, low and rambling, in the Spanish style, with attractive décor and a cool interior. Two very large dogs were penned into a courtyard. The cavernous building did not have the feel or appearance of being inhabited as someone's home.

Malcolm explained that Pablo had inherited the house from his father – Pablo pointed to a framed photograph of an elderly gentleman – but did not live in it because he had accommodation in the university. Felix took the lead in showing us round, in his gentle, bashful way, occupying no space, in contrast to Malcolm who always filled his spaces. 'This is where I sleep', said Felix, smiling with happiness as he showed off a neat, small bed. Its immaculate folds and perfectly positioned small teddy bear suggested the attentions of a maid. 'And this is where Malcolm sleeps!', Felix announced proudly, guiding Liz and me through into a master bedroom with a grand high bed, equally tidily maintained. 'We do our work through here', and he showed us a double-aspect room with picture windows and long work surfaces along each aspect. Malcolm appeared and explained that the two enormous computer screens at his workstation were beneficial for aspects of his work. Actually the set-up was similar to what I have now in my study at home, but at the time it seemed surprisingly high-specification, tech-savvy and business-like.

We were shown the grounds. Outside, the air was heavy with the scent of citrus blossoms: every breath was like sniffing a bottle of perfume. I was surprised that the grounds were so thickly planted, and that they were surrounded by densely wooded hills – surprised only because I was still wrestling with my mental concept of what a 'ranch' ought to be like. The citrus fruits were of many varieties that we do not have in Britain; the trees were laden with them. Liz tried some; I could not, but instead I was given a freshly plucked passion fruit which tasted much better than the ones in shops at home. There were also palm trees bearing large fruits, and agaves, and papayas, avocados and banana trees, which were all heavily fruiting. It was quite an experience to amble around this subtropical paradise. We were led to an area where the bird of paradise flowers grew. A hired hand was picking them in a leisurely manner.

Near the house, an old wooden cart stood decoratively on a slab of concrete, surrounded by cacti in large flowerpots. Back indoors, Malcolm suggested coffee. Liz and I both needed tea, and went to the kitchen to sort ourselves out. Felix came to make the coffee and to help us hunt in cupboards and packets; we chose the nearest approximation to proper tea we could find. Malcolm had settled in a great leather chair in a lounge area. He started talking about his plans and wishes for how the new leadership centre would be led and governed, but soon took the conversation on a more general path. All I can remember is that we discussed aspects of the philosophy of education; that Malcolm was erudite and charming; and that we ended up spending rather longer at the ranch than he had planned. So he announced that we should go straight to the university rather than back to our hotel first as had been his original intention.

The meeting at the university was to be with the rector, senior staff and some members of its council, so quite a significant occasion. 'It will be Pablo's meeting', Malcolm explained. He drove us there, in his car: an American model of unfamiliar design. When I took an interest, Malcolm said he didn't know much about it: it went with his job, he said rather dismissively. Like the ranch, I thought, still no clearer about his 'job'. What was clear was that he was a surprisingly keen and snappy driver: fast, assertive and accurate to the millimetre. He said he had trained in some kind of racing or rally driving when he was young. These technical skills combined with his hot temper made for an alarming journey. At one particular junction he had a furious altercation. He believed that the custom here was for turns to be taken, the traffic merging one car at a time, but a motorist was cutting in supposedly out of turn. Malcolm shot forward to show he wanted to block the other car's progress, shaking his fist out of the window and shouting in Spanish, making further jerking, ramming movements, stopping just short of actual collision. I was embarrassed to be in the front seat; I would rather have been somewhere else entirely.

At the university we trailed into an upstairs room set out as a boardroom; the rector greeted us briefly and got the meeting going. All the preliminaries were in Spanish, of which I have no knowledge. As Pablo spoke, introducing the project, I was surprised to see the rector and several of the other eight or nine dignitaries present concentrating on their mobile phones, thumbs a-twitching feverishly. What was this? Where I come from that would be pretty discourteous. Afterwards I was told that they were texting each other about us, about the line they should take. Then I was invited to outline the nature of the support our institution proposed to provide. There followed a discussion in a kind of Spanglish, all apparently supportive. Some further meetings for us were also discussed. The original schedule needed to be adapted. The rector said that after Liz and I had given the lectures we had planned for Wednesday morning, we would meet with the leaders of the upper secondary schools run by the university. Then in the afternoon we would meet the leaders of the schools run by the federal government. Malcolm and the rector ran through several other planned meetings, and it was confirmed that a press conference would take place on Friday morning. The meeting concluded apparently amicably: certainly Malcolm and Pablo considered the general mood had been positive.

Malcolm drove us back to our hotel, but had to take a circuitous route because the St Valentine's Day festivities included noisy demonstrations as well as street parties, and some of the main roads were closed. Night had fallen, so I got quite an atmospheric tour of backstreets which I would not otherwise have seen. Liz and I welcomed the opportunity to sit and have a quiet meal together, and to take stock of what for me had been a long and tiring day. My senses felt bombarded with everything that had happened since coming down to breakfast in this new country: the morning meeting, the trip to the building site, the amazing experiences of lunch, the ranch and its garden, and the afternoon's slightly weird, formal meeting. Liz had been looking up the meanings of Spanish words on the menu, so using that knowledge we each had a variation on the local fish, which was very good, a type of flounder. Mine came with tomato and pepper sauce, with olives and caper berries, plus rice and salad. I reflected that if today was typical, there would be a lot of time wasted hanging around socialising, but how could I do that when the others were often speaking rapidly and at length in Spanish?

That prediction certainly came true the next day, Tuesday. The 'breakfast' meeting started at 9am and ended at 2.10pm. Liz and I ate beforehand, piling our plates with fruit, which seemed good: in my case melon and strawberries were the main elements. When Malcolm arrived, the fruit got discussed, and Liz must have questioned something about washing it: whether that happened, or the quality of the water, perhaps. 'You can never wash a strawberry!' Malcolm opined, and proceeded to tell us about some dreadful complaint he had suffered because something harmful had got down into the pores of strawberries, underneath the seeds and hence impervious to washing. I thought of the pile I had just eaten and hoped for the best.

Our discussion started with just our immediate group, but it seemed hard to get much sense of direction. The part of the restaurant we sat in had picture windows on two sides looking out on to the busy street scene, which helped to pass the time. The key steps of our consultancy were reiterated and confirmed: our first report would concentrate on setting up the structures of partnership and firming up the concept of the leadership centre. Pablo and Ruben would come to London in May to learn first-hand how our leadership centre worked; Liz and I would return to Tepic in June to complete our analysis of the initial programmes to be offered by the new centre, which was scheduled to begin operating in September.

At 1pm a man joined us to talk about English-language teaching, which was quite a priority if local partners were planning to draw on the services of our institution. I felt a bit of migraine coming on: I was expecting it, these things are predictable and in this case it was the delayed effect of too much cheese. Malcolm was wearing a white shirt with red stripes and I made the mistake of looking at it. A splodge appeared in the middle of my vision and spread, so that after a minute or two the world looked like the screen of a television with no aerial. Voices faded into an indistinct murmur of meaningless sound, and I knew that if I attempted to speak I would stammer wrong, muddled words. So I just sat, not drawing attention to myself, and after about 20 minutes or so I began to get some of my faculties back. No-one seemed to have noticed, which summed up the level of communication generally.

Malcolm had booked us into a high-class fish restaurant in town for 'lunch' at 2.30pm. He explained that this was an opportunity to meet an important ministry official 'who spoke excellent English'. The official turned out to be charming and friendly, but there was a lot of background noise in the restaurant, and his excellent English was spoken with a thick accent, so I caught very little of what he said. As I do when in noisy crowded social settings, I looked attentive, smiled and nodded and hoped I said 'yes' at appropriate moments.

The meal started with various stodgy tortilla-style things with fishy fillings. Then came enormous platters of glorious fish grilled to a crisp over very hot charcoal: I guessed it might be Chilean sea bass. It was a pity this course hadn't come before the stodge. There was no vegetable, salad or fruit to provide balance, but I did tuck into the fish with enthusiasm. We got up from the table at 4.40pm (lunchtime in Mexico finished at the point I would be halfway through cooking dinner at home) to go back to the hotel, where we sat at our usual table for a meeting at 5pm with the president of the Parents' Association. The essential elements of that session could have been transacted in a quarter of an hour, but side issues got discussed at length, mainly in Spanish, which required us to sit there until 7.30pm. Afterwards, Liz and I agreed we didn't want an evening meal. We both wanted to think about the lectures we were presenting in the morning and had preparation to do. For my part I was worried about the suitability of my material.

I need not have worried. On Wednesday we arrived at the lecture room; no-one was there except a technician setting up the projector. A handful of people started to appear. I thought the standard of hospitality was pretty poor: for example, I had to make a fuss to get some water for the speakers. The rector, who was due to be here with his entourage, was apparently locked in a disputatious meeting with the unions. Malcolm said that a delegation from a university in Miami who had come for a scheduled meeting with the rector had gone away in disgust. Malcolm was still wearing his red-striped shirt, so I explained my problem and asked him to keep out of my sight-line. The lectures started 40 minutes late, without the rector's party. I went first, and unfortunately not until afterwards discovered a monumental failure in translation.

Quite early in my talk I explained that in the work we did, we supported leadership development at every stage of a teacher's career. The translator mistook 'career' for 'Korea' and assumed my lecture was about education in Korea, interpreting accordingly. The sparse, ragtag audience, if they listened at all, must have been completely bemused. No-one wanted to ask any questions. Liz followed, with what was to me a clear and interesting exposition of her main research specialism, which received an equally stony reception.

Then we were taken to a different room for the meeting the rector had promised on Monday, with the principals of the 15 upper secondary schools run by the university. It was by now past my normal lunchtime. I had had nothing to eat, nor even a cup of tea, since breakfast, and my head was starting to pound. There were about 20 people in the room, which was large and laid out in conference style, so they were spread around the edge, mostly out of my sight-line and hard to hear.

Someone invited each of the principals to talk about their school and situation. They did so, at length and tediously, with much basic factual information that did not seem important at this very embryonic phase of the project, but politeness required me to keep scribbling in my notebook. The issues the principals raised often concentrated on the inadequate state of their premises and shortage of resources, which actually told me a lot about where they were in their development as educational leaders. Some did not identify themselves as educationists, nor see the role as full-time: one was a medical doctor maintaining his general practice; another was a dentist running his surgery in a town near his school. Looking back later at my notes, there was, to be fair, quite a bit of useful and relevant information in these expositions, but at the time I felt deep dissatisfaction with the lack of opportunity to engage in meaningful dialogue, with the excessive time the meeting was taking, and with the lack of consideration for my comfort.

About halfway through this purgatory, at 2pm, everyone in the room except for the supposedly distinguished guests was served with a steaming mug of something. Malcolm remonstrated at this appalling rudeness and eventually, seemingly reluctantly, we were given a hot drink. My headache and annoyance were becoming obvious; one of the hosts shook a packet of foreign-looking painkillers at me in the way one shakes a rattle at a fractious baby. I demanded a comfort break. Some peanuts appeared, but when I crammed them eagerly into my mouth I found they were soaked in extra-concentrated lemon essence. The last principal completed his talk, then, as icing on the cake (which would have been nice) a sour old official related the history of the university and its predecessor college, starting from 1925 and being very thorough.

Mercifully the meeting finished at 3.30pm. I staggered out with the others; we were driven somewhere for lunch then back to a different part of the university for a meeting at 5pm with the leaders of the sector of schools run by the federal government. This was much better because it was free of the dead hand of the university and felt more like a normal consultation session. It was led by a dynamic and positive woman, Martha, from the relevant government department. I was allowed to give what I hoped was a rousing little address about the benefits of the planned leadership centre. The interpreter had not appeared, so a couple of willing volunteers did their best, but they didn't know the technical terms, and I couldn't understand their accent very well, which was a good formula for avoiding disagreement.

There were more such meetings. Thursday was full of them, and one blurs into another in my memory. One was supported by an extremely personable and helpful interpreter: she cast a warm glow over the proceedings. But towards the end, one of the delegates, referring to the proposed leadership centre, said, 'It's a nice idea, but it won't happen'. I felt surprised and annoyed by such certainty of failure, and piqued by such a complete dismissal of my own capabilities as a consultant. Of course it would happen: funds were sitting somewhere locally; key authorities had signed up to it; my organisation had been contracted to support the process, so why should it not?

Another meeting was similar to my first at the university: a long conference table packed with people, each of whom intended to introduce themselves at length before we could get down to doing anything useful. After formal opening courtesies, the delegate nearest me embarked on what seemed to me a summary of their life history and extremely general comments about their work. The other delegates listened respectfully. Then the delegate next to the first did the same, and then the next. I felt a deep gloom descend: what was the point of this? After an hour, these introductions had reached the other side of the table, and I was getting annoyed and frustrated. We had a schedule to keep to, and my organisation was charging a high daily rate for my time on the assumption that I would be doing something productive.

After another half hour or so, everyone had introduced themselves, and I was readying myself to start some consultancy, when the first speaker began again. This time the focus of the contribution was their school, but steering well clear of anything specifically related to leadership development. The delegate next to them did the same, and so on, all avoiding anything relevant. I called a halt to the proceedings before this process had reached the end of the table, saying that it had all been most informative and helpful but we could not possibly take up more of their valuable time.

Outside, Pablo berated me for not understanding or respecting Mexican culture. He explained that the group had been really helpful: they had tried to compress into a few hours a process which would normally take at least three days. This was about how the group related to each other, how they established norms, how they worked towards consensus. I am ashamed to say I was unrepentant, saying they could do all that on their own, or with cardboard cut-outs of us, and we could join them when they were ready to get down to business.

Graham Greene's memoir of travel in Mexico in the 1930s, *The Lawless Roads*, includes phrases which resonated with my sentiments: 'The age of Mexico falls on the spirit like a cloud' and 'You get used in Mexico to disappointment'. Another thing which hadn't changed much since Greene's day was the amount of hanging around because of changed schedules. Greene kept getting marooned in boring places waiting for a delayed plane or mule train, with so little happening that he filled the pages by recording his dreams. Since Monday morning, various adjustments to our programme had been needed, especially where ministry personnel ran into more pressing matters.

The rescheduled press conference did, however, take place on Friday morning. I have a tentative hypothesis that, when it comes to business in countries which struggle to achieve outcomes, greater emphasis is placed on enjoyable celebrations of initial stages: press releases to publicise intentions, or launch events to fete a plan. That way, they get some feel-good occasions. It was well attended: people want to be seen and recorded in case the project itself goes well. The university and the ministry had latched on to the term 'diagnosis': they wanted us to diagnose the leadership development the upper secondary schools needed. That would be the intended outcome of our next visit, planned for June. There were numerous speeches, Liz and I were invited to contribute comments, and a somewhat garbled version of the project found its way around the media – one English-language publication had the headline 'It makes a diagnosis of middle level education'.

We checked out of the hotel, and I left Malcolm to settle the bill. Overall I had been comfortable there, and in particular I remember it as the point where I started to consider showers as a satisfactory alternative to baths: praise indeed for the robust old pipes, slates and hot water. The happy glow of the press conference meant that we parted from Malcolm in quite an upbeat mood. The scenic drive back to Guadalajara had a certain freshness because we were looking in the opposite direction: the combination of terrain and vegetation was just as stunning.

That evening, although we were still on duty, Liz and I allowed ourselves a glass of lager and had a relaxed and pleasant discussion to draw together our conclusions and next steps. We agreed that our report would include detailed advice on a long list of matters that needed to be sorted out locally. On the table were pots of what I now know to be habas fritas, which of course I nibbled with the lager because they were there. In my ignorance I wondered whether the beans were cooked sufficiently, and even wondered, unjustly, whether they might have played any part in the prolonged and significant stomach upset I experienced in the days following my return from Mexico. I had only four days at my desk before setting off for Jeddah, so the state of my body was of some concern.

We wrote our report; everything seemed well with the world. Would this become the sustained partnership project we so sorely needed? The first bad news was that the university had refused to confirm Pablo's appointment as head of the new centre, and had not agreed any arrangements for accommodating the centre within the university. Then the visit to London was postponed indefinitely. Two factors became magnified in my reflections. First, the lack of evidence that, apart from Malcolm, any significant local power-brokers were really prepared to shoulder the responsibility for creating the leadership centre. Secondly, the massive shortcoming in attempting such developmental work across a linguistic barrier. I had no fluent Spanish speaker to draw into my team.

The invoice for the first stage of our work was not paid. Representations were made, and I wrote serious and formal letters to people in senior positions, but the bad debt remained and caused me periodic hassle until it was written off years later. Since I had avoided paying for anything, it was, from a business point of view, only the air fare and our time that had been wasted. From the viewpoint of my learning, I felt the price paid was cheap for the richness of the experience.

Chapter Six
Transitions in Jeddah, Karachi and Lahore

After returning from Mexico, I had three busy days in the office before setting off to Jeddah. This was for the final instalment of the work with Saudi school leaders: my second, and thankfully last, encounter with the group of male principals I had met in Dammam. There were some positives: we were to be based at the Jeddah Hilton, a venue I knew well and liked a lot. My team – Gordon, Margaret and Sveta – were colleagues with whom I enjoyed a relaxed amiability. It was a relief to be getting to the end of a project which had been problematic from the start: a year of negotiation and two years of delivery, without a major bust-up and with our organisation's reputation reasonably intact. I was discomforted by the stomach upset I had brought back from Mexico, but set off on Friday 25th February in the expectation of getting some enjoyment from the opportunity.

That didn't come – I didn't expect it to – from my working sessions with the male principals. Having got off to a bad start with them last time, things were only going to get worse. For a good many years I had been accustomed to working with groups who were respectful and courteous, helped by my organisation having given me a job title which made me sound very senior. I wished I had introduced myself more authoritatively when I first met the group: the complex management structures around this project had left them with the impression I was a mere contracted-in trainer. Arab audiences can exhibit the extremes either of charm or scornful disregard. This group took me right back to when I was a young trainee teacher being given difficult classes.

The project management company that controlled the contracts for the work had set up an organisation structure for the duration of the project; at this end-game stage the structure was visibly unravelling. As is normal in such companies, a tiny core of its employees was supplemented by freelance consultants who shouldered much of the burden of getting things done, of getting boxes ticked. I had done such work in my own freelance period and knew it was necessary in that role to be quite firm and focused: one's own payment depended on those boxes getting ticked. The two freelancers who worked with our team, Chris and Claire, had always been pleasantly professional and supportive. They were experienced educators with similar backgrounds to us.

Fran hadn't mellowed an iota: she needed to adjust arrangements for lunch in some way, and during a coffee break strode towards me with a glare of death. 'When is your group scheduled to break for lunch?' It was clear that while those were her words, she was not actually asking a question, so, 'Whenever you tell me', I wisely replied. The amiable companionship of Chris and Claire was all the more enjoyable by contrast. They would, of course, have been looking out for future assignments to replace this one. I did wonder if they were mindful that I ran a consultancy business for my organisation which had been quite large when they first knew me. In truth since my transfer to international work those wings had been clipped, and I felt it only right to let them know that it was unlikely I would be able to offer much work in future.

We took our evening meals as a group, including Chris and Claire. The hotel catering was as excellent as I remembered it to have been on previous visits: a wonderful buffet including regional and international cuisines, a sure recipe for gorging. But of course no alcohol, and while usually that did not bother me, just occasionally the forbidden thing seemed extra desirable. One evening I was sitting next to Claire; we were both replete with several starters, mains and desserts each, and somehow it arose in conversation how pleasant it would be to round off such a meal with a good whisky. Like poking an aching tooth, like people in privation wistfully remembering luxury, we reviewed various options and agreed that a smoky, peaty Talisker would have been particularly apt.

We had team meetings; as one of these broke up I said I fancied a walk by the seafront and asked if anyone wanted to join me. For a moment I hoped Sveta might, but quickly remembered the social inappropriateness of that in this place. Chris was keen for a breath of air; we set off. The hotel was a tower block, and from the bedroom windows the Red Sea coast looked not much more than a stone's throw away: a strip of glittering blue-grey water beyond palm trees and buildings covered with dazzling white stucco. I knew from previous visits that in fact it took a walk of about five to eight minutes to get there, along deserted dusty pavements. Deserted, because Saudis don't walk anywhere, nor do their planners take much account of pedestrians' needs. I never did find a good way of crossing the busy corniche boulevard. There were traffic lights at major junctions, but near the hotel dodging the traffic seemed the best option.

The coastline was artificially constructed. Beyond the road was a wide promenade, separated from the sea by an embankment of boulders. There was nothing out to sea, just sunlit water to the horizon. That may sound dull, but I loved this spot. When I first saw it, I was excited by the fact of standing on the edge of the Red Sea, with all its exotic and historic associations. In the evenings, local residents came with their children and set up cosy little nests among the boulders, with fine oriental rugs, blankets, games, lamps and Primus stoves, for a few hours of leisure in the cool part of the day. Dozens of scrawny little cats would come out from among the rocks to take titbits from barbecues and picnics. The people using the seafront in this way were almost entirely from the large immigrant sector of the population: Saudis were limited by their social customs from much involvement in mixed-sex public gatherings.

We agreed a direction in which to walk, and in the course of relaxed conversation Chris told me some things about his life. He and his wife had suffered a significant family tragedy, and moving on from that had caused him to adopt a particular approach to life. He said he had learnt that you never knew what might be waiting for you around the corner, therefore if there were things you wanted to do it was best to get on and do them while you could. That thought had prompted him to give up the security of being a school principal to pursue the nomadic wandering and variety of life as a freelance consultant. I found that view resonant; I think it encouraged me to continue taking opportunities for international assignments while I could. In recent times, now that doors have closed, I have caught myself reflecting, from the other side, on the wisdom of Chris's words.

I led the way on to a short jetty in order to watch the waves for a while. Where the sun shone through the rising crests, the water was a soft turquoise shade, and very clear. I had heard that the Red Sea has unusually low levels of silt because it does not have muddy rivers flowing into it. The onshore breeze, and the rhythmic breaking of the waves (not crashing – this was not the Atlantic), were relaxing. The timeless feel evoked reflection, including memories of my childhood fascination with the seaside. That train of thought, particularly of boyhood outings with a friend, reminded me of the simple pleasure of easy, undemanding companionship with a male of my own age. Working in a predominantly female profession, and in a culture both hierarchical and competitive, that was a surprisingly rare treat nowadays. I doubt that Chris was aware, that afternoon, how much I appreciated his company.

As I knew would be the case, Sveta was finding her work with the female principals enjoyable and rewarding. Towards the end of the three-day course we were teaching, one of her group invited my team to dinner at a restaurant. This principal had raised the prospect of some future partnership: certainly a good rapport had been established. The five of us arrived by taxi. The restaurant was a single-storey structure around a tent-covered central courtyard dining area, like a marquee at a wedding reception. That meant that the way in was like passing through the outer wall of a castle: of course, our hostess took the lead, checking in with staff in a hot busy passageway, and we were guided through to the cooler, spacious tent which, not being visible from the outside, came as a pleasant surprise.

The dining area was set with heavy, practical wooden tables. It was early evening, still quite light, and the place was perhaps one-third full. The groups of diners were a mixture, including families and women-only groups; I didn't notice other Westerners but there were probably some later, when it got busier. The women wore black abayas and headscarves, and a minority wore niqab face veils, yet the atmosphere was one of merry enjoyment. In particular I noticed a group of young women near us smoking fragrant hubble-bubbles, chattering and laughing, flashing their beautiful eyes at each other, enjoying their night out pretty much as girls would on a boozy Friday in an English town centre.

That merriment was infectious; in our own small party we were delighted to have reached the end of a challenging assignment, and delighted to be treated to such enjoyable entertainment. Our hostess sat at the head of the table, with Margaret and Sveta on her right and left hands, and Gordon and I next in line. 'Saudi champagne' was ordered, and arrived with a flourish in a great metal jug: sparkling apple juice with a fruit salad and ice cubes bobbing about in it. Personally I would have much preferred the apple juice on its own, but this presentation was considered suitably celebratory.

Food started to arrive: delicate pastries with a tangy, white, cheesy filling, then kebabs, salad, rice and flatbreads. The ovens were visible – right by the tables – and every so often a long plank-like sheet of metal was drawn out, covered with flatbreads, which were tipped off on to a wooden table and brought to diners straight away by staff who seemed gleefully proud of them. The combination of heat and freshness, and enthusiastic presentation, made them especially appetising.

The restaurant filled up to a noisy bustle, the night was dark, and various forms of lighting glowed and flickered. Staff moved around carrying buckets of wonderfully fragrant, smoking incense, which apparently helped to keep insects away. Now I need to explain that I love incense, the smokier the better. From early in adult life we kept supplies of frankincense at home, and burnt it occasionally in tea strainers and other improvised arrangements. It may sound weird, but on the morning my daughter was born, when I got home from the hospital my first act of celebration, even before opening wine, was to make clouds of smoky fragrance. Later, in more prosperous times, I invested in a brass censer on its swinging chain to do the job properly. So, on that wonderfully atmospheric Arabian night, what to others may well have been an intrusive nuisance was to me the icing on the cake. While the food was relatively simple, and the conversation largely inaudible, what made the evening a special memory for me was that it was *different* – completely different from anything I had experienced previously in Saudi Arabia.

A fitting ending: there were no prospects in the pipeline for me to do further work in Arabia. I did in fact return some years later, after I had retired, to run a course in Riyadh, standing in at short notice for someone who had died, but I was not to know that. The actual moment of goodbye was when I got rid of my Saudi riyals: for the last four years they had, along with US dollars, been a currency of which I kept a permanent cash stock. Walking away from the exchange booth I felt bereaved of a relationship with a strange and fascinating culture.

*****

Back in London I had the pleasant task of getting ready to return to Pakistan, to teach the courses which had been planned with Taymur, Colin and the Commander the previous November. This was a bit of an experiment for all of us: something to try out and learn from as part of an intended long-term relationship. My aim had been to move away from what I thought of as the 'colonial' approach – British 'experts' flying in to tell Pakistanis what they should be doing – in favour of a respectful partnership, learning from each other, helping to develop local expertise and confidence. I had hoped to enlist some of the local school leaders and trainers as associate staff of my organisation, and to coach them in our methods of teaching. I took steps in that direction, inviting expressions of interest, but after a while Taymur advised me the system just wasn't ready for that. People such as himself and Colin were too strongly associated with their own schools, within a competitive system, to be able to assume the identity of associates of my organisation. In addition, local trainers had their own reputations and agendas: if they were given teaching roles, the participants would question whether it was really my organisation's programme they were paying for. So, with some regret on my part, we had to fall back on the traditional model of a single presenter working with a large group of participants.

The plan was for two courses to run at the same time. The Pakistani partners had originally wanted a three-week block of activity, with the courses being run in Karachi, then Lahore, then Islamabad. Personally I didn't want to commit to such a long visit, and I knew that back at the office there would be concerns about taking staff to Islamabad, so our partners agreed that Islamabad was a step too far on this occasion. While I would teach the programme on leadership, I needed to staff the programme on teaching and assessment; finding a colleague with the right skills and availability was expecting quite a lot. Eventually it was agreed that Tina would come with me to Karachi; we would return to London, and then after one week Tamara would come with me to Lahore.

Tina and I caught a 8pm flight from Heathrow on Tuesday 22nd March 2011. It was my first experience of flying on an A380 Airbus: the enormous double-decker. I don't think I had checked beforehand what kind of plane it would be. There seemed to be a tremendous crowd of people waiting for the flight, and when the flight crew boarded there was a great army of them. The announcements included statements like, 'Now boarding rows 80 and above'. I was in row 50 and assumed I would be at the back, but was in fact well forward on the lower deck. I had hated the old jumbo jets for their uncomfortable 'flying dustbin' experience, and it was a pleasant surprise that the A380 had sufficient power to offer a smooth ride, in comfortable roomy seats, and with various modern refinements. It was an overnight flight to Dubai; my rest was disturbed by some not very educated men seated nearby who talked loudly and wanted to obtain as much free alcohol as possible.

The flight was late leaving Heathrow, and landed in Dubai about ten minutes late, leaving us 45 minutes to transfer to our connecting flight, which left at 8am. That seemed as if it ought to be achievable, but Emirates had a strict rule about arriving early for boarding or being left behind. This rule was expressed in terms which put all the responsibility for lateness on to lazy, idle, thoughtless passengers, notwithstanding that on this occasion it was caused by Emirates' own schedule and pilots. Thus we were debarred, and had an unplanned interval in which to drink an expensive cup of tea and to text Taymur with our revised schedule.

The benefit was that I had the opportunity to find out a bit more about Tina, who I didn't know, as she and Tamara worked in a different department. She was American, about my own age; like me she had a daughter who was both 26 and a Durham graduate. She had joined our organisation relatively recently, having previously worked in a national agency concerned with regulating school qualifications. She was recovering from recent significant surgery which caused tiredness and occasional discomfort.

Taymur had received our messages; he and Colin met us at Karachi and took us to the Avari Towers Hotel, where the staff were as hospitable and charming as I remembered. Once again the costs of our rooms and meals were waived by the proprietor. In my tired and slightly apprehensive state, it was relaxing to watch about 100 red kites circling and soaring outside my bedroom window, as if they were welcoming me back. We went to the Commander's house to run through the arrangements for the following day. The courses we were teaching covered three full days, from Thursday to Saturday.

The venue for the courses was Avari's Beach Luxury Hotel, which was a cheaper, less plush facility within the Avari group. The course participants were lodging there, and for the teaching rooms we had two first-floor function rooms on the same site. These were side by side, the size of assembly halls. At my request the rooms were furnished with round tables, to enable some interactive table-based activities.

Taymur had driven us there, but as usual, I didn't know where I was. I had no large-scale map, and trying to get my bearings in the sprawling mass of Karachi was not easy. When I went outside to look around, and to enjoy the pleasantly warm spring sunshine and cloudless sky, what I found was well-maintained gardens beside a large, mainly enclosed body of water.

The hotel seemed quite large, of modern construction and very smartly maintained: the residential block was four storeys, cream-painted; the function rooms stood separately as a two-storey, white-painted block. The gardens included extensive neat lawns, flower beds, and many palm trees with tall pale grey trunks growing at drunken angles. There was also a tree with a massively thick short trunk and dark green leaves like a rhododendron. Neat paths with street lamps completed the scene.

The body of water looked, to the east, like a lake fringed with vegetation. To the west, the scene was more obviously industrial, including a substantial road bridge and a forest of dockyard cranes. Later, much later, when I had leisure time for research and reflection, I learnt that the water was the irregularly outlined mass of Chinna Creek; the hotel was on the northern shore, facing south; I was looking across to Kiamari Town; and the bridge was Jinnah Bridge, which led to a major area of wharves. To the east of the hotel was the naval officers' residential quarter; the hotel was almost next to Captain

Sajid's school, which I had toured on my previous visit. At the time I did not realise how close-knit was the network of people with whom I was interacting.

Having most recently had an assignment in Saudi Arabia, and coming now with a female colleague to teach in another Muslim country, part of my subconscious had been telling me that Tina would work with the women, and I with the men. Even though I knew really that was not going to be the case, it was still quite refreshing to find that both groups were predominantly female, and the women wore the bright colours of South Asia rather than the black of Arabia. The mood was one of goodwill and happy expectation: the participants were aware of the aim of a long-term partnership relationship. There were, nevertheless, more than 60 of them in my group and it was a long teaching day, not ending until 5.30pm, so I found it hard work to maintain a sense of pace, variety and involvement. Overall, however, it seemed to be a good day.

Tina's experience was similar. We had been invited to an evening function, I think by the British Council, but we agreed it would finish too late, so instead Taymur took us to the rooftop barbecue restaurant in town where we enjoyed a roasted leg of lamb.

On Friday both Tina and I settled into working with our groups. My group was mainly made up of proprietors, principals and other senior leaders of independent schools. As well as being respectful, pleasant and happy to engage, they also gave me the impression that they were, overall, much better read, and less argumentative, than an equivalent group would be in the UK. Although there was a good level of interaction, mainly in table-based discussions, it was difficult for me to get much real insight into the issues that troubled them in their work. The group also included a local trainer whom I had regarded as a potential associate. He was keen to offer his insights, which, while obviously including an element of self-promotion, provided a change of voice and a local perspective that I welcomed.

The lunches provided in the training rooms were workaday, economical fillers: typically a meat curry, rice and naan bread, mainly taken standing around in informal conversation. There was some intermingling of the two groups during these breaks; a number of institutions had sent representatives to both courses.

That evening, Taymur and Colin took Tina and me to one of the international hotels in town which had a good Pakistani buffet on its top floor. It was my first and, as it turned out, only visit there: needless to say, some hearty gorging took place. I had already learnt that in Pakistan eating, eating well and eating a lot was an important element of being socially entertained: a cultural tradition I was happy to honour. As well as a range of stews, biryanis and dhals, Taymur urged me to try a rich soup of bone marrow which he said was traditional, and had enjoyed often as a child. The juice reminded me somewhat of oxtail soup; one got at it around a pile of short sections of bone.

Saturday was a busy day. As well as teaching the last day of the course, we combined the groups for a discussion about future plans, posed for official group photographs, had interviews with journalists, and started on an initial perusal of the feedback forms.

Kiran had been attending Tina's course; she had spoken to me a couple of times during breaks, including mentioning her intention to visit the UK to attend a conference in Cardiff. As well as the official group photograph, a lot of other photography was going on. I was used to this: often delegates wanted pictures for their school newsletters. Among that general activity, Kiran wanted a photo of the two of us; I obliged, and as she posed on my left-hand side I felt a movement and was pretty sure her right arm had come loosely around me for the purpose of improving the composition.

Tina and I were keen to get to the privacy of our rooms as soon as possible, for light room-service snacks and some rest: we had to be downstairs and ready at 3am on Sunday to be driven to the airport. Our flight was due to leave at 5.45am, and to arrive in Dubai at 6.45am (local time); our main flight set off at 8am and was due to land at Gatwick at 12.30pm. Travelling westwards across time zones gained me time, but did not, of course, shorten the actual tedious duration of the journey. Karachi's departures terminal was not the most relaxing place at the best of times. Tina was tired and uncomfortable; she had no ongoing commitment to the project, and our long pre-dawn wait was a bit of a cheerless drag, but fortunately the flights and connections worked smoothly.

*****

I caught up with other work matters on Monday; on Tuesday I was booked to give a speech in Leeds, so it was convenient to spend the rest of the week relaxing at our second home on the Yorkshire coast. I set off back to Pakistan on the following Tuesday (5th April 2011), catching a flight at 9.10am from Heathrow's Terminal 4, scheduled to arrive in Abu Dhabi at 7.15pm, allowing ample transfer time for the connecting flight, which was due to leave at 10.45pm and to arrive in Lahore at 2.55am on Wednesday.

My colleague for this trip was Tamara, a big, tall woman full of well-researched, original ideas, which she expressed through her writings and lectures rather than in casual conversation. She was self-contained, keeping social interaction to a minimum, at least with me: an undemanding, enigmatic companion. The flight to Abu Dhabi was tedious because of turbulence and very slow service. There was no rush to transfer as we had several hours to kill, which I filled with an Upper Crust baguette and several cups of tea.

As we approached the departure point for the second flight, we encountered an enormous group of returning Umrah pilgrims, mainly elderly and very bad-mannered. They stuck together as a single, seething mass, barging, shoving and trampling anything in their path. Predictably, they carried great piles of baggage, much of it balanced on their heads, including great canisters of holy water. So I wasn't looking forward to the ride: our progress up the boarding steps was dangerous, crushed and repulsive. At the last minute, the welcoming member of the cabin crew took pity on us, scribbled on our tickets and directed us to the left into business class, where we were the only occupants. That was a wonderful moment of relief, followed by nearly three hours of Ritz-quality comfort, pampering and fine dining.

We were staying at the Avari Hotel in Lahore, and the hotel had sent a minibus to meet the flight. On that first arrival in the middle of the night, I could not form much of an impression of the city, nor of the hotel, except that its dimly lit check-in area seemed bigger, older and grander than the one in Karachi. That impression was confirmed when I got to my room, which as well as being spacious had a slightly faded grace and charm. I noticed the bowl of floating rose petals, and that it had a bath rather than a shower; I went straight to bed at 4am and set my alarm for 9am.

Wednesday afternoon was memorable: a stunning and thoroughly enjoyable introduction to the attractions of the Old City. It counts among the top few highlights of my international travel experience, and marked the start of a lasting affinity I felt with Lahore. Taymur had arranged a guided tour with a guide from the local tourist board.

As well as Tamara, Taymur, Colin and myself, two course participants from Bangladesh were also included. We were shepherded into a minibus and set off for the old fort and Badshahi Mosque. This treat was unexpected; I was sleepy from the overnight flight and disorientated from being in a new location, so the tour took on a bit of a dream-like quality.

I learnt that Punjab province was the most fertile region of Pakistan, and that Lahore, its capital, had been the seat of power of the Mughal rulers of India, which explained the grand scale of the antiquities. What is always described, somewhat modestly, either as 'Lahore Fort' or 'the old fort', is in fact an immense complex of pleasure palaces built in the 16th and 17th centuries with great skill and artistry. After we had parked and entered the postern gate, the first feature that amazed me was the Picture Wall. Although parts of the masonry were now somewhat faded and crumbling, this massive external wall was ornamented from bottom to top with rows of recessed picture frames, arched in the Islamic style, each filled with intricate colourful mosaics.

The walk around the fort could be taken clockwise or anticlockwise, and I am glad that on that first occasion the guide chose the clockwise route. That started with the Elephant Staircase, which we ascended. The first flight of this broad, low-gradient staircase ran up the inside of the Picture Wall, into which a number of recessed balconies were set. Returning royalty with their retinue would ride their elephants up the stairs, and people welcoming them in the balconies would shower them with rose petals. The staircase then took a right turn up to a high, level surface around which a dozen or so significant buildings were sited.

These buildings were spaced out, well apart, around a formal garden which once would have contained water features, all now dry.

The buildings were of different shapes, built at different periods – a sleeping chamber, a pavilion, a hall of mirrors, a ladies' mosque, a royal bath and so on – but what they had in common was a breathtaking standard of decorative craftsmanship. Many surfaces were covered in mosaics incorporating mirror fragments, in bright non-figurative geometric designs. Many more depicted swirling floral designs in vivid colours, including bright lapis blue. These decorated surfaces were absolutely smooth and finely finished; despite their location on a hilltop exposed to the elements, it was hard to believe they were hundreds of years old.

The guide directed our progress, pouring out vast amounts of information, then led us through a different gateway from the one we had entered into a formal garden which we crossed to enter the Badshahi Mosque. I had to leave my shoes in a pile with everyone else's and walk long distances in my thin socks. The mosque was built in the 17th century, of red brick with white marble domes. Its massive central space had tall minarets at each of its four corners. I was struck by the thoughtful cleverness of the architects: the guide said that each minaret tilted very slightly outwards, so that if they were damaged by an earthquake most of the falling debris would avoid the worshippers. He explained that the main building of the mosque had been designed to amplify the voice of the preacher. Back at the fort I had seen delicate lattice-work masonry like honeycomb, in which every cell had a carefully shaped interior to give cooling ventilation without a draught.

After the mosque, we were taken through a park where I was interested to see cannons with the old British foundry marks. We passed some trees that had massively protruding buttress trunks, like great sheets of wood holding them up. I saw unfamiliar birds perching under the roof above an open walkway: finch-like, with dark backs, pink stomachs and white rumps.

We passed into the Akbari Serai: an enclosed area where the surrounding wall incorporates 180 arches where travellers could rest, shelter and cook in safety. Tamara strode ahead: with cultural sensitivity she had chosen a white outfit with a brilliant emerald-green scarf that could have become a headscarf had occasion required. I liked her choice because, being short-sighted, it meant that I had no worry about becoming detached from the group. I was, however, pretty tired, and I fell asleep in the minibus both on the outward and return journeys, so it was a relief when two further attractions planned for us were cancelled. We were to have been taken to a museum and to the zoo, but the museum was closed because someone important was visiting, and then it was too late for the zoo.

The hotel, seen in daylight, confirmed my first impression: it was grand and luxurious, with extensive, impeccably maintained gardens. The lawn opposite the front entrance had masses of flowers: not in flower beds, but in flowerpots clustered into rectangles like guards on parade. The door staff, who all seemed to be very tall, wore traditional Punjabi costumes with headdresses topped with stiff pleated plumes like folded napkins. There was an extensive foyer lounge; between that and the main eating area there was often an elderly violinist playing. These were not Western melodies or a musical form that I recognised, although it may have been rooted in South Asia. He would strain from his instrument a flow of mournful, evocative sounds of which I grew strangely fond.

The hotel had several restaurants, and that evening was also offering a barbecue in the garden, which Taymur suggested we try. An open-sided tent, like half a marquee, housed a number of grills;

the dining tables were set out on the lawn. The offerings included very enjoyable lamb, chicken and fish kebabs; the weather was warm but overcast, and overall the experience reminded me of a high-class summer garden party in England.

In the morning I found the breakfast buffet in an anteroom at the end of the main eating area. A separate section to the right on entry presented a Western-style continental breakfast with breads, pastries, spreads and so on, but I normally avoided it. The shape and appearance of the bread looked right, but it had an odd, cake-like texture and didn't taste quite right for morning toast. The main corridor of the buffet had an overall Pakistani flavour: I enjoyed nicely puffed-up puris and cooked vegetables. The table at the far end presented a Japanese-style offering, from which I took pickled ginger and some other bits and pieces. Tea, poured at the table, was a very strong, acrid, tarry fluid; drinking it took courage and determination. I assumed the normal way of enjoying it would be to dilute a small quantity with hot milk.

One of the many advantages of having the Lahore Avari as our venue was that we would be teaching the course in two of the hotel's many function rooms, without the need to commute to another site. The room allocated to me was spacious and well equipped, and the group of participants were enchanting: a joy to work with. There were, however, only about 40 participants in each of the two groups, and from my experience I guessed that the income for this activity would not cover its cost.

Perhaps because of the smaller size of the group, they were willing to talk, and were pleasantly lively, with an element of friendly competitiveness between the men and women. Some of the participants managed large chains of schools, and some were from the military sector of education. I thought that if just one such participant followed up this course with some bespoke provision for their group of institutions, our presence here could be counted a significant success. Tamara did achieve that breakthrough, and the feedback from her course resulted in her coming back subsequently to run some courses in the teaching of maths.

On the second day of the course, Taymur told us that he had ordered a car for 5.30pm to take us back to the old town, and that afterwards we had a dinner engagement with someone from Cambridge Assessment International Education. So at the end of the teaching day I changed quickly into a cream suit, and piled into the back of a smallish car with Taymur and Colin; Tamara sat in the front. She said she needed to buy an 80th birthday present for her mother. Taymur said, 'I know just the place', and took us to a traditional crafts centre run by his sister.

The driver parked outside what appeared to be a shop; on our way in we passed a young uniformed security guard proudly wearing a revolver. Inside, part of the space was devoted to displays of books and artefacts for sale, and part was laid out as an area for the teaching of practical crafts, especially calligraphy. A small group was in the middle of a class as we came in.

This was the Hast-o-Neest Centre for traditional arts and culture. The name relates to the concept of 'doing things beautifully', and the centre promotes research and study of traditional intellectual thought, as well as arts and architecture. The organisation has been doing its promotional work since 2006; this shop had opened the previous year, 2010. More recently it has grown from a 'centre' to an 'institute'. Of course there was a fair bit of chatting as Taymur caught up with his sister and she enthused about her work. I didn't mind spending some time in such a fascinating environment, and although it had been a long time since I had felt moved to buy a souvenir, I bought a small, delicately wrought copper box of 'pandan' shape, which in fact was a squashed hexagon. Pandan leaves are long and thin, but may be folded around a filling and cooked, so perhaps the shape referred to those parcels. The exhibits also included some delicate watercolours, and some fine ink miniatures in South Asian style that one of the guys in the centre produced, and which sold for high prices in New York. During this browsing time, one of the members of the calligraphy group produced a wall poster featuring Tamara's mother's name in Urdu calligraphy.

The street scene in this part of Lahore was pure South Asian: the roads were a jostling mass of mechanised rickshaws, light trucks of local design, a few donkey carts, and motorbikes usually carrying two or three riders. The way they swerved and weaved conveyed a kind of joyous exuberance. The buildings were mainly mature, with few high-rise blocks. I felt a contrast with the parts of Karachi I had seen, with its modern commercial developments and Western vehicles. Other scenes in Lahore, of a city where streets were tree lined, where bookshops, art and culture seemed prominent, made me think of Paris. That may sound a crazy comparison to anyone who knows both cities, but I found it recurring, and it was to do with mood: here was an old place with an old culture, confident about its identity, relaxed and enjoying the things it enjoyed.

Taymur was keen to show us Cooco's Den. At the time I had no sense of where I was: each experience, each visual image, was new and strange and not connected into an overall pattern. We came to a narrow street with buildings along one side: these were old, many storeys high, and with rugged irregular frontages. Beams and masonry stuck out here and there, in odd patterns and balcony-like structures.

We were guided in to one of the most extraordinary museums I have experienced. The building dated from the 16th century; it had been the working base of Cooco (Cuckoo), who was a famous prostitute. This area had been Lahore's red-light district until comparatively recently. The building was now owned by a renowned living artist, whose mother had been a sex worker here. A great many of his paintings – a kind of Lahore equivalent of Toulouse-Lautrec – were displayed: the proceeds of his work supported charities devoted to the welfare of sex workers. Apart from the paintings, the building was left just as it had been, with the décor and furnishings dating from the 1500s.

I was amazed that we could just wander around; in hindsight I guess Taymur did some discreet transaction with the guy at the door. There were ancient couches and beds, some with posts and canopies, and deeply carved wood and marble. We started to climb up very steep marble spiral staircases, but Tamara said she had no head for heights and found a seat where she could wait for us. Eventually we came out on to the roof of the building, passing a lot of ancient, decorative, deeply carved woodwork of a style that could have been found anywhere between Jeddah and Bangkok.

Taymur drew my attention to the view; I approached the parapet, and there before me was the Badshahi Mosque, its minarets floodlit, under a velvet ultramarine sky with a crescent moon lolling backwards. The fort was beyond. Looking down, I saw a scene of everyday life: someone was doing something with a horse, making it trot around in a circle at the end of a long rope; chickens were scratching about; squatters were settling down under canvas hovels. Nearer to, street traders were active. This top floor was a restaurant, but Taymur explained that at present the kitchens were not operating, so street food was winched up in buckets which swung about wildly on ropes and pulleys. I kept looking back at the mosque; my initial stunning sight of it had been unexpected because I had not known that this building was so close by. A warm breeze blew; appetising aromas drifted up from the street-food vendors below. Drinking in the panorama, I could not remember having seen anything more beautiful: a sight etched into my mind forever.

It was time for our dinner engagement. We made our way back down, collected Tamara and found the car. We were squashed together and made fast, swerving progress. Taymur wanted to show us a school, but it was too dark to make out more than some large red-brick buildings behind trees. That is how vague I was about it at the time: it was not until three years later, when he took me around it, that it became clear that it was Aitchison College, the school he had attended.

The street seemed very dark when we got out at the restaurant, which was called Salt'n Pepper Village. On the way in we passed pens and cages with chickens and other animals waiting to be enjoyed: the preference is to eat meat very fresh in Pakistan. The staff greeted us in a dark interior lit with an assortment of lanterns, candles and flickering flares which, with the general hubbub of excitement, gave the place immense atmosphere. We were guided to a candlelit table where we met our host. He was a pleasant guy who chatted about this and that: Cambridge Assessment International Education (universally referred to by its old name: Cambridge Examinations Board) is one of the most popular examination boards in Pakistan and the meeting seemed to be for general catch-up and relationship-building.

The restaurant was busy with extended families enjoying their Friday night out. Staff marshalled activity, and at a certain point told us we could get our food, which involved going into a rectangular central kitchen and buffet area. This was as dark as everywhere else, but the improvised assortment of lighting was supplemented by numerous piles of bright red glowing charcoal, underneath seething cauldrons and skewers with a wide variety of offerings. It was a good meal, in a great atmosphere. About a year later I was back in Lahore working with a different client who took me to the same restaurant, and only then did I realise that the exciting atmosphere I had enjoyed so much was the result of a power cut: they happened so frequently in Lahore that no-one had thought to comment or explain.

We saw other sights: I can't remember why we were in the locality, but we crossed the River Ravi, and I was excited to see that significant tributary of the Indus. The water was low, making a somewhat braided channel; great expanses of pale sandy banks were populated with hundreds of squatters' simple shelters. In contrast to that scene of very low water level, we were taken to a part of the town that suffered badly in the floods to which the region was prone. Beside an ancient and massive wooden door was a rectangular slab of stone with neatly painted horizontal lines, each marked with the letters HFL (High Flood Level) and a date. Some were a bit faded, but I could see October 1955, August 1973 and September 1982. All of the lines were higher than Tamara's head. More recent floods were marked in a different place: in fact many such markings were made by the property owners. The way that Taymur pointed them out seemed to imply a down-to-earth, matter-of-fact acceptance of these periodic disasters. That, and the current vibrancy of the city, spoke of depths of resilience which I took to be a reassuring strength.

The third and final day of the course, Saturday, finished happily, but we were aware of a need to rethink the format and content before making a future offer. We needed to find a format which would pay its way, and a method of working which would draw more on the knowledge and interests of participants. Tamara and I left the hotel at 1am on Sunday to catch a flight at 4.25am to Abu Dhabi. Despite the uncivilised hour I felt upbeat about the prospects for the next stage of the project, as if we were on the cusp of something yet to be defined; and the mutual commitment to a long-term relationship seemed to be holding firm.

Chapter Seven
History and Hubris in Lucknow

In Chapter One I introduced Lalita, a senior academic member of our organisation, who was well connected in India and increasingly based there; also Hilary with whom I did a teaching assignment in Delhi. In the summer term of 2011 I was made aware that Lalita was looking for suitable speakers for an event to be held in Lucknow in October.

She wanted one speaker on education leadership, and one on early childhood education, and proposed me and Hilary respectively for these roles. We were both to have speaking slots at an event called the Education Leadership International Roundtable, and Hilary would also contribute to an early years education conference immediately beforehand. The venue for these events was called the World Unity Convention Centre.

I accepted the invitation willingly: Lucknow would be a new experience, and professionally such engagements helped to build profile. I respected Lalita's judgement and didn't need to know any more. In a meeting with one of our organisation's top managers, looking at diaries, I mentioned that I would be in Lucknow on a certain date and he said with an amused twinkle, 'Aha, so you are visiting the largest school in the world!'

The point of that comment became clear when the visa request letter came. These conferences were among various sidelines run by a school that announced itself as recognised by Guinness World Records as the world's largest school in a single city. The founder and proprietor of this great enterprise was Lalita's father. The school had a large number of campuses spread across Lucknow, and to me seemed similar to the chains of independent schools under tight central management which are common across South Asia. The distinction appeared to be one of nomenclature: calling it all one school enabled the claim to be made. It is interesting what accolades people value.

We were to be lodged in an on-campus hostel next to the conference centre. Hilary travelled earlier than me because she was involved in the preceding event. I arrived on a flight direct from Muscat to Lucknow; my lack of need for local internal flights marked me out as an awkward anomaly in the minds of the organisers. I had decided to travel very light. As well as the short duration of the visit and the limited nature of my responsibilities, I was feeling a bit of an old hand at this game now: a bit more confident and self reliant, more trusting that everything would go smoothly. So I had the clothes I stood up in, and a small leather holdall with minimal extras. No laptop: my presentation was on a data stick in my pocket. Thus lightly burdened I emerged into scorching mid-afternoon sunlight in Lucknow on Thursday 13th October, after having travelled for nearly 24 hours: I had set off for London's Heathrow Terminal 3 at around tea-time the previous day. I was looking forward to a smooth transfer to the hostel and some rest and privacy there.

At the terminal exit, I hoped to see someone holding a square of cardboard with my name on it: that was how things normally worked except when I was meeting someone I already knew. I was a bit surprised when a woman placed a garland of marigolds around my neck – albeit somewhat worn and droopy, having already seen some service – and guided me along a strip of red carpet towards a few more people, armed with spotlight, camera and microphone.

Another woman, holding the mike, accosted me with the question, 'What particular aspect of our early years education are you most interested in learning about?' Well aware of being a tremendous let-down, I explained that I was not attending the early years conference: that I was a speaker at the leadership roundtable. Faces fell; they didn't waste any more time on me.

A minibus took me the short trip to the hostel, which was next to the conference hall. Two women met me outside, where the minibus had stopped. The more junior one asked, clearly expecting the answer 'yes', whether I would like to come straight into the conference hall to join an act of celebration taking place. To her obvious disappointment, I explained that I wanted some time to myself to rest after my long journey; that the event in which I was involved did not start until the following morning, but I would look in later. During this conversation, I was distracted by an enormous screen, covering the whole external wall of the building facing the road, bearing an image of my colleague Hilary being interviewed upon her arrival a couple of days previously, drowned by a commentary along the lines of, 'Experts from all over the world come to learn from our educational practice'.

Meanwhile, the more senior greeter was preparing to show me to my accommodation, and noticed me picking up my light holdall. 'No! We'll see to that!' she commanded, turning on a nearby male minion with a look of death, furiously pointing at him and at my bag. He scuttled forward with a manner of cringing apology; I felt deeply embarrassed that he might assume I was the one expecting him to carry my bag. We proceeded up a staircase, and I was puzzled to see another nameplate on the room door as well as my own. Inside, the facilities were basic, to the point that I didn't see any great merit in staying there for very long. So I caved in and went to see what was going on in the conference hall. It was a massive space with a very large stage. Most of the available wall-space seemed to be covered with screens like the one outside, big enough for a drive-in cinema, which at all available moments during breaks between speeches broadcast self-aggrandising propaganda.

The main body of the auditorium was set out with tables fully covered to the floor in the style of an altar cloth, but in this case printed with the logos and titles of the two events. The chairs were made of brilliantly glossy silver-grey plastic, shining like pearls. At the front was a row of easy chairs for distinguished guests, to which I was directed.

At 5.30pm the assembled company was guided on to a fleet of buses for a 'Lucknow bus tour', which would end at one of the school's other campuses where dinner would be provided. The vehicles were ordinary yellow school buses of local design. This would be interesting – I had never ridden in one before. And interesting it was, but not for the merits of the scenic tour. We boarded in daylight, but night fell early, and most of the ride was in total darkness, clogged among dense traffic congestion. Vehicle headlights provided the only scenery, and hooting and engine noises constituted the only soundtrack. What was interesting was how collisions were avoided, which had puzzled me previously. Early in my travel experience I had appreciated that there were particular skills in driving in congested Asian cities.

In this instance, the bus had in effect three drivers: the actual driver behind the wheel kept his eyes glued to a large door mirror, while a second man stood as lookout in the front left corner, and a third stood in the open door (which let in rich fumes) facing the rear, poking his head out slightly when circumstances allowed. The three of them kept up a stream of terse communications: they were obviously practised at it, and the driver must have had complete trust in his assistants' guidance.

After an hour or so of this interesting demonstration of skill, we debussed at another school – sorry, I should say another campus of the one very big school – which on this occasion was serving simply as a feeding station. Nothing else happened there to justify the journey. Dinner was a buffet, served outside under open awnings, which with the lights and the smell of food seemed designed to attract as many insects as possible. Entomology was one of my boyhood interests, and I retained a passing knowledge of UK insects and which ones are harmful, but Lucknow's were in a superior league of which I knew nothing. I experienced a mixture of interest and alarm each time one dropped on to my head or scuttled over the rice on my paper plate. The food was welcome because I was hungry, and because I like Indian food, but it wasn't great. Typical of conference catering, cheapness and bulk took priority over finesse. The only 'meat' dishes seemed to be rice cooked in meat stock and decorated with sharp bones.

The journey back to the hostel was quicker because the traffic had thinned. I dozed for part of the way: not even the hard, upright, shaking seats could entirely counter my tiredness. Back at the hostel, my room was hot and housing numerous insects. The metal window-frame didn't fit properly and left insect-sized gaps, so I had to accept that my initial plan, to attack and clear the intruders, would be futile. Unusually, I hadn't brought any night attire. I tried to sleep. Periodically, insects dropped on to my naked body: I would feel the heavy pin-sharp claws of beautifully iridescent beetles, and the lighter, feathery touch of more dangerous-looking Hymenoptera. Morning came, after what I will always think of as my night in the insect house of a zoo: not strictly true, but unlike anything before or since.

My nose guided me to breakfast on the ground floor of the hostel: doughy breads and oily vegetable concoctions. On the way out, the hostel manager accosted me self-importantly to tell me my room-mate would be moving in this morning. I reacted angrily, telling him I was not prepared to share a room. 'He is British, I thought you might like to share with one of your compatriots.' How dare this silly little man make such an assumption: I was there as a distinguished visiting speaker, did he have no idea about how I should be treated? I reiterated my objection; perhaps in the heat of the moment I might have said I would prefer to sleep on the pavement. One of the conference organisers was called; also Lalita herself appeared; another room was found into which I could transfer. They flapped about helping, and were amazed that I was travelling so light. As soon as I was on my own, I checked how well the window fitted its frame, and was greatly relieved to see that it was insect-proof.

I had a chance to see more of the campus in daylight. It was enormous, and immaculately maintained. White four-storey blocks were separated by vast green lawns. Along corridors and external walkways, every available surface was covered with educational displays and uplifting exhortations.

The conference ('Roundtable') at which I was speaking lasted for five days – I would be leaving at the start of the third day – and according to its publicity would involve 2000 participants. Certainly the hall seemed pretty full. The opening formalities took a full two hours, including performances by school staff and children, an elaborate lamp-lighting ceremony in which I was asked to take part, and a session on expectations in which Lalita's sister took a prominent lead. It was interesting to see the two of them interact, with sisterly rivalry which played out on the world's stage. I learnt during informal chat that her sister had been appointed to an international role, based in America, for which Lalita considered herself to have been more relevantly qualified. Lalita then gave the first formal lecture: the first time I had seen her perform. As expected, it was informative and well researched. Other inputs followed.

Lunch was efficiently distributed in cardboard boxes, containing a reasonable picnic, followed by an extended and very tedious interlude outside under the blazing sun. The first activity was a group photograph of the assembled delegates: a common occurrence at such events, but this one seemed to take a long time to get everyone arranged. The hot sun shone, my head flushed and sweated, and knowing this organisation's thirst for self-promotion made me resent the discomfort more. The photography was followed by a press conference. Everyone remained a captive audience on the uncomfortable tiered benches while the cameras rolled and the management boasted about their achievements. Some of the questioners may have been genuine journalists; I doubted whether all of them were. My speaking slot was immediately after this parade-ground ordeal, which had already overrun by half an hour. If the delegates were anything like me, moving straight from here into the relative cool of the conference hall would cause a proportion of them to fall asleep after my first few sentences.

I had been allocated an hour; I didn't use all of it. The technology worked smoothly, I outlined my evolving thinking, and at the end of the afternoon several people came to me to express interest. There weren't any tea breaks: wisely the organisers had chosen the more efficient method of serving tea at people's seats during the sessions. This involved staff obsequiously crouching between the rows, shuffling along dispensing the refreshment. The tea was a beautiful thick cardamom mixture: hot, black and invigorating, and in every way to my liking except that it was served in tiny coffee cups when I was yearning for a mugful.

The last session of the afternoon was a 'cultural programme', taking the form of eight consecutive performances by students of the school, involving groups from six of the campuses, spreading over a good couple of hours. This was somewhat in excess of any in-conference entertainment I had experienced previously. The performances were polished: probably the same troupes were wheeled out each time visitors needed to be impressed. Two themes predominated: the first was the school's very strong commitment to a multi-faith ethos, which I could applaud without reservation.

The second was the school's equally strong commitment to promoting world peace. A key, and I gathered oft-repeated strategy to that end was for the children to write to world leaders along the lines that they wanted world peace, and what were they going to do about it? Of course the children were guided by their teachers to make these overtures; nevertheless letters from children elicit a different response from the one that you or I might get if we made similar requests. The kind responses given by some of the famous recipients were captured by the school's media and milked to the full. The commitment to promoting peace was prominent in the school's mission statement, but I never really found out how far that went beyond simplistic aspiration: whether the curriculum enabled students to make mature judgements about the causes of conflicts and the obstacles to their resolution.

Dinner was served outside by the pool, at the conference centre. The format and menu were similar to those of the previous evening, but here there was the added interest of insects which are attracted to water. Next morning, one of the conference organisers, called Rani, approached Hilary and me and asked if, after lunch, we would like her to take us to some of the interesting places in Lucknow: an offer we eagerly accepted.

The morning's presentations proceeded, some quite interestingly, interspersed with the usual promotional films from the school's vast store. In one of them, a kind of glorious finale, the commentator in a voice of fanatical dedication was concluding, 'All of this is the work of one man...', and there he was on the screen: a high-angle shot of the great founder-proprietor, a little old man in a brown suit, marching across a parade ground holding a banner on a stick, followed by marching ranks of children: king of the kids. 'One man, who has the vision, the devotion, the commitment... ' (and many other qualities), 'One man, who has never taken a day's holiday...' Really? What a bore for his family. The boss must have either written this script himself, or at least approved it. It was slightly nauseating to see the presentation of what was almost certainly a very good school being marred by such hubristic twaddle.

Rani took us to her car: she sat in front with the driver. Soon I was able to drink in the environment. The street was lined on both sides with mature deciduous trees with large emerald-green leaves. On one side, a dozen or so green and yellow mechanised rickshaws were parked haphazardly; white-clothed men sat and stood among them in patches of shade. The road was full of cars and motorbikes, and some bicycles. We turned into a more open, sunlit street with white stucco houses along one side, fronted by a few metres of scrawny grass and shrubs, before joining a more major road which ran straight and passed under several bridges. We were behind a great crowd of motorcyclists, overtook a donkey cart, and passed a street trader sitting in the dust and fumes beside a barrow of vegetables. We passed a side street: one side of it was jam-packed with parked bicycles, the other with vending stalls made crudely from poles and scraps of corrugated iron, leaving just enough room for single-file traffic. Dozens of electric cables curved across the road at a height of 5 or 6 metres. In places where the traffic was proceeding slowly, people walked freely in the road: sari-clad women and men in Western-style shirts and trousers, none of them in a hurry. We passed many such scenes, mixing clutter and colour, tradition and modernity, of which I could never tire, and in due course arrived at the Residency.

The ruined site of the Residency was preserved in its cannon-battered state as a sombre memorial to the great suffering of the Siege of Lucknow in 1857. Hilary was excited to be making this visit: as we moved among the exhibits I gathered that the place held some special significance for her family. It was clearly an emotional experience for her. We took our time: there was so much to absorb.

The site was extensive, incorporating the main residency building, along with a large house identified as 'Dr Fayrer's' and St Mary's Church and cemetery. The grounds were well kept, with carefully mown lawns, neatly swept paths and trimmed hedges, but parts had been deliberately allowed to take on a wild character. Bushes had been left to grow big and untidy in the cemetery, and some views of the main residency showed the ruins rising out of long grass. It was a nice touch, creating an eerie, haunted feel. All of the buildings had been extensively damaged by cannon fire, with great holes in the parts of the walls which remained standing. The museum was constructed mainly at basement level. Around the edges were some of the cannons used in the defence. I looked at the British foundry marks on their dark bronze barrels. Some had been new at the time: proof-marked 1854 and 1856.

I was not paying respects to a dead ancestor as Hilary was, and I thought I would be able to look at the site and exhibits with detached objectivity, but the atmosphere of the place was too strong: it demanded engagement. The three principal considerations for me were the duration of the siege, the level of suffering it occasioned, and the tragic avoidability of the whole thing had the British shown more respect to their hosts.

Lucknow had been the capital of Avadh, a kingdom ruled by a succession of highly cultured nawabs noted for their patronage of art, music and fine buildings. The British East India Company deposed the last nawab in 1856: to modern eyes, an act of oafish high-handedness which must have been deeply shocking to the local population. The Indian Mutiny occurred the following year. In July 1857 the British population of Lucknow sought refuge (presumably with their Indian staff) in the Residency. Sir Henry Lawrence, the local commander, had prepared for a siege which he believed would be relieved in a couple of weeks. More than 12 weeks later, a relief force led by Sir Henry Havelock broke through to the Residency, but then became trapped inside. The siege continued a further seven weeks until finally relieved in mid-November by Sir Colin Campbell. Over the five months of the total operation, about 2000 of the besieged people died from artillery action, cholera, typhoid and malnutrition. The number of Indians who died in the conflict has not been recorded.

The Residency building had been designed to incorporate a basement level, to provide a cooler environment in the summer heat. During the attack, it provided the safest area for the women and children; the extreme overcrowding down there must have added to their woes. The plaque beside St Mary's Church, which now stood only about a metre high, explained that the surrounding cemetery was created during the siege. Enormous numbers of corpses were dumped there during the night with minimal ceremony.

At the end of our tour of the Residency, Rani led us across Mahatma Gandhi Marg to stand on the banks of the River Gomti, a major tributary of the Ganges. I was delighted to see such a major Indian river, all the more so because following our previous contemplations the scene conveyed a distillation of tranquillity and Indian-ness. The greenish water flowed lazily between grassy banks dotted with bushes. The river was wider than British rivers: nearer to estuary width, although this one was still a long way from the sea. A dozen or so black water buffalo bathed, some submerged to their horns, while others made leisurely progress to the shore. Several monuments were in view, including a small temple-like structure built in the middle of the river. Rowing skiffs were moored along the bank. It was mid-afternoon on a sunny day: the light was hazy with a slight umber tinge above the horizon.

Next, Rani took us to the Bara Imambara complex, an enormous spread of ceremonial halls and mosque. I write that as if I knew where I was and what I was doing, but at the time all was shrouded in the usual blur and bewilderment of guided sightseeing in the course of working visits. After parking, we went through an entrance, and I was immediately struck by the size, graceful proportions and elaborately carved decorative stonework of the ancient edifices. At a certain point, progressing from secular to sacred ground, shoes had to be taken off and left among a hundred other pairs dotted about on the sun-baked pavement. Would I get them back? I had no other footwear with me.

The mosque was stunning in its scale, elegant proportions and ornamentation. My only real comparator was the Badshahi Mosque in Lahore: this was just as impressive, but had a completely different character. It was somehow more 'Indian', in the ornate style of its carved stonework, and, despite its great size, it had a more intimate, welcoming feel. I had not previously fully appreciated the significance of the minority religions in India: certainly this visit brought home to me the importance of Islam in Lucknow and the other city-states that had grown out of the Mughal empire.

Our itinerary concluded with a visit to the National Botanical Gardens. During conversations in the car, I gathered that despite her senior position in the school, Rani's current attachment was temporary. She had a professional background in something different – it might have been stockbroking or merchant banking – and she was planning to move into something to do with books: opening a bookshop, or writing, or both. At the time we made a vague plan to keep in touch, but did not.

The National Botanical Gardens were, of course, full of plants, most noticeably great banks of brightly blooming flowers. The metal railings and neat walkways made me think of Kew in a hotter climate. The combination of flowers and sun was attracting many butterflies. In part of my mind I was a boy again, with my butterfly net, whiling away summer days in a world of my own. Another part of my mind told me continually that I was a long way from home, in Lucknow, totally dependent on someone I had met only recently. Why did it all feel so normal and natural? Here and now, it was Saturday, so not strictly speaking a working day, but all the same, ambling in this environment with pleasant companions, it was hard to remember that I was doing my job.

That night, I found myself in a conversation with Hilary and Lalita in the corridor outside my bedroom. They had come to say goodbye, as I was off in the morning: Hilary was staying longer. I had been a bit surprised to see Lalita's situation at first hand: back in the office, when people talked about her being deployed on liaison work in her home country, I hadn't realised that involved a return to the family nest. I felt moved to challenge her on whether this was what she really wanted to be doing with her life, and how much academic research she was able to achieve here. Privately, although it was none of my business, I also wondered how much return our organisation was getting for her salary. She admitted that often she spent the mornings dealing with her father's correspondence. I gave her a peck on the cheek and wished her well, and left her looking thoughtful: I didn't think that she had been challenged to reflect on her priorities for quite a while.

My flight was due to leave at 7am on Sunday morning, and I needed to confirm arrangements for getting me to the airport. I found the hostel manager – it was the same guy who had been so keen that I should share a room. I told him I needed to leave at 5am at the latest. No, he explained in his superior manner, the airport was only five minutes away, so it would be fine to leave at 6am: he would arrange the taxi accordingly. 'But I am supposed to check in two hours ahead', I protested. 'No, it is only one hour for domestic flights.' 'I am flying internationally.' 'But you will be going to Delhi first, or another Indian city: that stage is domestic.' 'No, I am flying direct from here to Muscat.' Finally, reluctantly, he conceded, while clearly regarding my route as irregular and disreputable. It was a relief to see the driver there on time, and satisfying to get airborne. Reflecting on how some of my preconceptions of the trip had turned out to be false, I thought that perhaps I would not travel quite so light in future.

Chapter Eight
Bogotá and Santa Marta: a Breakthrough

After my trip to Lucknow, which as always seemed to have lasted much longer than its actual duration, I had two weeks before setting off to Colombia. That turned out to be a week and a half of frenetic meetings and activity to keep the rest of my job under control, and a couple of days doing as little as possible at our Yorkshire house.

Back in the summer, I had received a brief e-mail offering the prospect of a consultancy opportunity in Colombia, brokered by a Colombian called Melba who was registered with one of my colleagues as a PhD student. After the briefest exchanges in the department – this was how these things happened – it was agreed that I should meet Melba to find out more and to take whatever action seemed appropriate.

I had no prior knowledge of her ethnicity, age, professional standing or areas of interest. The person who came and stood in the open doorway of my office was a smiling and heavily fragranced woman, middle-aged, with a short, soft, ample figure and, I guessed, predominantly mestizo roots. Her relaxed and sunny disposition enabled us to enjoy a pleasant rapport from the outset.

Her professional work had covered several aspects of school leadership and improvement. In addition, she had specialised knowledge of teaching English as a second language, and her work in that field had brought her good standing with the British Council; she was also on friendly terms with people in the Colombian Ministry of Education, through a combination of professional and personal links. Senior people in the ministry knew of our organisation, and of Melba's link with it. They were looking for an organisation of our kind of standing to develop a programme to teach coaching skills. The ministry planned to appoint a cadre of people to be change agents ('*formadores*'), who would coach education personnel to help them to improve the quality of teaching throughout Colombia.

This was an interesting and ambitious project: one I was delighted to get involved with professionally, and also very attractive because it offered me a first opportunity to work in South America. I made the usual business arrangement with Melba, and the process of liaison and preparation began. There was the familiar problem of a language barrier, and the rather larger problem of Colombian bureaucracy which was truly Byzantine. Every piece of business correspondence had to be vetted by the Colombian Embassy in London; we had to appoint a Colombian lawyer in Bogotá to represent our interests; we had to prove that our organisation did indeed exist; the director of our organisation had to prove his existence: these are just a few illustrations of a deeper quagmire.

I also had to field questions coming from within our organisation about the extent to which the government was actually in control of the country, and a range of related risks. I was no stranger to such situations, and Melba's reassuring involvement was like a soothing balm.

After much interaction, it was agreed that I would go to Bogotá with Melba, in her new capacity as a member of my team, to conduct a short consultancy to cement the partnership, and to agree what the coaching programme would include and how it would be organised. I had already agreed internally that my colleague Gordon, who specialised in coaching, would do the detailed design if we got the green light, and between us we identified a team of course presenters who would work under his direction.

I travelled to Heathrow on the evening of Saturday 29th October, and on Sunday morning flew by Lufthansa to Bogotá via Frankfurt, which felt like going a long way round. The timings were better and the cost lower than the other option I was offered with Iberia via Madrid. It was my first experience of Lufthansa and I was impressed – I don't think it was just my imagination, based on stereotypes – by their smooth efficiency. The woman in charge of the cabin wore a military-style uniform and exuded quiet competence: neither the aggressive gaoler attitude of some British Airways staff, nor the smiling geisha manner of the air hostess tradition. The plane started moving dead on time, and taxied fast around a curving route to the runway, then straight into take-off without pause. The long-haul flight took 12 hours, which with the time difference meant that I landed in Bogotá at 7.35pm.

Melba was there to meet me. I don't know what I would have done had she not been: my mobile phone didn't work on that side of the Atlantic. She guided me out to a taxi, and to a Holiday Inn near the airport which she had chosen as my lodging place. By London time it was the middle of the night, so discussion about our work was left for the morning.

On Monday 31st October, my first view of Bogotá, from the window of the taxi in which Melba was briefing me, was slightly masked by early morning mist. My main impression was of busy, grid-pattern roads, through tracts of concrete low-rise buildings, almost East European in their grim monotony. Everywhere I looked, the scene was backed and overshadowed by the Andes, whose tops were hidden in a leaden blanket of cloud. Of course the street scenes I was glimpsing made up just one small segment of the outskirts: Bogotá is a rambling metropolis of nearly seven million people, built at an altitude of 2640 metres: the world's third highest capital city. The only ones higher are also in the Andes: La Paz in Bolivia and Quito in Ecuador. There was no time for sightseeing built into the schedule of this short visit: Melba said that there would be the chance for that pleasure on a subsequent trip.

We came to the ministry: a slightly higher-rise concrete block, and passed through the reception formalities, which were administered mainly by young women in military-style uniforms, and involved entries in log-books and examinations of laptops. Upstairs in the office there was a bit of a party atmosphere because a number of staff had dressed themselves up in Halloween costumes and make-up, and had festooned suitable decorations around the place.

The morning began with briefings: first a two-hour session with Monica who, with her assistant Angelica, explained the programme for transforming the quality of education. Then an hour and a half with Claudia who went through the national plan for teacher training. Both of these women spoke good English; they would have been in mid-career, the high-flying, up-and-coming change agents. From my perspective as an old man they seemed young and lively. Both exuded confidence and energy, and emphasised the importance of training the trainers to support change through enabling, coaching methods.

Without getting sidetracked into a boringly professional voice, this approach was immensely attractive to me. At the heart of most understandings of 'education' is that people should be enabled to make informed choices about their ongoing development and direction in life: in the trade we talk of giving learners agency. Yet most of the education reforms of recent times imposed by governments around the world have been implemented in a very dictatorial manner: you must do it this way because we say so, which clashes with the whole purpose of the enterprise. Here at last was a government committed to improving education using truly educational methods. I was impressed and excited. But not totally surprised: I had several times worked with groups of senior education officials from South America (although not including Colombia) attending my sessions in London, and I had noticed that educational philosophy had a stronger place in their hearts than came over when I dealt with officials from other continents and regions.

My programme in the afternoon included a session with the vice minister, who was an amiable middle-aged man wearing a cardigan. 'We are fighting a war here, you know', he explained fairly early in the conversation. As usual I had not done much background reading before this visit, and my impressions of Colombia and its troubles were derived from British news coverage. So I knew that two long-standing issues bedevilled attempts to apply normal government: massively powerful and violent forces controlling the drugs industry, and politically motivated armed insurrections of one shade or another. I knew that, as was so often the case in troubled countries, the impact on the ground varied markedly on a regional basis, and that the Foreign Office advice at the time deemed Bogotá an acceptable place for me to be working.

Only much later, after reading Tom Feiling's *Short Walks from Bogotá*, did I appreciate how deeply the troubles had been embedded right across Colombian society. His knowledge of the country had been built up between 1999 and 2005, gained in front-line situations as he researched the cocaine trade. He made a film, and wrote a book on that subject, and then, after a five-year break back in England, he returned to the country in 2010 to find out how the 'new' Colombia was faring in its more peaceful and optimistic phase. His accounts of conversations all over the country portray a lasting legacy of loss, grief and suffering, and the impossibility for many of escaping the permanent brand-marks of alignment with one or other faction during the troubles. His fieldwork was contemporaneous with my little bits of consultancy.

The foreign affairs journalist and security expert Frank Gardner also wrote about his two visits to Colombia in his travel memoir *Far Horizons*. His first, in 1996, was a trekking expedition in the mountains, which involved flying from Bogotá to 'the tiny coastal airstrip at Santa Marta, where a hot wind was blowing in from the Caribbean'. Gardner described the risks to visitors at that time, and the level of violent crime to which the population was subjected.

He went back in 2008, wheelchair-bound following the severe injuries he sustained in an Al-Qaida attack in Riyadh, to do a piece for the BBC about kidnapping. Kidnappings in Colombia had reached a peak of 3500 a year in 2002; by 2008 they were falling to about a tenth of that figure, averaging a mere one a day. Gardner saw the security forces training; he interviewed people on all sides including former kidnappers; and despite careful precautions narrowly avoided his team being robbed of their recording equipment.

The amiable guy in the cardigan elaborated two points about the struggle relevant to the project. First, the provision of school education had been much disrupted in the worst-affected areas. I knew what he meant. I had seen the effects of the long conflict in South Sudan: infrastructures wrecked, teachers not paid for years, everybody distracted. The second point concerned where I could be taken to in reasonable safety to see a school system typical of those the project was most intended to help. Thus decisions had been taken, and arrangements planned: I was to go to Santa Marta in the morning.

That involved catching a shuttle bus at 6am from the hotel to the airport for a flight due to leave at 7.31am. We assembled: a delegation of five. Angelica was in charge, supported by two very pleasant young colleagues: Yenny and Nicolás, the latter being the designated interpreter, although the others spoke English quite well. The small plane sat on a runway amid lush green grass. Beyond the perimeter fence was a dark green mass of mixed woodland, and in the distance, humpy-topped mountains, slate grey in the morning light. We took off on time, I got views of the mixed industrial landscape around the airport, then we followed the valley of the River Magdalena, which had been a major thoroughfare throughout much of Colombia's history.

The scenery was spectacular, and my companions were delightful; my heart danced with joy. The sky was mainly clear, dotted with fair-weather cumulus clouds, and the visibility was excellent, as if the air was clean. The plane started off flying in the valley, so I was looking level or slightly upwards to the horizon. The valley sides were covered with dense dark green forest; above that the Andes rose on both sides in spectacular jagged peaks. As the plane climbed, I saw that the relief was more complex: not a single valley, but a series of interconnecting lowlands broken up by ridges. The lowlands showed a mixed land-use pattern of agriculture and some sizeable settlements.

Further on, the landscape became even more rugged, and I saw a number of lakes. The difference in altitude between valley and peak was enormous, and continued right to the sea. Indeed, I understood that at Santa Marta the mountains rose higher than behind any other coastal city: the Sierra Nevada de Santa Marta reached 5809 metres. As we approached the coast, the valley bottom broadened into a great expanse of different greens; the sides of the valley were forested at the lower levels, and signs of mineral extraction became more evident. Melba quoted me some facts and figures about the size and range of Colombia's mineral exports, including to Britain. Suddenly we were over the coast: there was my first aerial view of the Caribbean Sea, where a mineral-carrying ship was getting loaded up at the end of a long jetty. We flew along the coast at a height well below the mountain tops. The settled coastal plain looked very narrow: not much more than 100 metres in places. The settlements included a few high-rise buildings.

The 700-kilometre flight lasted an hour and a half, which was long enough to allow for informal social interaction. The strongly positive impression I had gained of Angelica in the formal setting of the ministry continued to grow. She wanted everything to go smoothly – she was hungry for professional success – and I sensed that she was enjoying this trip almost as much as I was. She was engaging, intelligent, and very attractive: dark Spanish with blonde hair. Yenny, who looked mainly Amerindian, was personable and eager to please, and I think in charge of tickets and practical arrangements. Melba was her normal sunny, unflappable self, so in all it was one of the nicest flights I can remember.

The drive from the airstrip into Santa Marta was also a pleasant tourist experience. The car turned on to a coastal road, heading east. The sea, to our left, was dotted with many cargo ships heading west, a scene that reminded me of a familiar view in East Yorkshire: specifically, standing on the Spurn Peninsula and seeing the merchant ships queueing up waiting for pilots to guide them up the Humber Estuary. The sea was blue and the sand pinky yellow, set back from the road behind a few metres of long grass in flower – blobs of fawn-coloured fluff swaying in the breeze – and trees, in some places dotted sparsely and in others forming thickets. There was a dominant species which I could not identify: greyish trunks grew at low angles, perhaps because of prevailing winds, and the pinnate leaves were smaller than ash, but larger than acacia. The space between the road and the sea widened, and under the trees was a row of what looked like market stalls, constructed of poles and tarpaulins: I could see tables and chairs beneath one of them.

The coast had a series of small bays separated by points; we came to a much bigger bay, where grass and trees were replaced by a paved promenade. Across the bay a line of white tower blocks stood against dark hummocky hills. Then, ahead, a greater concentration of white buildings came into view: we were arriving at Santa Marta. The road curved south, away from the shore, and we saw the town across an expanse of lush green grass and scrub.

Heading inland across the coastal plain, we soon passed an ungated level crossing. A motorcyclist crossed at the same time in the opposite direction. The track ran arrow-straight towards Santa Marta; it looked like a toy-train set, although it probably carried heavy wagons laden with minerals. There are just over 3300 kilometres of railway in Colombia, of which only 150 kilometres are of standard gauge: they carry coal from the Cerrejón coal mines to Puerto Bolivar. The rest is 914 millimetres (3 feet) narrow gauge, of which 500 kilometres is disused. There are now no passenger trains except the Turistren between Bogotá and Zipaquirá. So the track I was looking at seemed small because it *was* small.

Near the crossing, a grand house in luxuriant gardens was enclosed by a white stucco wall exhibiting a local design feature. The pillars incorporated into the wall at intervals to strengthen it were topped with miniature square roofs of red pantiles. There may have been a practical reason for that design: short heavy showers occurred at intervals. We drove beside a hillside covered in lush green bushes and small trees, among which cacti poked up their tall columns. I had seen the same pattern of vegetation in Mexico, which had dispelled my assumption that cacti only grew in deserts.

Colombia has 32 administrative divisions ('departments') and Santa Marta is in Magdalena. Our first work engagement was to visit the local director of education, to exchange courtesies and to get his formal blessing to go ahead with the visits that Angelica had arranged with him. The first visit, which was to occupy the remainder of the morning, was to a school in central Santa Marta of 1700 students, where I was to see the secondary phase provision. The rector, Calixto, explained that the school itself was 106 years old, and that it was housed in a national monument which was in poor condition.

The building was in a classical style, with Corinthian columns, balustrades and porticos, painted strikingly in mustard and white: the mustard was peeling off everywhere I looked.

It was a new experience to see a school operating in what felt to me a bit like a dilapidated old castle: crossing an inner bailey, mounting deeply weathered stone steps to watch a lesson on Columbus taking place inside a turret. Another lesson was being held under the trees. It was a warm climate and there was a blending of internal and external space, with no walls separating classrooms from adjacent open-air corridors. The premises were packed quite densely with students. There was a lively buzz of engagement, although the teaching methods were basic and formal: I saw a fair bit of dictation. A noisy lesson about the revolution was nearing its end; the female teacher seemed to be enthusing the students to adopt a revolutionary attitude. We spoke briefly at the finish; she added a final comment under her breath. I asked what she had said. Reluctantly, Angelica explained, 'She said will he come back and marry me?'

Next I was taken to lunch at a small two-storey restaurant near the city centre. Showers of warm rain continued to punctuate the day. The restaurant was in a narrow side street crowded with people and cars, with a dense untidy cobweb of electric cables overhead. Mature trees grew out of the pavement at intervals, further restricting the space. We passed a noisy bar on the way to our reserved table upstairs, then crowded around its polished dark wooden surface. I did not gain much of an impression of Colombian cuisine during that first visit: most of the food I was given was canteen-style, starchy and bland, but always welcome, because working heightens my appetite. However, I became quickly aware of the place of Coca-Cola in national life: the sweet, purple-tinged rice on my plate now, alongside some stewed meat, had been boiled in it.

As a child I had not been allowed cola drinks. On the very few occasions, such as at a school party or at a friend's house, when it seemed obligatory to try a little, I distinctly remember three successive sensations. First, the guilty wickedness of supping forbidden fruit; secondly a weird but strangely alluring flavour, and finally, a few seconds later, a truly alarming attack of sugar and acidity on my teeth and gums. My thirst and my need to avoid citrus fruit drinks (the only alternative) prompted me, in Colombia, to try cola again, after an interval of 45 years. A pint tumbler arrived, full of dodgy-looking ice cubes, and the first six gulps were delightfully quenching. The flavour was fine; this is not so bad, I thought. And then the effect kicked in, heightened by my having suffered receding gums for many years.

There was some free time after lunch before we needed to go to the second school; the women thought (rightly) that I might like to see the sea. On the way to the car we passed a crowded square with white stucco buildings and many mature trees growing out of the pavement. We were driven past a large, well-tended ornamental garden; for a while we were behind a picturesque, crowded double-decker bus with open sides. Another shower spattered down as we passed more squares, more imposing white buildings and a round bandstand area surrounded by palm trees, and came to a parking place near the shore. I was led through bushes and coarse grass, over an uneven surface of earth, rocks, roots and sand, to look at the Caribbean Sea from its southern shore. Another significant step for me: another badge screwed on to the walking stick of wandering.

The sky was blue and the sea sparkled, and the sand was yellow; but at this point it formed only a narrow strip as the shoreline here was mainly of wave-smoothed rock. Coastal natural features have a certain universality; the backshore vegetation we had come through might be of different species, but in form, appearance and feel on the hand, could have been on the Spurn Peninsula. The location was so exotic for me that some part of my mind expected the landscape to have strange fairyland qualities: its familiarity was disconcerting.

Someone suggested a photograph; Nicolás produced a camera and took a snap of me with the three women in a line among the backshore scrub, with the sea behind us. The onshore breeze was strong at that time of day. There was me in my black suit; the women were smiling for the camera but also laughing about their battle with the wind, hair disarrayed and light summer blouses buffeting.

The afternoon's school visit was in Ciénaga. The town and municipality were next door to Santa Marta, but the school itself was out in the rural fringe, reached after a drive through suburban sprawl, past fields, along roads edged with dusty red earth. The edges of towns displayed an odd mixture of modern commercial buildings among rows of tatty, thrown-together shops with an almost shanty-like character. One was selling masses of great green plantains under crooked sheets of wavy corrugated iron. Road surfaces ranged from broad expanses of concrete blocks to beaten earth, rutted and puddled in places: the sporadic showers continued. Even down some of the poorer-looking streets, it was not uncommon to see trees and shrubs neatly clipped, on stretches of verge maintained as gardens.

The school had over 2700 students; it was housed in fairly new buildings. After brief introductions to the rector (who was a civil engineer by training) and some of his senior staff, Melba and I were to sit in on a sequence of classes for primary-aged children. I assume that Angelica and Yenny spent the time talking with the rector about the project.

We saw four classes, spanning the first four grades. By modern global standards, the quality of teaching was poor in all of them. With a startling sense of time-travel, I was seeing the practice that would have been typical in an averagely poor English primary school between the late 1950s and early 1970s. There were periods of time when the children were not directed at all; then, when the teacher did direct a teaching or learning activity, it was left very much up to the children to choose whether and to what extent to engage with it. The pupils spent much time off-task, and often ignored the teacher's instructions without any consequence. In the youngest class, the number present varied, as the children seemed free to wander out of the classroom unsupervised. One lesson covered the fight for Colombia's independence, like the lesson for older students I had seen in the previous school.

After seeing the lessons, we rejoined the others and I had the opportunity to put some questions to the rector. Which I did sensitively, knowing how irritating it can be when consultants arrive from an alien planet, but it became clear, as I knew it would, that the rector saw his duties beginning and ending with putting a teacher into every classroom and providing a functioning building.

Our return flight left at 8.05pm; there was time to eat and Angelica directed us to a restaurant alongside the terminal. We sat outside around a rough wooden-slatted table, spotlit among ornamental shrubs which cast interesting shadows. The food was a basic but welcome filler: breaded chicken, potato wedges, a bit of salad. A cat came hopefully to the table: the others ignored it; it identified me as the one to come to, and was friendly. I fussed it but did not feed it.

There was much to ponder during the drowsy flight back to Bogotá through inky-black sky. While we were all tired and nodding off at intervals, the mood was very positive, with a sense of momentum and warm collaboration. My reflections on the day concerned the relationships between place, time, and movements of people and ideas, which I was exploring in my professional writings. Here, as in numerous other countries, an educated, globalised political elite made three- or five-year plans to bring about a scale of change which had taken 30 to 50 years to achieve in England and other mature school systems.

To change attitudes and expectations so quickly was a daunting task, but not impossible. Whereas the Western systems had evolved at their own pace, for those coming new to the game there were models and templates to copy, a load of scientific knowledge, modern communications and modern understandings about how to manage change. Importantly, there was also a cadre of clear-sighted young media-savvy professionals who would not take 'no' for an answer, of whom Angelica was one.

After a late night and an early start, my work on Wednesday began with my giving a lecture to a group of about 50 assembled by the ministry, supported by simultaneous translation: a two-hour slot starting at 8.30am. The second half of the morning was a working session with the first group of designated *formadores*, in which Melba and I were to gain a clearer picture of their prior knowledge of the coaching process, and their views on specific needs and issues to be addressed in the training. As usual, language was a hurdle (as distinct from a barrier): a number of the group had a good level of English. At one point, one of the participants asked, 'What language is this session being conducted in?' 'Spanglish', another good-naturedly replied.

After a late lunch, Melba and I worked on our report, which needed to be e-mailed to Angelica by 5pm ahead of formal presentation to the vice minister the next day. We did our work at the hotel, and at the end Melba suggested a celebratory drink of the local rum, which sounded appealing. I said I wanted it straight, which was just as well, because Melba explained that had I not done so it would have come automatically drowned in Coca-Cola.

On Thursday morning we had a series of meetings at the ministry which, among other things, finalised practical and contractual arrangements for the next phase of the project. Gordon would finalise the course materials to take account of what I had been told. He would then come in December to train the small group of *formadores* who had already been appointed, and again in January with his team to work with a larger group. Quite a lot more work would follow, and I was delighted to have helped to broker such a significant assignment.

My flight left at 9.45pm, arriving in Frankfurt at 3pm on Friday, and thence to London at 4.55pm. As I passed through the formalities at Bogotá's El Dorado airport, an official had noted my business suit and started patting my pockets, asking hopefully if I was carrying more than 10000 US dollars.

Chapter Nine
Innovations in Karachi and Delhi

After getting home from Colombia, I had four days in the office to set in place everything that had been agreed about our project there, and to turn my attention to Pakistan. It had been arranged that I would go back to Karachi, to visit Taymur in order to spend a few days planning the future development of our project, and then to conduct a short two-day developmental workshop. Administrative staff in the office found it hard to understand the nature of my activity in the few days before the workshop: was it consultancy? Where was the income to cover fees for that? No, I explained wearily, I will just be getting on with my normal job, but I will be doing it in Karachi rather than in Bloomsbury. My hosts were covering air fares and expenses, and Mr Avari was once again providing free hotel accommodation. They remained mystified, although numerous colleagues in other departments regularly based themselves in their regions of interest for much longer periods.

The other slightly strange feature of this visit was that I spent the preceding Friday to Monday at the Black Swan Hotel in Helmsley, one of our regular haunts. The idea was that a long weekend in the North York Moors in mid-November would be refreshing and relaxing. As was the case, but the transition back to working mode on Monday felt weird. The hotel coped with my surprising request to print my boarding pass. I was dropped at the breezy little train station in Thirsk, where I shivered on the platform in my lightweight suit, thinking that the announcer should say, 'Thirsk, next stop Dubai'. I flew from Heathrow at 4.55pm on Monday 14th November, arriving in Dubai at 3.25am on Tuesday, where I had time to kill before my 8am flight to Karachi.

The flight landed at 10.55am, but the entry formalities took ages. Taymur met me and drove me to the Avari Towers hotel, where I just had time to check in and have a shower before rejoining Taymur, now with Colin also, for lunch and a planning meeting. Previously there had been talk of a possible day trip to Islamabad on Wednesday; that had depended on particular people being available, and was not now considered practical. So the talk was of preparations for the workshop, the future direction for the development of our project, and the important business of what meals to have where.

Regarding the workshop, having reflected on the short courses we had offered previously, I wanted to find a way to break out of some of the expectations regarding short courses offered by visiting 'experts'. I was eager to be part of a more empowering process, one which would help the participants to build the skills and confidence to develop local self-help strategies that could become self-sustaining. As a first step on that journey I had put together a two-day programme that Taymur and his associates had titled 'Making it stick: embedding a learning culture into professional school life'. My two aims were to add depth to professional conversations, and to add criticality to professional reading.

Back in my hotel room at 5.30pm I started a somewhat sleepy e-mail session, writing home to comment that the cosy bed in Helmsley on Sunday night seemed a long time ago; that the capacious one in my room looked inviting, and that the break in the Moors had worked well for me in being more relaxing than the usual last-minute frenetic activity in the office. Reviewing work e-mails, I saw that my book had been favourably mentioned in the *Times Educational Supplement*. That news was like a shot of adrenalin.

This was the book I had been finishing in Cyprus; it had been published a couple of weeks previously, to my great delight. I worked alongside colleagues of my own age whose numbers of published books ran into the 40s and 50s, and which were automatically cited in every relevant Masters dissertation. I was well aware of the modest status of my own achievement in comparison. But having come late into an academic environment after a lifetime spent doing other things, and having distilled into the book ten years of my own work and reflections, of course I was proud of it. It was also relevant to the workshop I was preparing. In the same batch of e-mails I saw that I was to write some short articles about the book for magazines; at the time this felt a bit of a chore, because I wanted to move forward to a new writing project.

On Wednesday morning, filling up my plate at the breakfast buffet, I decided to accede to the urging on the place mats and try the local lamb brain speciality. It was unexceptionable but left me with no desire to eat it regularly. The texture was not new to me: when I was younger, before the days of mad cow disease, I had tried breadcrumbed calves' brains in Spaghetti House.

We spent the morning at Taymur's school, where I met some of his senior staff who had responsibilities for staff development. I needed a volunteer for the opening session of the workshop on Friday, and that person needed to be visibly genuine, not someone who other participants might regard as a previously groomed performer. So I couldn't start with Taymur or Colin. Fortunately one of his senior staff, called Samia, volunteered to be the guinea pig in this risky experiment: she was willing but visibly anxious, which was actually ideal.

Taymur pondered aloud where to go for lunch. Colin said, 'Well, you can come to my place if you like', and that was agreed. In my naivety I felt touched by the kindness of such a personal invitation. I imagined we might chat in Colin's kitchen while he put plates out on the table and assembled a homely snack. I was thinking of an occasion in my freelance years, collaborating with colleagues, all of us used to working in our homes. On that particular occasion, I was in the home of a retired headmaster, with another man who was tall, jovial and laughed loudly. We bunched around the computer, getting the work done, then our host took us to his spacious, traditional kitchen. Seated around the scrubbed wooden table, we ate a lunch of homemade soup, bread with mackerel pâté, some other bits and pieces, and a great deal of good-hearted gossip. The tall man demonstrated how to fold and burn the wrapper of an amaretti to make it perform as a hot-air balloon. Foolishly I imagined some similarly informal, relaxed encounter might be about to happen.

In fact, 'my place' meant the principal's residence at Colin's school, at which we arrived through an impressive archway and courtyard. He led us upstairs to a small dining room which was furnished, looked, smelled and sounded very much like a school canteen. A member of staff appeared, to whom Colin explained, 'There are three of us for lunch today'. Plenty of food arrived. The main course was a leg of roasted meat: Colin thought at first it was goat, but later concluded that it was probably lamb.

We talked for a while then I went back to the hotel, which took a long time because the traffic was so thick, for a shower and relaxation. Taymur, as a hospitable host, had asked if I wanted to go and look at the seafront, but I had sensed that he was busy and I also had things to get on with, so I suggested we defer that until a future occasion.

We went out for dinner somewhere in town; I got back, at 10.30pm, to the sound of a band playing loudly under my window, so there was no point in going to bed. I attended to e-mails until it stopped at 11.45pm. In the morning, the news was that there had been trouble on the seafront the previous afternoon.

We had set aside Thursday to talk about issues which I knew were bound to be tricky. The first concerned possibilities for accreditation, that is to say, possibilities for local participants in our activities to gain the certificates, diplomas and higher degrees that my organisation awarded. This was always on the agenda when international partners sought to work with us: how could they gain access to our qualifications? The possibilities were always disappointing, being more complex and much more expensive than people supposed. It sounded so logical to get a group together locally, for us to fly out and teach them there: surely that would be economical? Well no, because of the strict regulation of the activity. Each person would have to be individually admitted and registered, each would have to pay the full overseas student fee – an enormously prohibitive cost for most teachers in Pakistan – and each would have to go through a Home Office procedure even if they had no intention to come to the UK. These problems were not insurmountable: we did teach groups overseas but these usually depended on heavy official sponsorship and guaranteed numbers. In the context of our project in Pakistan, the most practical way for people to get our qualifications was to enrol individually as open learning students, as Taymur himself had done.

There was a more specific, and equally perennial, interest in the teaching certificate (PGCE). Could people study for it locally, and if they got it, would that mean they could come and teach in the UK? Well no again, not in any simple or automatic way, because to teach in a UK state school requires 'Qualified Teacher Status' which is awarded by the UK government alongside the PGCE.

I did my best to navigate these issues, trying to assuage the frustrations by emphasising the activities and pathways which were possible. I got a clear impression that if the right business model could be found, there would be willingness locally to make substantial investment, even including buying sites and building teacher training facilities.

The other thorny issue concerned exclusivity: our partners had set up a charity specifically to enable our presence and activities in Pakistan, and they hoped that we would recognise them as our sole and exclusive agent for such activity. We did not, as a matter of policy, enter exclusive partnerships for good reasons which I won't bore you with, but there was also a more practical obstacle which our partners found harder to grasp. For us, any such agreement would be internally unenforceable. It would be natural for people like the Commander, used to the Pakistan Navy and the business world, to assume our organisation was a tight entity which would speak and act with one voice. In fact our organisation was (at that time) a loose confederacy of departments, within which world-class experts ran their own affairs and teams with a high level of independence, within a competitive culture. Great swathes of the organisation would see no reason to constrain themselves for the benefit of 'my' very small venture in Pakistan.

We did, however, achieve a bit of a breakthrough in thinking about where to take our project. We hit on the idea of reconceptualising the activity from 'short courses' to 'conferences'. The essential difference was that the conferences would be locally owned, with the expectation that the participants would be actively contributing and taking charge of their own learning. The inputs from myself and my colleagues would be redesignated as 'keynotes' from visiting speakers, but there would also be other inputs from local speakers, and short papers and contributions from delegates. The conferences would be regular (we thought twice-yearly), and intended to generate a sense of belonging: a learning space that delegates would look forward to returning to periodically. The model in my mind was the annual ICSEI conference that I describe in Chapter Four. The thought of helping to create a modest version of something similar for the South Asia region was inspiring.

So after a day of intensive discussion, I rested in my room looking out at what had become quite a familiar scene. While the different rooms in which I had stayed had different outlooks, the birds provided a constant feature that in my experience was distinctive to this place. Red kites and hooded crows – at least a hundred of each – performed an elaborate ballet. Watching them was as soothing and therapeutic as a spa treatment.

On Friday morning we assembled in a function room the hotel had made available to us, where a good-sized group hummed expectantly. I had published the learning aims of the workshop, but not any detailed programme: I wanted flexibility. Most of those present would have expected me to begin by giving a lecture. Instead I asked Samia to come forward, and positioned our two chairs carefully so that she was looking at me, with the group only in her peripheral vision, so as to steady her nerves.

I asked her to describe a development she had led in the course of her work, beginning with a simple narrative of what she was trying to do, and what happened. We got going, I used prompts and encouragement. After the narration, I explained that I called this technique 'telling the story four times', and led her back into the narrative but this time looking at the issues, obstacles, fears and motivations that she had encountered, and how she had handled them. Next I got her to explain those things using ideas from some selected theories of change. Finally, I asked her to think about features of the working context: what would others need to know about this particular situation in order to judge how much of it might be relevant to their own situations?

It worked. After listening in rapt silence, several other participants volunteered to be interviewed. Partly because, as always at such events, there were some who loved an opportunity to talk about their achievements, but that did not detract from the learning aim, which was to bring more depth and insight to professional conversations: how to describe, and what questions to ask.

The other highlight of the day was a session I ran on developing critical reading skills. On this, the cultural context made for a different starting point. I had found that South Asian school leaders tended, on average, to do a great deal of serious reading, and to remember it, but not very critically: things published by experts were to be absorbed like nourishment. By contrast, in Britain, very little professional reading is done in schools except where people are preparing for a qualification, and it can often be taken with scepticism, which is different from criticality.

So I explained the techniques and gave opportunities to practise them, but I made one error of judgement. The literature was (and still is) completely dominated by Western writers; I was keen to encourage writing in the region, and so wanted to find and showcase an article in a reputable journal by a Pakistani author. There was only one recent example: it was quite interesting and relevant, and good enough to have got into the journal. The analytical skills I helped the group to apply to it did, however, lead them to identify a lot of questions and shortcomings as well as strengths. Although that was the point of the exercise, I felt bad about it, wishing that I had got them to pull apart something written by a Western expert, and then used the local example in a wholly positive way. Later the author of the article heard I had used it, and asked me to support her academic promotion, which I did.

On Friday evening, there was a dinner at the Commander's house, starting late by my normal schedules and therefore likely to finish very late indeed. He had moved, but from previous experience I was pretty sure his house would have the feel and ambience of a minor stately home, and his entertainment would be packed with influential people, very good food, and a variety of alcoholic refreshments. All were so, but I was tired after a full day, and expecting a bit of a rough time from the Commander regarding the progress of treaty negotiations with my organisation. I needn't have worried: I had forgotten the business astuteness which had attracted us to working with him in the first place. He guided me away to a small side-room, and sat me down: just the two of us. I braced myself. Then he said, 'We know that you are on our side. All I ask of you is that you get us the best deal that you can'. That was it, then I was released to rejoin the party.

The space was dominated by a striking woman, who had somehow managed to position herself under the one bright lamp in the room. 'Let me introduce you to my mother', Taymur said. Mother? Sister, surely. The woman in question was nearly my height, had pale skin, and blonde hair in a short, curled style. She was beautiful to begin with, and beautifully made up. She spoke in a strong, sonorous voice with an interesting timbre; her manner was talkative, bold and flirty.

Perhaps she had been told to charm me, in which case she carried out her brief to perfection. I learnt that she ran a successful fashion business and, later, that she was much involved in the Pakistan Fashion Week in London. Typical of her occupation, her clothes were dramatically stylish. She preferred military government to the current lack of law and order. 'In General Zia's time I could walk through central Karachi in shorts!' was her conclusive argument. I was dragged away, and told to circulate myself into another room where people were expecting to meet me, where I encountered half a dozen earnest headmistresses. I buckled down to my job.

On Saturday the workshop included discussion regarding the proposed series of regular conferences. Taymur's team had decided to offer some free places to representatives from The Citizens Foundation to enable them to participate in this workshop. It was agreed that free places would also be made available for the conferences and be extended to enable some participation from the government school sector. The possibility of participants writing short conference papers about their work was also discussed.

Kiran was one of the workshop participants. At our meeting in March, she had mentioned that she planned to attend a conference in Cardiff, and that we could meet up in London. That did happen, following some e-mail exchanges. Attempting to be a kind, caring host, I had asked whether it would be her first visit to London. No, she had replied, her parents owned a flat in Park Lane, which put me in my place. As the date drew near, it became clear that she would be on quite a tight schedule, fitting things in on her way to Cardiff. In the end she chose Selfridges department store as the venue for our meeting. It was a place I knew well for relaxing retail therapy, but it felt distinctly odd wandering through that ambience for the purpose of a professional meeting. After some texting I located her in the food court: she was waiting for me at the top of the escalator in an elegant white outfit, and with a whole row of posh shopping bags. We had a simple lunch, which she insisted on paying for, and discussed her idea for a small research project she was keen to undertake.

That was back in the summer; earlier in the autumn she had contacted me on another matter. Her father ran some sort of bank, in which she held a nominal position; he had been taken ill and she had needed to take on significant responsibilities, but some of the staff did not accept her authority. She needed coaching support, and didn't know who else to turn to. Executive coaching was one of my fields: we had a couple of telephone sessions. Now in November it was no surprise that she volunteered to produce a conference paper on her research. Several other participants made similar commitments: we were on our way. On Sunday morning, at the Commander's house, we took stock of how the project was developing, and set the dates for the first conference: 6th to the 8th of March 2012, in Karachi. I caught the 2.05pm flight from Karachi, changed at Dubai and arrived at London's Heathrow Terminal 3 at 8.15pm in an upbeat frame of mind.

*****

I was in London over the mid-winter period, while Gordon worked with the *formadores* in Colombia. My first trip of 2012 was to Delhi, to carry out a long-awaited, much-rescheduled assignment commissioned by the Central Board of Secondary Education. The CBSE is a long-established official body in India: in its own formal language, 'an autonomous organisation under the Union Ministry of Human Resource Development, Government of India'. Its main function is as a school examination board, serving both independent and government secondary schools, but it also offers a range of related services to the schools using its examinations, including professional development activities. CBSE had approached my organisation wanting a five-day training programme for principals of independent schools across India in strategic management and leadership.

This was an attractive invitation because of the official standing of the customer, and because it became apparent during the discussion stage that they understood and wanted good quality. They were confident that there would be good take-up of the opportunity, and were prepared to price it at a level which would enable us to include the features we considered helpful to a good learning process. So in addition to the full five days of face-to-face training, they were happy for us to organise pre-course and post-course tasks for the participants, and they also put in place a selection procedure. Their intention was to limit the number of participants to around 40: in fact the group turned out to be 46, which was manageable.

The colleague I chose for this assignment was Carol, with whom I had interacted a fair bit in relation to work in the UK. She had not previously worked internationally, but I knew that she was an excellent presenter and manager of classroom activities and discussions; I liked her a lot and found her very easy company.

In these auspicious circumstances, we set off on Saturday 18th February, which happened to be my partner's birthday: not the first to be disrupted by my work. I met Carol at London's Heathrow Terminal 3 and we caught a 9.50pm flight to Delhi. During the flight, Carol was sociable and I learnt a little more about her. She told me she had grown up with a crowd of brothers; this explained why she was so confident and at ease in dealing with male colleagues. In fact the way we got on over the coming week had a touch of brother–

sister camaraderie about it: she was friendly, tactile, and happy to talk about quite personal things in our off-duty relaxation, but without the slightest suggestion on either side that any boundaries would be crossed. I couldn't have wished for a more enjoyable companion.

The one slight puzzle in the otherwise very efficient arrangements concerned where we would be accommodated. One of the participating schools had been designated as the venue school, where the teaching would take place. That was just a name and address to me: I had no idea of where it actually sat within greater Delhi. A different school was given responsibility for hosting us: for managing our accommodation and general well-being. I hadn't seen any need to question or examine the particulars. We must have been told the details of the hotel: that was something I insisted on as part of the formalities of getting clearance to travel on behalf of our organisation, but I hadn't researched it.

It turned out that the hotel in which we were lodged, the 32nd Milestone Hotel in Gurgaon, was very near the host school, whose principal, the fearsome Dr Indu, almost certainly used it on a regular basis. She seemed determined to exercise close control over her hosting function – perhaps some local politics was involved – notwithstanding the impracticality of this arrangement. I came to understand, from later assignments, that Gurgaon is a separate town, not even within greater Delhi: our lodging there necessitated between half an hour and an hour's commuting through rush-hour congestion at the start and end of each day.

Dr Indu had on her staff a man called Randeep: his actual role and status I was never told. He met us at the airport on Sunday and took us on the long, long drive out to our remote and miserable destination. I am sure that he meant well, and it became apparent that he acted under the very close supervision of Dr Indu, frequently reporting by telephone, but I found his demeanour extremely irritating. He had an over-confident, sing-song voice, and a manner that clearly said, 'I know best, I am in charge, my opinion is much more important than yours!' He deposited us at the hotel, making it clear that if we needed anything changing there, he would happily bully the hotel staff accordingly. His parting declaration was, 'I am not expecting the course to begin tomorrow, no, no teaching tomorrow, but you can visit the venue in the morning', before tripping off self-importantly to report his mission accomplished.

His last comment seemed weird; fortunately I had e-mail connection and reported it to our contact at CBSE, assuring her of our flexibility should they really have decided to compress five days' work into four. It was later confirmed that Randeep had misunderstood, and that the work would proceed to schedule.

Meanwhile we were making the best of the hotel. There was nothing specific wrong with it, except that it was in the wrong place and of a distinctly lower grade than I would have expected when travelling officially. The beds were covered with an assortment of unattractive, well-worn fabrics, and neither Carol nor I were clear between which of them we were supposed to sleep. Flushing the toilet required a special knack: a sort of twitching movement. An ancient electric socket was falling out of the wall; I managed to fit an adapter into part of its obsolete design, although it was a bit wobbly. The tepid bath water was brown and sandy, smelled of drains, and ran away before there was enough to use. The wing of the hotel containing the bedrooms was near a flyover carrying a major road, which remained busy all night, and on which a proportion of the drivers enjoyed sounding their musical horns.

Carol and I met in the breakfast room at 7am on Monday, to make the best of its limited offerings and to discuss the day. Randeep picked us up at 8am, demanding to know whether we had any complaints. No, we lied, we were fine, thank you. The grey wintry morning did not make the area look any more attractive: a soulless concrete suburb that could have been anywhere in the world. The traffic was, however, distinctly Indian: congested, noisy, fumy, horns blasting, a mixture of different types of vehicles getting in each other's way. When we crawled into the metropolis the scene became more and more like my mental image of Delhi, with higher-rise buildings of different ages, street enterprises, and men squatting on the strip of brown earth between the carriageways.

We came to the venue school. It was a modern brick building, three storeys high, with some pleasant architectural features and spacious grounds. My later research showed that it was in the Hauz Khas Police Colony area, near Mayfair Gardens, on the southern fringe of Delhi. We were directed to a fair-sized room laid out with round tables, and well equipped. It was crowded with people talking, milling around: the normal hubbub at the start of such an event. The participants included a proportion from the farthest corners of India; they wanted to talk to each other. The group included 19 men and 27 women. One of the men was Pankaj Das, from Assam, who I had met on my previous visit to Delhi. He came to greet me, and over the next few days discussed further his wish to bring a group of his staff to the UK, which did eventually happen.

We had been asked to design five full days of training, so we had assumed, perhaps unrealistically, that we would be able to get down to business on time. Instead, extended opening formalities were required, under the direction of a man representing CBSE. These included speeches, a lamp-lighting ceremony and a song. Carol and I were given fragrant flower arrangements, which we took back to our hotel rooms at the end of the day.

Eventually we got going, and started to establish the rules for how we would work. Quite a few of the group were lively, had a lot to say, and didn't understand about taking turns, but we soon settled into a good positive relationship. One of the issues in the kind of work we did was how to manage our intellectual property. Obviously those who paid a lot of money to listen to us got full access to that; the question was how freely it got spread more widely. CBSE had published the full detailed content of the five days on their website; I was a bit put out to see that it stayed there for years. One of the group was a Saudi man – I think he ran a Saudi school in Delhi, and from later conversations it seemed he owned a group of schools in Dammam. During a break he discussed the possibility of us going to Dammam, but as a cheaper alternative he also video-recorded all our presentations, saying it was just to help his memory.

Carol's sessions were first-rate, as I knew would be the case, but it was still inspiring to see the virtuosity of her performance. During a break following one of these, she told me how much she had had to adjust her assumptions. The people we were working with were high-achieving and very well qualified: most had doctorates. They were very well read, and modern in their thinking. Their schools had a standard of facilities, equipment and resourcing beyond that of state schools in the UK. Carol said that her expectations of what it meant to provide a development programme in a so-called developing country had been jolted.

Lunch was served in a pleasant staff restaurant area. It was, however, the same every day: a very hot and very oily vegetable curry, with rice, and quite interesting desserts, followed by the passing round of a box of fennel seeds to assist digestion. Inevitably the character of the main dish had its effect on my system. The toilet was in a round, turret-like building that I got to know quite well. On about the third day, a group of women showed me that they had brought in plastic boxes of their own food. 'We are Indian but we are from the different regions of India; we don't want to eat such hot spicy food every day', they said, with some concern for how I was coping.

Meanwhile, Randeep continued to think up ways of adding to our discomfort. On Wednesday morning, during the drive from the hotel to the venue, he asked if we would be willing to address the morning assembly at his school, the following morning. Clearly, the request had come from Dr Indu; clearly it could not be refused. It was one of those tests which school principals worldwide like to set for those who presume to teach them: so, you think you can teach us something? Let's see what you can do. My organisation's reputation required that I fulfil this duty.

He also offered us a scenic tour of Delhi after the end of the teaching day. This I was more concerned about, because we were busy, we were there to work, and he didn't appreciate what we had to get through each evening to be ready for the next day. Conscious that it was Carol's first visit to Delhi, I reluctantly agreed, subject to the tour lasting no more than one hour. I explained that we wanted to have dinner at the hotel, followed by a working session. Fine, he said, despite having no intention of complying, because he was not picking up what my words really meant.

When we arrived at the venue school, Carol was whisked away by a group of women, eventually reappearing wearing a sari. Which she did very well: it really suited her, although she explained later when we were on our own that her first attempt at fastening it to herself had been a dramatic failure. I was very glad that there was no male equivalent.

At the end of the day's work, Randeep collected us like a jailer: just one hour, I reminded him. I later discovered that the area around the venue school was actually quite interesting. It was near the Mehrauli Archaeological Park, and various other sites that it might have been quite pleasant to see before night fell. But no, we had to set off towards the standard sites of central Delhi. On the way, he stopped at a kind of craft market, so that we could do our gift shopping. The stalls were set out in a park with trees and flowering shrubs. I was interested to see flocks of green ringed-neck parakeets shrieking in the trees, just as they do in London parks. It was also nice to see monkeys in the trees. Neither of us wanted to buy anything, to Randeep's obvious bewilderment.

Next he took us to the lotus-domed Bahá'i house of worship: a spectacular feature set amid formal gardens. Carol was still in her sari, swishing along confidently, apparently not at all concerned that it might fall off. I was in a business suit with heavy, highly shone black brogues. Daylight was already fading. 'You can go in if you like', Randeep advised. 'But you would need to leave your shoes outside.' Mindful of how the time was passing, I seized on that excuse, pointing at my footwear, saying that if I took them off it would be very difficult to put them on again.

Back in the car, it was pitch dark as we edged through congested traffic towards Connaught Circus and India Gate. I said I needed a toilet. Randeep parked near India Gate, and led me past the guttering memorial flame to a facility. Then for a long time we edged along in a traffic jam in the darkness, any sightseeing clearly out of the question. Over two hours had elapsed; I was getting annoyed. Randeep kept making phone calls, reporting in to Dr Indu.

He stopped the car, got out and went to the boot. He opened the passenger door and passed in some picnic offerings wrapped up in foil. Most of it I had to reject because of my food intolerances: the orange juice, the orange, the chocolate bar... There was some small item I ate, an unpleasant cake or something, but I was furious with the assumptions he had made. He remembered I had said I needed to be back in time to have dinner in the hotel, so he had produced this alternative, as if to say, 'There, you don't need your hotel dinner!', in his complacent, self-satisfied manner. Hunger, discomfort and frustration brought out the worst in me. I found myself thinking, 'Does this silly little man really think this is an adequate alternative to the sort of dinner an English gentleman likes to sit down to at the end of a difficult day?'

Randeep said that his school would like to give us some craftwork made by their students. Yes, lovely, we said, while I worried about the capacity of my small suitcase. A further telephone conversation ensued. We had been in the car for over three hours as we finally approached the hotel. 'Not so late, not so late!', Randeep insisted in his piping sing-song. We staggered in wearied relief to the restaurant to relax, to get back to normal, and to start to address what we had to do before going to bed.

The first issue concerned the school assembly in the morning. Dr Indu had e-mailed: it was sent mid-afternoon but she must have known we were to be kept captive until bedtime. She wrote, 'The topics are how to compete with oneself, and how to raise the bar of excellence. The duration of the talk is 30 minutes, from 08.00 to 08.30'. Carol and I agreed to share the task and take one topic each; there would be no time to review and co-ordinate, we would just have to hope that there would not be too much overlap between the two contributions. I thought that

30 minutes was far too long for a speech to a morning assembly; at least two different voices might make it bearable.

The invitation came with no contextual information. I assembled some ideas for an uplifting homily on the theme, which I could deliver in a statesmanlike manner as a visiting dignitary. I attended to the most urgent messages regarding work in London, then at last slipped between the rough, stale uninviting bedclothes.

In the morning we were taken the short distance to the school, met formally in reception, and guided through and out the back to the playing field. It was vast, sunlit, flat, short-mown and parched with great patches of bare earth. On it stood the entire school population, in straight lines, standing to rigid attention, from tiny nursery tots to young adults. The lines were well apart. Metal poles bore loudspeakers. There were some words of introduction, which confirmed what I had guessed: the public address system was ineffective – weak, distorted and echoey.

I started to speak, while inwardly angry on behalf of the children at the stupidity of such a set-up. Did Dr Indu and her senior team seriously believe that the same address, delivered in these conditions, could be meaningful both to 4-year-olds and 18-year-olds? I completed my homily on time, although I am sure that to the students the 15 minutes felt like an hour, then Carol took over. The gamble paid off: there was no significant overlap between our contributions.

Back in the administrative part of the school, Dr Indu said, 'You want us to give you some of the students' craftwork', in quite a cross tone, as if this had been an unreasonable request from us, rather than our polite acquiescence with an offer the school had pressed upon us. We were given a bulky collection: my selection included a wooden picnic table with a painted tile top, which only fell apart recently, and a framed paper sculpture of Ganesh which is on my study wall as I write.

Our duties at the assembly meant that we arrived late for the day's teaching. The programme included what we termed a problem-based learning task. This had to be undertaken in groups, and led towards each group presenting its solution to the problem on the final day. We had introduced the task on Monday, and allowed time in each day for the groups to work on it. By Thursday this was reaching a serious stage as each group worked on its presentation. As I knew from previous experience, it was difficult to judge how well the groups were addressing the task: the lively hum of conversation could be deceptive.

Another normal feature of this stage of the course was that individuals now felt able to raise with us issues and prospects for possible further work with them, or for their academic advancement. One such was Dr Anita. Generally, the women in the group engaged with us as one professional to another, with gender being irrelevant. Dr Anita differed: she was a charmer. Comely and personable in the Indian tradition, with round cheeks and full mouth, long eyelashes and big liquid eyes, she slinked towards me sinuously like a tigress, ignoring Carol. I don't think that was entirely because of my seniority. We talked of various things, on several occasions. She made no secret of how she employed her charm: 'People have been very kind to me', she explained, when talking about several beneficial opportunities that had come her way.

The issue of the moment was that she had arranged an audience with someone important, at the end of the working day. So after the session Carol and I were taken on a long, congested drive to the offices of the Delhi Public Schools Society. We were led upstairs and shown into a waiting room, while Anita slunk to and fro checking arrangements and availability. She beckoned us along the corridor and into the room of the chairman. He was a grand old gentleman, who gestured that we should occupy the chairs in front of his desk. Anita disappeared. We explained what we were doing, and a little bit about ourselves. The chairman outlined some of the priorities for professional development among the group of schools he represented. His manner was courteous, intelligent and engaging, with a touch of humour. Anita came back into the room, and I am sure that the old gentleman perked up noticeably in her presence. He threw me somewhat by asking if I had been in the Indian Civil Service. I didn't know whether it was a joke, or a compliment, or whether he had overestimated my age by 40 years. That evening was the last time we would dine in the hotel; we lingered over it in a spirit of amiable joviality.

The group presentations by the participants on Friday morning were outstanding: the highest standard I had seen. With one slight exception they were full of sensible content, thoroughly prepared and expertly presented: real team efforts, which were most impressive. The final working session of the day involved explaining the post-course task, which had to be completed in order to get the certificate, completing a personal action planning task, and feedback forms: all very positive.

We were to attend an event in the evening. I didn't know the details, only that we would be given dinner in a club by someone senior in CBSE. We were ushered to a car and off we went. After quite a while, and quite a long tour of varied urban landscapes, the driver admitted that he wasn't quite sure of the location of our destination. He stopped and made a phone call. Of course I couldn't help: I didn't even know its name. This illustrated one of the common risks and stresses of these trips: that of not knowing vital information. Suppose the driver ran off and left us… suppose there was an accident and the police got involved. 'Where are you going?', they would ask. I don't know. 'Who are you meeting there?' I don't know.

Fortunately we did eventually arrive in the right place and were guided to an upstairs restaurant, to a table with some dignitaries. The professional conversation flowed smoothly and pleasantly enough. The senior figure, our host, was very proud of the club's collection of scotch whiskies, and pressed me to try this and that, which I did willingly. On our flight back on Saturday, the cabin crew handed out tubes of Love Heart sweets, which Carol and I played with stupidly like children.

Chapter Ten
Karachi and Punjab: Contrasting Settings

That was February: I spent the last few days of the month resting on my own at our Yorkshire house. My diary for March was filled with travel adventures: first, back to Karachi for the first of our new-style conference programmes. Then I was to start a new project in Lahore working for the government of Punjab province, before ending the month in Brazil.

Since my last visit to Karachi, work on supporting a series of locally owned professional development conferences had been ongoing. A vital part of that had been finding a colleague with the right expertise in methods of teaching, who would enter the spirit of the project and commit to supporting it long-term. Thus I met Eleanore, with whom I forged an enduring professional partnership. She threw herself into the work, contacting the conference organisers, arranging reading material and devising her sessions. The conference would run for three full days starting on Tuesday 6th March; we met up at Heathrow to catch an evening flight on the preceding Sunday.

On this, my fourth stay in the hospitable and elegant environment of the Avari Towers Hotel in Karachi, I was at last getting a better sense of its layout and how it fitted into the lie of the land. The views from bedroom windows at the front and back of the hotel suggested a fairly flat landscape, and belied the change in elevation on which the hotel was built. The main reception and the high-rise residential block were part of the way up the slope; many of the facilities, including all the function rooms, were at lower levels. These rambled down the slope in a series of stages like canal locks: small shops, display cases, meeting rooms, a Chinese restaurant and, somewhere in the depths, a gym which I had no desire to find. There was a second, lower-level exit for vehicle pickup, on a drive that linked by a swirling route to the one with which I was more familiar.

The hotel's general manager was more often seen down here among the commercial facilities than in reception. He was an amiable, talkative Scot called Gordon. He had a forthright manner: on my first or second visit somehow we got to talking about the minibar items in the bedrooms. 'I don't charge for them', he said. Of course they didn't include alcohol. 'The whole lot only costs…' (I forget the small amount of rupees). 'Charge a fair rate for the room and then no extra charges.' He went on to give a spirited impression of checking out in hotels that take a different view: 'I just need to phone housekeeping to go and check the minibar… oh, it seems that a small packet of nuts needs to be added to the bill, just a moment and I will reprint the paperwork…' My previous visit had spread into a Sunday morning, and I had guessed he had chosen the background music wafting through the loudspeakers. It was an orchestral version of tunes from *Hymns Ancient and Modern*: a nice touch, meaningless and hence unobjectionable to all but its intended beneficiaries.

Another time I was on the fringes of a conversation where he was talking about a spate of traffic-light robberies – they went in phases – where at a red light, someone would poke a gun through the car window and demand wallets and mobile phones. He was recounting the talk he had given staff that morning: 'Make sure you carry an extra old wallet with just some low-value notes in, and a cheap old phone to hand over if you have to; I'll be checking to make sure you have them!' Such sound advice: it had never occurred to me, but on all my subsequent travels I did exactly that.

The conference ran smoothly and had a good, positive atmosphere from the outset: it was uplifting to see the stage of development the project had reached. One of the local contributions was particularly memorable. It was a presentation by a young man called Zain, about change and the future, and its tensions and opportunities. His professional standpoint wasn't clear – much later I learnt that his work had something to do with design and architecture – but his aim was to stimulate, and that he did splendidly. Quick-talking, jokey, whacky, provocative: alongside his talk he flashed many images to illustrate the impact of technology on culture. One was a photograph of a row of women in the most fully shrouding burkas, sitting in front of computers surfing the web.

Eleanore liked to be independent in the periods we were not working together, so I didn't see much of her. Later, when I knew her better, I understood that she valued a bit of time to herself as one of the advantages of overseas assignments. Tuesday evening was an exception, because she had arranged to meet up with an old friend who, by what at first seemed to be an odd chance, also knew Taymur. His name was Hek; among other activities he published textbooks, so his knowing Taymur was not odd after all. The four of us ate dinner together, at a restaurant I hadn't been to before. We had an outside table, perhaps because Hek smoked heavily. Hek kept up a stream of lively, controversial conversation, spanning local issues, politics back in the UK, and anything else which caught his imagination. The core of the conversation was Eleanore and Hek catching up, but the atmosphere was jolly and engaging for the whole group; we finished late.

Captain Sajid was one of the conference participants: he had supported all of the project's events. He was a centre of attention, in his modest way, because a few days previously he had experienced a traffic-light robbery attempt, which had not gone quite as intended. The robber would have seen a small elderly man in civilian clothing, and must have been surprised to have ended up in custody. Sajid explained, 'I smiled at him, got out of the car and gave him an old phone: not my BlackBerry. I kept smiling and that confused him, which gave me the chance to break his balls and take his gun away, then I held him until he was arrested'.

One of the distinguished guests at the conference was a man called Mohammed, who worked for the government, and chaired a committee made up of all the school examination boards. On Wednesday evening, the Commander was hosting one of his parties. That afternoon I passed Mohammed in a corridor; he mentioned the event. 'Do you think he will give us some beer?' he asked. I was a bit thrown as to how to reply. It was a certainty that the Commander's residence would be awash with alcohol, but I didn't want to get anyone into trouble. I gave a neutral reply, and walked along chatting; Mohammed was limping and complaining about an injured knee.

That evening at the Commander's house, Eleanore went off to do her own networking, which, as it turned out, she did most effectively. I paid homage to the groaning buffet. There was an enormous flatfish, a turbot or something similar, kebabs of different kinds, flatbreads, salads, rice: the overall character was more Middle Eastern than traditionally Pakistani, and most enjoyable. I might have had a drop or two of wine with it. Part-way through the evening, I was joined by Mohammed, who plonked himself down near me, and wanted conversation, although his voice was a trifle slurred. He had clearly discovered the joys of wine, in the manner of a teenager at his first grown-up party. And also like a teenager at a party, he wanted to talk about women in the way farmers might discuss heifers, which wasn't to my taste. I tried to divert the conversation to admiring the artworks and carpets surrounding us. The Commander's wife circulated, dutifully hostessing. When she got to Mohammed, she said, 'Now, I'll bring you a nice glass of lovely fruit juice'. 'Wine!' he insisted; she went off tut-tutting. The original plan had been for Mohammed to share our taxi back, but I was a bit bothered. If we were questioned by officials while he was trying to stand or walk, perhaps we could say that his leg had got a lot worse, but that might not fully explain his condition. In the end the Commander got his chauffeur to take him. The next day, Mohammed in conversation with Taymur commented (seriously, neither joking nor ruefully) how terrible it was that some people went to parties and got drunk, which was disgusting and something he would never do.

Meanwhile, more pertinently, on Thursday Eleanore was outlining some next steps with the group. In her sessions, she had modelled the styles of teaching and learning she was advocating, and had arranged for some of the conference participants to work on projects in their own schools to apply these techniques. They should then record the results and present them at the conference in one year's time. She offered e-mail support in the meantime, and also offered to get some of the project reports published. This was a breakthrough point in the development of the project. On Friday morning, we were picked up at 3am to go to the airport, arriving at Heathrow at 1.50pm, tired but thoroughly satisfied with the progress made.

*****

I spent the following week in London, packed with meetings, juggling various responsibilities, before heading back to Pakistan on Saturday to begin a new project. This was in every way a fresh departure. My five previous visits to Pakistan (four to Karachi, one to Lahore) had been initiated, organised and supported by Taymur and his associates, and everything about them had reflected the comfort and gentility of the independent sector. The work was under our own design and direction. My new project contrasted in all respects.

A long time previously, at least 18 months, perhaps nearer two years, I had been put in touch with a Punjabi man enquiring about a possible project. I had the impression he was youngish, acting as a middleman broker, and probably registered for PhD studies at our organisation: that is how a lot of these contacts arose. The contact was by e-mail. The Punjabi government was interested in developing a scheme to register and license teachers, and wanted external support; he had been directed to me. At that early stage it wasn't clear to me even whether the project was in India or Pakistan, and I started off looking at information about the Indian state of Punjab before realising that the enquiry concerned the much larger Pakistani province of Punjab. I wrote a brief paper – just a few pages – outlining some do's and don'ts, key issues and how I could help if they wanted me to. The guy acknowledged it but I never heard from him again.

Then, recently, I had been telephoned by someone working for one of the big project management companies, and it soon became clear that the enquiry concerned exactly the same project. This company wasn't the one I dealt with in Saudi Arabia, but it operated in a similar fashion. During my freelance years it had kindly given me work, but dealing with it as one organisation to another was a longstanding nightmare. In our business it was impossible to avoid working with this particular company: periodically we convened summit meetings to try to thrash out rules of engagement, but these were generally ignored. We were prepared to work in partnership, but the company just wanted to cherry-pick the expertise of our staff as if they were freelancers, with no regard to their status as our employees. On several occasions, having promised partnership, the company had won bids on the strength of the expertise of our staff, and then had not given those people anything like the level of involvement originally promised. Where they were used, they were 'used' indeed, as if they were hourly paid contract cleaners rather than world-famous experts.

So I was on my guard. The man explained that this project formed part of a much larger programme of World Bank-funded activity to improve education in Punjab, which the company was project managing. Their problem was that they couldn't find a credible expert to support the teacher registration and licensing scheme, and for that reason it was nearly two years late getting started.

In the tick-list culture of such companies, 'credible' meant someone who had done the same thing before, achieving all success criteria, with evidence to prove it. I explained that what the Punjabis wanted to do had not been done before in any country in modern times, so no-one could produce that kind of track record. Alongside my day job, I was president of a professional body working on related matters, which had, for over a century, acted as a repository of information on many initiatives to develop teaching as a profession, so I knew a bit about it. The caller said the company wanted to employ me; I replied that the only way I could help was for the company to contract with my organisation for the provision of a consultancy service, which I would lead but I would also involve other members of my team. Reluctantly he agreed; we arranged a meeting at the company's head office, an hour's train journey from London, to sort out the details.

In that meeting, among other things, more details of the project emerged. For some reason (it seemed bizarre to me) the package of activity they had hoped one single consultant would undertake included drafting the legislation for the creation of the statutory board that would oversee the teacher registration and licensing process. No wonder it had been difficult to find the right person! By lucky fluke (because it didn't feature in public statements of my skills), I had studied administrative law and had worked in Parliament both as an official and as a lobbyist, and was adept at, and liked, legislative drafting. It was agreed I would make a short initial visit to find out what had been done already and what the next steps should be. Another thing which became clear in the meeting was that the company hadn't softened its style, and that I wouldn't be getting much in the way of comfort or hospitality.

Accordingly, when I left Heathrow for a flight direct to Lahore at 3.55pm on Saturday 17th March, it was with Pakistan International Airlines (PIA), a carrier that British organisations didn't normally use because of its low standards and poor safety record. I was the only non-Pakistani on board. The plane was old, with scuffed, grubby upholstery, and everything about the journey seemed tired and tiring. It landed in the very early hours of Sunday morning, and I was driven to Hotel Sunfort.

This was another signal that no red carpets were going to be rolled out for me. In my meeting at the company's office, I had mentioned that I had stayed at the Avari Hotel on my previous visit to Lahore. The man had said, 'We will lodge you in one of the hotels we use regularly for consultants of your grade', with the clear implication that 'my grade' wasn't anything remarkable. Lahore's elegant boulevards were still just a maze to me: I hadn't sorted out the city's topography, especially not in the dark. In fact, we were heading further south: whereas the Avari rested its genteel presence opposite the large park which housed the Lahore Zoo, in the Mozang Chungi area, the Sunfort was near Liberty Market, in the Gulberg III district. The outside of the building looked fine; my subsequent research revealed its standard daily rate was less than half that of the Avari. At check-in I was shocked to be asked to pay, myself, upfront for accommodation. I had expected either that the hotel would bill the company, as client, or that the company would have arranged for me to receive an envelope of cash to cover such expenses. My remonstrations were in vain: fortunately I carried enough US dollars to make the required payment.

I was handed an envelope: it contained not cash, but a handwritten note from a consultant, who had been assigned to be my minder, assistant, mentor, companion, whatever, saying we would meet later that day. Her name was Rosemary; she came to the hotel late morning. I was up but barely awake. She was tallish, I guessed quite a few years older than me, with thin fair hair, a slightly weather-beaten complexion and a wiry physique; her movements were just a shade stooped, stiff and careful. She wasn't really supposed to be attached to this project: the person intended was on holiday – I never did meet them. Rosemary was an old Pakistan hand, telling me she had spent several years in the wild mountainous north of the country. Clearly she was a self-reliant survivor, whom nothing would faze; she had a calm, open manner and I found it easy to relate to her from the outset. The fact that it was not her project probably helped: she had no axes to grind. Our talk soon revealed that I should have received a great pile of documents: vital pre-reading. None of it had come; it was the first I had heard of it.

Rosemary suggested we go to the Avari for lunch: she had a car and driver outside. That act of kindness was more significant than she might have realised, because being transported into that familiar environment, with strongly positive associations, uplifted my spirit. The violinist scraped his dolorous sounds, and Rosemary advised me that the company was just trying it on by putting me in the Sunfort: in future I should insist on staying at the Avari. I learnt that she had a property in a pretty part of rural Ireland, looking out over water, but didn't get to spend much time there. We talked a little about the project, but we were both feeling our way.

After lunch, Rosemary took me to the company's Lahore headquarters, a two-storey suite of offices. The ground floor and stairwell were panelled in dark heavy wood; the first floor was a lighter, largely open-plan set of workstations. The building seemed to be uninhabited, except by the office manager: meeting him was the main purpose of the visit. A retired colonel, he was a little man with glasses, crisply spoken, exuding efficiency. He had a desk on the ground floor: 'I designed it this way', he explained. 'Upstairs is for the professional consultants; all the administration is downstairs so it does not disturb their work.' We sat in front of his desk and he went through some basics of induction, giving us folders he had assembled himself containing information and contact details. They were largely wasted on me: this was years before I acquired a smartphone, and my simple mobile could receive texts but did not work in any other way in Pakistan.

I think I did once know the Colonel's name, but wouldn't have been so familiar as to use it. Rosemary usually addressed him as 'Colonel Sahib'. For all his senior commander persona, what I saw of his work seemed to be low-level clerical. Something needed to be arranged regarding times and destinations for car drivers: he did it there and then while we sat and waited. 'I take the action in front of you, then you know it has been done!' The most welcome benefit of the barren ghost-office was that it had internet connection, which enabled me to send a message home and catch up with e-mails.

The Sunfort claimed to be connected but it didn't work for me until near the end of my stay. The hotel was staffed with brash young men. I didn't mind that: it was preferable to the insincere show of servility I had sometimes encountered in India. To me these lads represented modern Pakistan, and we interacted as we might have done in London.

Shortly after my arrival I had tried unsuccessfully to use the hotel's phone to establish contact with the company I was working for on this project. One of the hotel staff came to help (which he didn't do); I unwisely mentioned in passing that I couldn't use my mobile phone in Pakistan. 'We'll put in a local SIM', he said, snatching up the phone he saw on my bedside table and making for the door. 'Give that back, it's not a real phone, it's to give up if I am robbed!', I remonstrated, wrestling it out of his hand. It was, technically, a real phone, but it was one I had been given in Saudi Arabia, supposedly for local use, but the start-up instructions were in Arabic and I had never got it going. I had encountered this mania for putting in local SIMs before: didn't people realise that if they did that, I would be cut off from the rest of the world trying to communicate with me?

By Sunday night, I thought the message would have got round that I didn't give tips. I do sometimes, and when I do I like to tip like a gentleman, but only at the end of an encounter, otherwise it opens a floodgate of expectation. I didn't feel moved to tip in this low-grade establishment, especially as I was still smarting from having to part with so many dollars for my stay. When I had arrived, the young man showing me to my room, insisting on carrying my small bag, had clearly expected something, and when I hadn't given a tip, had asked for one, which I regarded as bad form, and made my view clear.

Ever since I had been pestered by a stream of staff visiting with needless enquiries, and hopeful expressions. 'Any laundry?' 'Minibar top-up?' 'Is your room alright?' Which it wasn't, but I couldn't be bothered to explain: I got the impression from some of them that these were the only English phrases they knew. I had just closed the door on one such enquirer when 20 seconds later two different young men came in, made a great theatrical show of putting down some silly impractical slippers and discharged half a can of air freshener, all the time grinning excitedly as if the smell of it was sending them high. And no, I hadn't done anything to warrant such excessive purification.

The electricity would go off for several minutes with great regularity: that wasn't the hotel's fault, but one of the lovable characteristics of Lahore. The hotel had, however, connected all of the room electrics to a single switch operated by the key fob. No separate switch for the air conditioning or the main room light, nor for the bedside light, so the choice was between sleeping cool but with all the lights on and a lot of noise, or hot, quiet and in the pitch dark, having to grope all the way to the door to switch anything on. The room had a shabby, unpleasant bath with no plug: my travel plug worked well enough. One night a very noisy extractor fan came on in the bathroom and wouldn't switch off; it finally stopped at around getting-up time.

Despite these privations, I was happy – elated, even – to be doing the work at all: advising official authorities on a topic I understood well, with every prospect of a continuing project. I also felt that working in my own right with the government of Punjab would give me added status and authority in relation to our other ongoing Pakistani project. The work started properly on Monday morning with a drive to the offices of a government department called the Programme Monitoring and Implementation Unit (PMIU). Rosemary's driver was a proper bodyguard: an ex-army sharpshooter who filled the whole saloon with his air of protective competence. In the back, Rosemary explained that PMIU co-ordinated all activity supported by foreign aid, and that, not surprisingly or unusually, the departments involved resented its interference with varying degrees of intensity.

There I met Dr Farah. Fluent, intelligent and thoroughly organised, she introduced me to key members of her team, and set about explaining the wider context of my project. She had been waiting a couple of years for this induction session: she must have said all this many times previously in relation to the other strands of the programme. Her role would have involved frequent presentations to politicians, senior civil servants and World Bank officials. Even so, I was impressed, almost stunned, by the content of her presentation.

Since the start of the programme, a massive investment had been made in communications technology, to provide computer connections between every school in the province and the central headquarters. The schools had all been set targets for improving key aspects of their work, and their progress was monitored on a monthly basis. These performance measures were shared among all headteachers to encourage a competitive spirit. To achieve this in Punjab, with its mountainous terrain and under-developed management systems was astonishing, and contrasted strikingly with the state of affairs I had learnt about in Karachi, where the provincial government of Sindh had not seemed to know or care whether its schools were functioning at all. In fairness I should add that on the specific topic of teacher certification and licensing, Sindh was ahead, having already established the Sindh Teacher Education Development Authority (STEDA), which I used as a reference point in my work.

I knew the guy behind all this computerisation and performance management: he had been very influential in shaping the education policies of the Blair government in the UK before going on to make similar interventions around the world. Methods that had been deeply resented in the mature school system of England clearly had greater utility here.

Dr Farah's presentation made no reference to the strand of work I was to support, nor did she seem to have much of a view about it. Towards the end, when we were talking informally, the conversation turned to the range and complexity of international aid going into Pakistan, and the manner in which it was used. Dr Farah expressed anger. 'People talk about World Bank funding as if it is a gift! It is a loan, this is our own money!' Her frustration concerned how directive were the strings attached, and how much of the money went into the pockets of Western consultants and project management companies. She probably counted me among that swarm of locusts, although I largely shared her view.

There was another side to it. In one of my discussions with Rosemary about how the consultancy might unfold, I had used the expression 'capacity building', which was a convenient shorthand to describe the process of building the skills and confidence of local leaders. She leapt on it and warned me not to use that expression. 'World Bank and other aid agencies produce great thick project plans', she explained. 'Some people don't actually read them; they get their staff to do word searches for certain phrases. "Capacity building" is interpreted as code for shopping trips to London, Paris and New York, and "local resource personnel" is code for sinecure positions for family and friends.' I thought her view was cynical, until the following year when I worked with a project in which that was absolutely the case.

We drove the short distance to the Directorate of Staff Development (DSD); Dr Farah and her deputy Sohail came too. We were led to a lounge with easy chairs. The only representative of DSD was Nadeem, the programme director, whose purpose was to brief me about the two strands of the project: teacher certification and licensing, and continuous professional development, which fell within his directorate. He kept his explanation fairly cool and factual; the atmosphere of the meeting suggested he wanted to minimise Dr Farah's engagement, and to appraise me before deciding how accommodating to be.

When that had finished, my usual lunchtime was long past: no arrangements had been made. Rosemary took me back into central Lahore to the English TeaHouse. She explained that it was just somewhere handy we could go without pre-booking; she was apologetic about it, assuming I would regard it as being in poor taste, somewhere an Englishman would not want to go. I loved it, mainly because I was hungry and we were served quite quickly, but also it was quite an artful pastiche: the style of the wooden chairs, the layout of bits and pieces on the table, and the way things were done, were all pretty accurate representations of what it was trying to be.

Rosemary gave me spoonfuls of advice, like a benevolent governess. She didn't hold with the modern fashion of drinking water all the time: 'Your body will tell you when you need it'. One of her tips, I can't remember the context, was that audibly blowing one's nose was considered as rude in Pakistan as audibly breaking wind.

She also advised me to play down, in fact not mention at all, my position as president of a professional body concerned with teacher professionalisation. I had thought that a worthwhile and relevant credential, but she said, 'They assume it must be some teacher training college, and the people in charge of school education in Pakistan despise teachers'.

We had a meeting scheduled for later in the afternoon back at DSD, for me to be briefed by two of Nadeem's staff: his deputy, responsible for quality assurance, and the course co-ordinator who organised the professional development programmes for teachers. On the way, I found myself developing an appreciation of what I perceived to be a characteristic typical of at least one sector of Pakistani society: a kind of military orderliness. Generally, things ran to time; generally, environments were kept clean and tidy. There was no specific trigger: the scene was drab; the official buildings we approached were utilitarian blocks painted white a few years ago, neither new nor old; the grass verges were neat but not manicured. Perhaps that was what resonated.

Our session was with just the two men: both courteous and helpful, but I had visited enough ministries to find it odd that here the organisation I was supposed to be supporting was so veiled from me. That never changed. The quality assurance guy had the systems on his laptop: he showed me the same sets of data that had featured in Dr Farah's presentation. The system allowed him to analyse it in various ways. All very impressive, but I did start to wonder just how far all this had penetrated into the bloodstream of the organisation: how widely this information was being used as a management tool. I think it was the sight of one guy bent enthusiastically over his laptop while his colleague seemed detached. Clearly, international consultants would be banging the drum, but conceivably most of the civil service might be carrying on as before.

I got part of the answer when the course co-ordinator explained his work. He described a basic, ultra-traditional model: headteachers told him what their priorities were for training courses for their staff, and he put together a programme of courses which as far as possible responded to those requests. Just as it was 50 years ago in England: a culture of administration, not leadership. Inevitably, the resulting pattern of courses would reflect pet interests, favouritism, strong personalities, trade union politics and headteachers' complacency about areas of their work which were mediocre. Modern school systems use professional development as a tool to drive change: the two guys were sitting there together, and to me it was obvious that the performance issues on the quality assurance guy's laptop should be having an impact on the programme of training courses to be offered. I smiled politely as I made my notes, murmuring appreciative noises: change is best led respectfully, in small steps, when the client organisation holds all the cards.

We called in at the office at the end of the day. The Colonel told me that from tomorrow, I would have a different driver. He made clear that he was just a driver, not a bodyguard: yet another example of how the company cheese-pared on its commitments to me. The driver's name was Nizam; the pickup was timed for 8.40am, and I was assured that he would be outside my hotel, standing by the car, from 7am. 'Because that is what he does.'

Shortly after 7am on Tuesday, from my bedroom window, which overlooked a cobbled parking area in front of the hotel, I saw a smartly dressed man polishing a saloon. I guessed, correctly, that this was Nizam; I admired his diligence, and wondered why he chose to minimise his time at home. He took me to DSD, where my job for the morning was to listen to the opinions of some representatives of the higher education sector. There were four of them, and also in attendance were the two guys from DSD I had met the previous day, and Rosemary.

This was beginning to feel strikingly similar to my work in Mexico: a heavily chaperoned 'consultation' session in which it was clear I was expected to listen and make notes, but not to initiate any investigatory or developmental consultative action. They droned on, covering predictable ground, the hours passed, and my hunger started growing to the annoying stage. That was another unfortunate similarity to Mexico: a pattern was setting in of very late, inadequate lunches.

Rosemary and I went back to the company's office, where some food was ordered in: it was after 3pm when I got to eat the bland, unappetising snack. I met the consultancy team leader: he was Chinese, and based in China, but came here from time to time, dipping in and out, covering longstanding vacancies. The company would be taking a massive cut from the World Bank funding for its services, but it seemed that at every point those services were a fraction of what would have been promised: the balance added to the profits gathered in at the UK headquarters. I remembered Dr Farah's words: 'It is our money!'

He had a brisk, bossy, no-nonsense style: his main concern was whether the boxes would be ticked, the tick-boxes that released each tranche of funding. I had picked up that one of the biggest obstacles to the teacher certification and licensing project would be strong opposition from the politically influential teachers' trades unions. Did the planned workstreams include a strategy for dealing with that? The team leader said, 'China is a very authoritarian country, we don't have any trade unions, so I don't tend to give that much consideration'.

I would be giving a lecture the following morning, and the last task for Tuesday was to go and look at the venue, which was the Royal Palm Golf and Country Club. I had suggested this lecture during my visit to the company's UK headquarters. It wasn't one of their precious 'deliverables' but the man had seen the benefit of offering this as a free extra: normally my organisation would charge a lot for it. My own motives were mixed. The word 'consultant' covers such a range: international experts, facilitators, project managers, back-room analysts, all of varying qualities. I wanted to establish at the outset that I belonged to the first category. Dr Farah had embraced the idea enthusiastically and had arranged the venue and gathered an audience. I had given plenty of lectures without seeing the venue in advance, but the offer having been made, it was a welcome trip out. Rosemary and I set off. The country club was set in an extensive golf course just to the north of the canal, a short drive east of the Avari Hotel. I use these landmarks as references because I never did manage to fix in my mind the location of the company's local office.

During the drive, there was a prolonged delay at the approach to a junction: police cars were involved and we were surrounded by stationary traffic. Conversation wandered along various paths. Rosemary asked about my personal set-up: I gave the basic factual information, which actually conveyed very little because every relationship is unique. A bit later she asked whether I had ever felt the need to play the field. I didn't want to engage with the question honestly. Being a long way from home, with someone likely to be a passing acquaintance, can lubricate the loosening of the tongue, the sharing of confidences, but I baulked: there in the car, and here in this memoir. Rosemary offered some information: 'I did feel such a need, and that is why I am single now'. Lamely, and with an attempt at light-heartedness, I said that I hadn't really had any offers, which, at least in relation to recent years, was pretty much true. She wasn't ready yet for me to kick the ball into long grass. 'The man has to make the first move', she advised, as if I were young and innocent. I looked away; after a few moments of silence, she reiterated, 'It really is the case that the man should make the first move'. I didn't want to meet her eye in case she thought I had mistakenly interpreted her comment as an invitation. Outside the car, horns blared, and the police did whatever they were doing; inside we were frozen in a tableau. I stared ahead, taking in Nizam's inscrutable back and fixed focus on the road; the air was thick and still. I knew that Rosemary was willing me to look at her. The traffic ahead started moving, and three sets of lungs audibly returned to their normal activity.

The next morning I was pleasantly surprised to see that Dr Farah had gathered an invited audience of 45. She had also arranged a video recording, so my contribution was more of a freebie than I had really intended, and I had to get dazzling spotlights adjusted, but it is always nice when people take an interest. I spoke for about an hour, but from my point of view the most valuable aspect was the discussion afterwards. Many of the audience were happy to participate in questions, comments and debate: it was the first time I had felt able to have a proper conversation about the project. That was the other advantage of the lecture format: clearly I was in charge of the discussion session, from which I learnt a lot that was of relevance to the report I would need to write.

We went back to PMIU for a meeting also involving DSD representatives to review the current position and for me to outline proposals for the next steps. They were considered acceptable; I would write them up and the first block of proper fieldwork would take place in a few months' time. So far, so good. During this process, Dr Farah asked one of her staff to order in some 'lunch' – it was again well after 3pm. What arrived, eventually, were boxes of Kentucky Fried Chicken, with various side orders. I had never eaten it in the UK so could not make comparisons: this version was lukewarm, and oil had penetrated between the coating and the meat, but hunger lowers the threshold of what is eatable.

Our work being done, Rosemary suggested we have a gin and tonic at the Avari. This was another of her gifts of helpful local information and advice: this time a pleasant practical lesson. I had no idea that alcohol would be available at the Avari. We went there, and she led me to an unmarked door in an upstairs corridor. Inside, a space the size of a hotel bedroom was fitted out as a bar. It was silent and deserted, but the sound of our entry brought a member of staff from an inner room. He bore an air of silent disapproval of the whole business: he inspected our passports, sold us what we wanted, and scuttled back to his privacy. We sat at a small table in this guilty, shameful speakeasy, which sucked out of me any sense of joy or relaxation. Rosemary explained that there was a system for foreigners who drank: she had to get a doctor periodically to certify that she was addicted to alcohol.

Rosemary took me back to the Hotel Sunfort (my flight was the following morning), and got out of the car to say goodbye, standing on the cobbled parking area. I gave her a light embrace and a peck on the cheek, with which she engaged happily, while giving me a final lesson in cultural norms: 'Now you have scandalised the neighbourhood!'

Chapter Eleven

Working Holidays in São Paulo and Bogotá

I arrived home from Lahore on the evening of Thursday 22nd March, spent Saturday running a seminar, and Monday in a string of meetings which finished at 7pm, then made my way back to Heathrow to catch a 10.35pm flight to São Paulo. I kept repeating that in my head: I was so excited to be going to Brazil! The previous August I had hoped that this might be the year in which I penetrated South America. The first step on that quest had been the project I had set up in Colombia, which was going well, and there was every reason to suppose that a justification would arise for me to go back to visit it in person before too long. In September, I had received an invitation to give a keynote address at a conference in São Paulo, which I was delighted to accept, and that was what I was heading to now.

It was a three-day event, from Wednesday to Friday; I was to give my lecture on Wednesday afternoon. It was a one-off engagement: there was nothing to negotiate and I did not expect any business development opportunities to arise. So apart from the lecture, I was basically on holiday, which was a pleasant feeling at the end of a busy month.

The flight landed on time, at 6.05am on Tuesday, and I went to the hotel where I was to be lodged, which was also the conference venue. It was the Maksoud Plaza, a five-star hotel one block away from Paulista Avenue, the financial heart of Brazil. The conference was run by a commercial conference-organising company: my dealings were with Sonia, its director. It was costing them a bit to get me here; I hoped they would find my contribution worthwhile both intellectually and commercially.

A few years previously I had shocked some in my organisation by advocating the charging of realistic market-rate fees for contributions to events run commercially. The traditional practice had been to charge the actual costs of staff time, as if they were contributing to an academic research seminar. 'Do the maths', I said. 'They get 600 delegates, and charge each of them £400 for the day; deduct the cost of room hire, lunch and marketing and they are left with a generous margin. The keynotes by experts are what sell the event: there is no need to give them that for so little.'

I hadn't done the maths for this event, but certainly felt at ease checking in, exploring my room and the catering facilities: all pleasantly five-star quality. My room was on the twelfth floor of a tower, probably about halfway up, and offered good views. My first proper look at São Paulo was dramatically enhanced by a tropical thunderstorm. I can call it 'tropical' because the Tropic of Capricorn runs through the northern part of the city. It was intense: lightning struck with ear-splitting cracks and ultra-bright flashes which kept on coming every few seconds. Because of the height of my viewpoint, I was looking down on lightning as much as up: an unusual perspective. Wind roared; rain beat the windows and ran down them in sheets. Twenty minutes later, the sun was shining. The city was a forest of skyscrapers.

The conference didn't start until the following day, but a proportion of the participants were, like me, already there, and the organisers were set up with stands and registration desks. I made myself known; everyone was welcoming. The event was conducted wholly in Portuguese, with simultaneous translation to be provided for visiting speakers as necessary. From the list of delegates it was clear that the majority were from Brazil; the rest formed two main batches. Some were from other South American countries – Spanish speaking – and a sizeable group were from other Portuguese-speaking countries and territories.

This was interesting. Where do speakers of Portuguese go for their professional development? Portugal itself is a small country of ten million people. Angola has nearly 30 million, of whom the majority speak Portuguese as a second language, and a sizeable minority as their mother tongue. It is also the official language of Mozambique (population 26 million), and these two African countries were well represented at the conference. Numerous other countries and territories hold smaller pockets of Portuguese-speakers, which between them provided a handful of delegates. Brazil, by contrast, has a population of nearly 208 million, almost all of whom speak Portuguese as their native language: it is the giant of global Portuguese-ness.

My interactions were limited by the language barrier. The organisers and some of the delegates spoke English, but there were times when I nodded and smiled while pursuing my own lines of thought. My speech on Wednesday was simultaneously translated from English into Portuguese: always a hazardous process if the interpreters are not familiar with the technical concepts. Despite (or perhaps even because of?) that, it was surprisingly well received, given that I had no prior knowledge of the particular interests or professional contexts of this audience. Later I published it pretty much verbatim as a journal article. I had obtained the kit for simultaneous translation, having fought through a scrum that morning, and explained that I was a keynote speaker: the equipment seemed to be in short supply. So after my own talk, I sat in the auditorium looking forward to the next one, assuming that one of the channels on the kit would be an English version. Not so: my only options were to pretend to listen to the talk in Spanish, or to use the kit and pretend to listen to it in Portuguese. The kits would not be available on the following days.

For the rest of the afternoon, and on Thursday morning, I decided that a polite and suitable strategy would be to sit around in the concourse areas of the conference suite, getting on with my own work, and talking with whoever chose to accost me. There were quite a few, typically school principals who were competent English-speakers. These were good professional conversations: there was real interest in some of the things my organisation did, but in every case it became clear that the language barrier was a significant obstacle. I had no inclination to wander around downtown São Paulo on my own, and was content to sit it out, but to my pleasant surprise, Sonia told me she had set me up with a guide and driver for the afternoon. The guide was called Pedro; I met him in the foyer after lunch, and that marked the start of the craziest session of guided tourism I have experienced.

He began in dramatic fashion: 'I will introduce you to Brazilian culture!', he announced, then briefly surveyed the people milling around and led me to two women standing near the reception desk. To my surprise, he kissed each of them on both cheeks. To my greater surprise, they didn't object: if anything, seemed mildly pleased. In England, they would have been furious, and perhaps would have called the police. He told me to do the same, 'to experience our culture', which I did but in a less rough and slobbery manner, intending to show a bit of respect, which the women acknowledged with twinkly smiles. Or perhaps they were amused by my English reserve. Did he know them? Had he set them up beforehand?

He took me out to the car. I couldn't follow any of his instructions to the driver, but we came to a street in the central business district which I guess was probably Paulista Avenue. It was full of skyscrapers, but Pedro was keen to point out one of the few old buildings, a mansion in Iberian style (of course I mustn't say 'Spanish'). Pedro was dismissive about Brazil's apparently miraculous economic growth. 'Banking: it is all imaginary, based on speculation about speculation. Fantasy figures, nothing real underneath. None of it filters down to benefit the population.'

Next, he took me to an old building which, insofar as I could gather from him, was some kind of elite club for city bigwigs. I supposed it was a bit like the Athenaeum in London: certainly the feel and ambience were similar. (No, I am not a member: my knowledge of it is limited to one long and memorable evening as a guest.) It was becoming clear that Pedro was driven by some form of angry political consciousness. Knowing that I had lectured on education leadership, he said, 'The government here don't really want to improve schools: it suits them to have a lot of the population poorly educated'.

Pedro took me to museums and galleries. I don't know how many, because some of the different sites might have been parts of the same institution. Even later, having looked at guidebooks and websites, I remained just as vague about where I had actually been on that kaleidoscopic afternoon. It was an example of the sensual bombardment which Andrés Neuman so insightfully describes in his book *How to Travel without Seeing*. I am clear, however, that the itinerary must have included the Memorial da America Latina, where I met Gia, because of its unmistakably distinctive architecture, including a sinuous raised walkway and bridge.

Pedro led me into a spacious exhibition hall which appeared to be deserted, except by us and by two pleasant young curators sitting at a reception desk. Perhaps they knew Pedro from previous visits, perhaps they were captivated by his animation. Perhaps he had embroidered the truth and told them I was important, perhaps they were just bored and welcomed something to do. For whatever reason, after the briefest of conversations (unintelligible to me), they were happy to leave their desk and give me a proficient and informative personal guided tour of the exhibits.

They were both friendly. Maria was Amerindian, quieter and more reserved than Gia, who was African, noisy, outgoing and bursting with ideas and opinions. It was easy to see that she would resonate with Pedro. She was tiny, with an almost child-like physique, counterbalanced by enormous Afro hair, extending wider than her shoulders. I noticed that there hadn't been any kissing upon greeting, contrary to the earlier encounter, but Pedro was quite assertive towards the girls. At one point he moved them by the shoulders into a line with himself, to explain to me, 'We three represent the ethnic composition of Brazil: African, Amerindian, Portuguese. The races have not intermingled here as much as in some other Latin American countries'. People of African descent actually represent about half of the population of Brazil; by 'Portuguese' he meant the group who are predominantly the descendants of Portuguese men and local women. Similarly to the USA, Brazil experienced and encouraged massive European immigration in the 19th and early 20th centuries.

Maria and Gia were explaining some brightly painted sculptures by indigenous artists depicting the early colonisers: the faces were painted pillar-box red. 'They thought the white men were red, because they only saw them outside in the heat, with flushed faces.'

We walked across a glass floor looking down on an enormous map of Latin America. After some other general talk about jurisdictions and politics, I puckishly asked, 'Whose are the Malvinas?' That set

Pedro off: he explained, in his animated fashion, that he had been part of a group of interpreters at some peace-signing conference or other. 'I can confirm first-hand, my own eyes and ears, the Malvinas are British.'

There was an art exhibition in a building nearby. Maria and Gia said it wasn't in their territory but they would come with us anyway. The journey involved going over the distinctive walkway; the artworks were revolutionary in subject matter and enormous in scale. I gathered some of them were famous. Meanwhile, Gia's chatter about politics, art, education and life in general had become more lively. Her English was excellent, her ideas interesting, refreshing and enlightened, and I thoroughly enjoyed her company. She was planning to visit London in the near future, and hoped to enrol in some short courses while she was there. I mentioned some of the options I knew about; by the end of the visit it seemed natural to give her my card and invite her to contact me when she came to London.

Pedro hadn't finished with me. After the gallery, he had me driven past pleasant parks. He expounded his ideas about the unifying policies of successive governments, at one point waving a banknote and pointing to the illustrations on it. I had no notes myself: like the Queen, I required no money for my passage through Brazil. 'The banknote says it all', he opined. 'One language – Portuguese; one religion – the Roman religion; and one law – the Roman legal system.'

He pointed to a car moving ahead of us around a roundabout. 'That car belongs to the former royal family: they have a special number plate. We used to have a royal family here. They were deposed when we became a republic, but they still live here and have certain minor privileges.' Later I read about the strange relationship between Portugal and Brazil: for periods of history, the latter seemed not so much a colony as a sort of extended back garden. The Portuguese royal family based themselves in Brazil during the Napoleonic Wars, and when the king returned to Portugal he left his son, Pedro, behind as regent. Pedro, discerning widespread dissatisfaction in Brazil with its colonial status, declared the country independent and himself emperor. He reigned until forced to abdicate in 1831, whereupon he designated his son, Pedro II, as his successor. At the time Pedro II was a 5-year-old child who took no part in government. He reigned from 1840 with political astuteness until 1889, when a bloodless military coup created the republic. Pedro II died in Paris; his remains and his descendants were repatriated in the early 20th century. The former royal family currently live in Rio near the imperial palace, now a museum, where they enjoy a certain social standing, as well as their distinctive number plates.

Pedro (the guide, not the emperor) took me to the university where he was a part-time student. It was a private sector university, housed in a modern building: the foyer and concourse looked like a hundred others. On the face of it, it was an odd place to take me in his capacity as a tour guide: perhaps he just wanted to share a part of himself, which I liked. He rumbled with discontent about the role of the private sector in education, then took me back to the hotel. An interesting guy, with intelligence, depth and passion: guides and interpreters are often so much more than their role.

Back in my room, checking e-mails, there was one from Gia: 'Hi, I am the girl you met in the museum…' I left for the airport at 4pm on Friday, for a flight which left at 11.40pm and landed at Heathrow at 3pm on Saturday 31st March. During the long flight, I reflected in a state of peaceful exhaustion about the pattern of my life over the preceding six weeks. A week in Delhi, a week in Karachi, a week in

Lahore and a week in Brazil: different types of work, different kinds of client, and some new social interactions, interspersed with a total of 16 days, including weekends, to attend to everything else going on in my life.

Gia wrote a number of times in the lead-up to her visit, which did not take place until late June, after I had revisited her continent. I always replied in a professional tone, in the way I would write to one of my own students, but her own style was unique and initially disconcerting. Her messages were very brief, very informal in style: I mean exceptionally, loopily informal, and sprinkled with gushing endearments. I had never received such messages: things were done very differently when I was young. Rationally it was inconceivable that Gia could regard me as potential boyfriend material, so I learnt not to get flustered as I penned dry advice about hotels and courses. Gia taught me that some modern young women, especially if they learnt English for social purposes, adopt a style that it would be quite wrong to decode using the social conventions of 30 years ago.

On the date we had set for us to meet my diary kept filling up; I was rushed, and not completely certain she would see any merit in keeping the appointment. A little late, I emerged into the concourse of my organisation and looked for her among the many people there. Then I saw her, or rather her hair in the first instance: she was sitting outside under a tree. I was disproportionately happy to see her, and she was every bit as lively and interesting as I remembered. I took her into the park in Russell Square: I had planned fish and chips in the café there as suitably unpretentious and English. In the queue she explained she was vegetarian, and chose pizza and chips. She politely said it was a nice meal, although privately I guessed it was possibly the worst she had had for a while. Over lunch, she told me, shyly at first but then with joy, that while in London she would be living with her girlfriend, her female partner.

She was heading next towards Tottenham Court Road, and I asked if I might go with her part of the way as there was something I wanted to show her. We set off, and part-way along one of the side streets there was a smartly painted door, with 'Gia' affixed to it in stylish brass letters. We said our goodbyes. I don't know what Gia gained from that hour, but for me she had brought all the best of Brazil into Bloomsbury in a gust of pizzazz, and I walked back to my office with a lightened spirit. She had, incidentally, already seen the door.

*****

Meanwhile, during May, Melba had been busy setting up the means by which I could return to Colombia. The purpose would be to enable me to visit the ministry to keep in touch with our ongoing project, and to visit universities to explore possibilities for collaboration. A source of funding had to be found to cover the cost of the trip; Melba involved the British Council and also got me an invitation to speak at an event.

This concerned an organisation called Empresarios por la Educación, abbreviated to ExE: a group of successful business entrepreneurs who gave philanthropic support to education improvement projects. They had been at it for ten years and the event was to celebrate what had been achieved. The only specific input required from me by ExE was to speak for 30 minutes and be present for certain sessions. In return for British Council support, I had to participate in a series of liaison meetings. This was quite a pleasing offer: if such a modest contribution paid for me to have a full week in Colombia, perhaps I was starting to get started. Perhaps, even, I had begun to arrive. No, later I realised it simply reflected Melba's negotiating skills.

I travelled to Heathrow on Sunday 17th June 2012 to stay overnight, ready for an early flight to Paris at 6.40am on Monday. At this point I need to mention a development on the home front which impinged on my thinking during the trip.

Some years previously, my partner and I had negotiated where we would base ourselves in retirement. She had roots in north-east England, and had spent 30 years as a 'foreigner' in London, so it was fair that in the next phase I should be the 'foreigner'. We considered the environments, properties and prices in the places we liked, and balancing those factors against each other, agreed that our chosen location would be Barnard Castle, a small, pretty market town in County Durham. We knew it well, but in 2011 took the next step of spending a week in the town to experience what it would be like to live there, and to look in more detail at desirable locations and houses. I wanted space, and a suitable ambience for working and writing at home.

Our favourite street was Newgate, which followed the top of a river terrace eastwards out of the town. It had a variety of pleasant old town houses of different styles and sizes. We walked past one called Spring Grove at the end of the row, with a front garden facing towards the great chateau housing the Bowes Museum. The house seemed to be of a good size, with high ceilings, three storeys over a cellar or basement (there was a small window at pavement level) and of an eccentric and interesting design. There was a 'for sale' board outside, to which had been affixed an additional bar carrying the information 'Five Beds'. In the casual manner in which I have taken all the great decisions in life, I said, 'Well, that would do!' We did not plan to move until several years into the future, so the incident passed.

On the evening of Saturday 16th June 2012, I was involved in what, for me, was always the long and complex process of getting ready for a working trip abroad. We had dined and wined well on my last night at home. I could not settle to anything purposeful, and on a whim browsed the website of the estate agent in Barnard Castle. Spring Grove was still for sale. I wanted it, and told my startled partner, who was unimpressed. She did not think I was being serious, or if I was, that it would ever happen, but she did not veto the idea. The next morning I wrote a rambling e-mail to the estate agent, saying I was interested in buying the house, asking a number of questions raised by puzzling elements in the detailed description, and saying that I was that day setting off for Colombia, then China, but I would like a viewing when I was back in July.

Two factors which had been slowly boiling away in my mind prompted that impetuous action. Property prices in London had been falling, which with my lifelong tendency to live beyond my means gave me the feeling that the possibilities for moving might slip through my fingers. Secondly, I was finding the pattern of my working life tiring and stressful: the joy of travel was marred by having insufficient support with the rest of my work while I was away. Moving to the other end of the country would shake things up a bit and force some changes. I had no idea what the outcome would be, but the prospect was attractive and energising. That sense of impending change stayed with me overnight in the hotel at Heathrow, and for the next few days.

Monday morning started in the middle of the night, so that I could check in for my 6.40am flight to Paris, where I had an hour and a half to transfer without rush to a 10.40am flight to Bogotá. With the eight-hour time difference, it was 2.35pm when I landed at El Dorado airport. During the entry formalities, an official pleasantly asked me something I couldn't quite catch. After several attempts, he wrote it down: 'Are you German?' I had never been asked that before: 'Raphael' usually prompted other lines of enquiry, but perhaps 'Wilkins' sounded a bit Germanic, when combined with what was left of my sandy hair. Outside, Melba smiled her twinkling, slightly mischievous welcome and took me to La Quinta Hotel and explained what we would be doing.

La Quinta was an attractive boutique hotel. Melba's ability to organise such a pleasant holiday for me was impressive. In the hotel's own words, it was 'A marvellous blend of English mansion-style charm and contemporary design… housed in a beautifully restored private residence… the lobby features several intimate areas for socialising, with overstuffed armchairs placed invitingly close to the fireplace and a lovely wood-panelled library'. Just my kind of ambience. It had two other attractions important to me. Its stock range of teabags included English tea: generally in Colombia, any of a wide range of infusions are considered to count as 'tea'. Also, it had excellent Wi-Fi internet connectivity: the combination of e-mail, tea, overstuffed armchairs and Melba for company made me feel that the sun was shining.

I had gleaned a bit about Melba in our previous working encounters: my knowledge of her deepened during the social times on this trip. She loved travel, and was self-sufficient, quite happy travelling on her own. She had undertaken a long work assignment in China and had picked up a bit of Mandarin. She described a train journey she had taken there that lasted many days, sharing a small sleeping compartment with a stranger, an elderly Chinese man. 'On the whole journey, he never said a word to me, nor I to him.' This self-sufficiency extended to a lack of concern about material things. 'I am happy, I don't need anything.' On some of her visits to London she would leave her luggage in any of a variety of secure places she had established and spend the days in libraries and cafés. She was at ease with the ups and downs of the freelance life and was not bothered about a career plan. 'If there was nothing else, I could return to my family home.'

Ah! So there was a family home, which added a new perspective. I didn't pry, but gained a vague impression of some old-established estate, or ranch, or plantation, somewhere in the lawless forested mountains. Her father was an artist. 'He painted a portrait of me', she said proudly, producing a photograph of the painting. Her pride was justified. The painting, in traditional style, was expertly wrought: it could have hung alongside portraits of 18th-century queens in the National Gallery. It captured Melba at an earlier age, I guessed mid-20s, and combined a portraitist's skill in beautifying a faithful likeness with a father's love and pride.

Working days started early. On Tuesday I had to leave the hotel at 8am to be taken to the ministry, where Melba had arranged for me to meet Natalia, who was in charge of international co-operation. In the entry foyer my passport was carefully inspected and information about the visit written in logbooks. The meeting, which lasted over an hour, was pleasant and productive. Natalia was welcoming and lively, and keen to discuss the next phases of our project, which, as anticipated, was expanding to include new groups of participants. Natalia seemed impressed (as Melba had intended) that I was able to drop in like this while visiting Bogotá on other business. We arranged that I would go back later in the week.

Next Melba took me to the Gold Museum. She had intended to do so later in the week, but with calm efficiency decided it was better to fit it in now. She took me to the entrance, said that she didn't want to see it again, told me to prove my age to get concessionary admission, and instructed me to have lunch there. In I went, to browse around several floors filled with displays of gold objects. The only comparator which came to mind was the displays of gold objects from antiquity in the British Museum, which was near my office, and into which I wandered from time to time when I had nothing better to do. I was always struck by how bright and clean and new the objects looked, even though they were several thousand years old. There was a fair number of them, filling numerous showcases.

In the Museo del Oro the bright, apparent newness of the ancient objects was the same, but the sheer quantity was in another league. The museum celebrates the products of pre-Colombian cultures, and with 34000 pieces of elaborately crafted ancient gold, it is the biggest such collection in the world. Vast and vastly impressive: but after the initial impact I had a low satiation threshold and was happy to absorb a general impression. Having looked at an amazing artefact of one particular kind, I did not feel a need to devote the same level of attention to each of 200 similar items. Having browsed several floors, as soon as I decently could I went to the restaurant, where I enjoyed what was advertised as a local Colombian speciality: a sort of potato soup with sweetcorn, chicken and capers. Outside, Melba was watching out for me from a car; she took me to the offices of the British Council.

The first meeting there was a briefing and planning session led by Martha, who had written to me previously while making arrangements for my trip. A representative of ExE was also present. A pair who did most of the talking were clearly keen to practise reading and speaking English, taking me through my programme from the beginning, including the things which had already happened: 'Your flight will arrive at… you will be met by…'

The second part of the meeting was with Paula, representing a university called EAFIT (pronounced 'Effit', Melba had coached me), to talk about whether and how we might collaborate in course provision in the fields of leadership and coaching. The British Council was leading on this, putting forward its view on how British expertise might be drawn upon locally. Quite soon I sensed a growing bond of fellow-feeling with Paula as we looked at each other, each checking that the other was equally bemused as to why and how our institutions would do the things being suggested. Our polite participation continued for a tedious period, then Melba and I walked back to the hotel, where we had an early dinner of prawn risotto. 'Yes!' I thought, with a sense of achievement; not concerning the meeting, but the more tangible experience of having walked the streets of Bogotá and survived.

Colombia was full of surprises. From my conversation with the young women on the security desk at the ministry, I had learnt that a lot of people here get up between 4am and 5am, because schools start lessons at 6.30am and a standard office working day lasts from 7am to 7pm. Yet they don't go to bed until about 11pm, so I was puzzled as to how they managed. It was so different from my assumption – prejudiced and stereotyped – of a relaxed pace of life in a Spanish-speaking country.

Melba maintained a stream of soothing social interaction, into which she was happy to drop saucy double entendres, although boundaries were always clear. In the midst of this exotic setting and company, I was continuing an e-mail dialogue with home and with the estate agent about the house in Barnard Castle. It had emerged from my enquiries that the property had at one time been divided up. What we had seen offered for sale was the front part, arranged as a three-storey, five-bedroomed town house, behind which were two flats. The ground-floor flat had also recently come on to the market: by buying that as well, I would get the whole of the ground-floor garden frontage, providing an ideal working environment. I cleared my diary for three days in July, arranged viewings of both properties, and booked accommodation in the Royal County Hotel in Durham. Taking those actions about my future life while in Bogotá made the world seem smaller, but in a way more interesting: it was possible to be in two continents at once.

Wednesday was taken up with the event that justified my presence in Colombia. I was collected from the hotel by taxi at 7am and taken to the venue, the Club El Nogal. Also in the taxi was the other international speaker, who was from Chile. That interested me: I was booked to visit Chile at the end of July. The ExE event was on a high floor of a tower block, offering fine views of the Andes. The lift took me straight back to rare visits to department stores in childhood: in the corner was a small wooden high-chair occupied by a smartly dressed elderly man pressing buttons and opening doors.

There were opening addresses from the president of ExE, and a much longer one from Maria, the minister for national education. I had a headset offering simultaneous translation into English, although the standard of interpretation seemed a little rough. After a break, the festivities began: it was very much a celebratory occasion, even though the session was called an accountability report, implying objective evaluation. There were numerous video presentations made by schools which had participated in projects: all of them full of lively music, and smiling, singing students and staff, thoroughly pleased with themselves as if they had just won the lottery.

As an experienced evaluator, I found this frustrating and uninformative. If these were reports of projects that had received funding for specific purposes, I expected to be told the following: these were the objectives, these were the actions we took, this is how we measured the benefits, this is the extent to which the objectives were met, these are the things which went well, these were the challenges, this is how we are embedding the achievements, this is what we have learnt. There was none of that; no-one seemed to mind. There was quite a contingent from the ministry, including the vice minister I had worked with previously. He and his team were all wearing brightly coloured gilets, decorated with the logo of one of the ministry's programmes, which to my eye made them look like a gang of bandits. They clapped and cheered along, enjoying the celebration.

Before lunch, during an ExE business meeting, it had been arranged for me to meet a representative of a university called ICESI, which Melba had instructed me to pronounce 'eesessi'. It was a specialised institution which had been set up by business people. Over the lunch period I had to attend a discussion session, but without translation, so I put on my nodding, smiling act as if I had a clue what they were talking about.

My presentation was introduced very formally and politely. I spoke for the allotted time, followed by my Chilean counterpart. Further contributions from Colombians followed, but the translation was so haphazard that much of the session sounded like a babble of random words. That evening I enjoyed a tasty, succulent steak: good South American beef.

Thursday required another early start: I went with Melba to the ministry, arriving there at 7.15am. I had a most productive session with Natalia, agreeing dates for the next phases of our work. There was a session with some of the *formadores* I had met on my previous visit, and in response to their feedback, I agreed some changes to the content of our course. Natalia decided that the progress merited kiss-on-cheek procedures. I was there for my organisation, this was part of formal ceremonial, and of course I did my duty: someone has to take on these tasks.

Melba had a treat in store. We were going up a mountain, more specifically the Cerro de Monserrate in the Parque Nacional. The trip started at the funicular station; she guided me into the building, through the ticket hall, and into the car, ahead of which I could see its steep course proceeding up a tunnel. I had not been in such a contraption since seaside holidays when I was young: that was my only comparator. The door shut, it creaked into smooth, soundless motion: the tunnel was cool and dark. Light appeared and we emerged into bright sunlight. The steep mountainside was covered almost entirely in vegetation: trees, scrub and lush undergrowth clinging to its uneven surface. The most obvious contrast with any English funicular was the length of the climb: it went on and on, lasting far longer than I had expected, while the view became more spectacular. Melba and I were the only ones wearing business clothes: the other occupants of the car were casually dressed, chattering in holiday mood. Eventually the crest came into view, then the station, into which the car clunked. We emerged into noticeably colder air, at an altitude of 3152 metres.

There were buildings on the top, notably the Santuario de Monserrate: its gleaming white walls and tower were a feature of the Bogotá skyline. There was also a restaurant, to which Melba took me for lunch. My meal was a fish dish, nicely cooked. The fish dishes I had eaten during this trip all had different names, but I guessed that the fish was actually the same each time – probably Chilean sea bass – and that the names simply denoted various presentations and accompaniments. We ate in the open air, looking down on a slightly misty panorama of

Bogotá's sprawl across the altiplano. Our journey down was by cable car, which ran alongside the funicular. This was only my second ever cable-car ride, the first being when I was 15, with my mother in Austria. As it glided down, swaying slightly, above the crowns of the trees, I found it hard to believe the voice in my head reminding me, 'This is your work; you are being paid to have this experience'.

My next engagement was another meeting with a university, this time at its premises. Melba advised me that Los Andes University was old and highly reputable, one of the best in the country (coded message: behave yourself!); they were interested in expanding their doctoral level study within the field of education leadership. The venue was a mature building on a leafy hillside; in its quiet, carpeted, panelled academic interior I met Juni and Carlos. It was mid-afternoon, towards the end of a trip, following outdoor adventures and lunch: it was a credit to my hosts that I did not fall deeply asleep. In fact we had an interesting and enjoyable professional discussion. They spoke good English, and they knew about the organisation I worked for; for my part I had helped another university to address similar issues and had useful comments to contribute. The session had value in itself, but it was clear that the language barrier would severely limit any formal collaboration. That evening the language barrier also prevented me from checking in for my flight online: I could only find Spanish-language websites.

Friday morning was taken up with a series of meetings at the British Council, from which I would go straight to the airport for a flight to Paris that was due to leave Bogotá at 5.35pm. Travelling against the time zones, I would not reach Heathrow until 4.25pm on Saturday. At the British Council the discussions were led by Juan Carlos who took us out afterwards for lunch at a restaurant where we sat in the open air.

The business done, he chatted informally. Overseas, the British Council generally locates itself inside British embassies, often in its postal address referring to itself as a 'division' of the embassy. This reinforces the view, widely held among local populations, that the British Council is part of the UK government, which it is not. This arrangement does mean, however, that British Council staff often have close insight into the work of their embassy cohabitees.

Juan started chatting freely, first about how the staffing of the embassy had, at some time in the past, swollen to many times the size normally expected of an embassy in a country the size of Colombia. The clear implication was that the intelligence services had been assisting in the war against the drugs barons. Juan talked about the resources and capacities of the latter, including their ability to build and deploy submarines.

This was astonishing: at first I wasn't sure if I had heard correctly. When Frank Gardner turned to writing fiction in 2016 with his thriller *Crisis,* informed by his knowledge of Colombia, he told the world about these submarines in some detail: everyone knows about them now. But we were having our conversation in 2012 and it brought home to me what the security forces were up against.

On the other hand, there was a force for change at work on the ground, swinging things in the government's favour. In discussion with the *formadores* I had picked up on the brave commitment of local people to defy the criminals and work on the side of reform. One of the *formadores,* Victor, had been assigned to support schools in the remote and lawless Amazonas region. He spoke about the physical difficulties of meeting up for professional development caused by the terrain:

'We *formadores* travel by bus, unstable "crazy bronco" cargo planes and canoes, suffering extremes of temperature, unusual food and threats of violence. The starring role in this programme is the communities we support. Last month we finally reached a remote group of teachers, mainly from indigenous communities...

'We worked together for an entire week. It was rewarding to observe their commitment and the excitement in their eyes: they felt valued and important. One of the teachers told how he had rejected recruitment to an armed group. These communities in the past were forced to support corruption and conflict. Now we are convinced that as the programme moves forward, we will transform to a nation state with its own identity and with confidence in its citizens.'

Victor's passion and commitment, endurance of discomfort and danger, his belief in education as a force for change, and his pride in his country, seemed to me to capture and express the essence of Colombia.

Chapter Twelve
Autocracy in Guangzhou and Zhongshan

I came back to London for an exceptionally busy few days before setting off for China, on an assignment which filled me with unease because I knew it would contrast in every way with my pleasant stay in Bogotá.

In March 2010, I had been on a business development trip to Guangdong province, arranged and supported by the British Council. From that flowed what I understood to be a five-year contract to provide leadership development training to school principals. The training would entail an annual one-week course in Guangzhou in July, followed by another week's course with the same group in September in London. In July and September 2010 that happened passably well: I did the training with my colleague Gordon.

The issues from the outset included the tightness of the budget: the margin on daily rates was minimal, and the total size of the pot precluded us from building in what we considered to be good teaching and learning practices. The interfaces were weak: although the project had been set up by the British Council, the real client was a local university, where the key players were in a mindset of purchasing, procurement and compliance, rather than of professional collaboration. This was always a recipe for giving course participants conflicting messages and misleading expectations.

Then there was Joe, the senior manager in the local university, who 'owned' this project. He was an awkward loner, and an authoritarian bruiser: I pitied the young woman who worked as his assistant, to whom he barked orders as if she was a dog. He would say he had agreed to some arrangement, then change it unilaterally to bring it nearer to his own view of how things should be.

That applied to the professional work, but Joe also spent a period studying in London (one of the ways China rewards high-fliers); I supervised his Masters dissertation and his mulish attitude applied there also. In tutorials I would show him how to make his writing more reflective, acknowledging a range of opinions, and the limits of certain knowledge. He would get the point, his next draft would show he could do it, but then a later version would revert to dogmatic assertions. I suspected he resented my power to assess and grade his work, and that it might be in his nature to want to settle the score some day.

In the early months of 2011, discussions started with the British Council about the second year of the programme, and our preparations were quite advanced when the client (Joe's university) pulled out. So that was that, I thought.

In March 2012, when I was in Karachi with Eleanore, news came through that they wanted to run the programme again. I thought about how to improve on what we had offered previously. The Chinese school principals had been interested in how their UK counterparts worked. It was difficult to help them convincingly with that, because school leadership is fully devolved to schools in the UK, so really it needed a school principal to give their perspective and share some of the detail of their day-to-day operations. That was a feature of the London stage of the course, but if it could be built into the Guangzhou stage it would be good preparation and give coherence to the course as a whole. I suggested we take a school principal with us, which the

Chinese found a difficult concept as they had a narrow view of what a 'visiting expert' looked like.

Reluctantly they agreed, but because the budget was tight, Gordon would need to drop out, which he graciously agreed to do. As an additional economy, they also shortened the programme by one day. By now it was April, and quite challenging to find a school principal from among those involved in the London programme who would be happy to work with me, and who could free themselves for the dates in July. I found one; preparations proceeded, then at a late stage – probably when sorting out visas – the Chinese withdrew their consent for the school principal to come. It was just to be me on my own.

Meanwhile, I had been discussing with Joe some aspects of the programme. I wanted it to include school visits, with the intention of teaching the course participants some evaluation techniques and setting them the task of applying them to a real situation. 'I'll arrange that', Joe insisted. I thought he wanted to minimise the cost of my time; I didn't believe he understood what I wanted to do, and hoped I might be able to improvise when the time came.

There was yet another cause for my disquiet. On the previous course in July 2010, British Council staff had taken a close interest, and as part of that they had looked after Gordon and me. For example, they had changed the hotel from the one the university preferred, the Zhujiang Hotel, to the Jianguo Hotel, where Western visitors would be more comfortable, and had adjusted some unnecessarily taxing aspects of the schedule. This time, after the initial brokerage, the British Council seemed much more hands-off: they were content that Joe would arrange everything and look after me appropriately. Lyn at the British Council had arranged my flights and had sent me local contact details but, breaking my organisation's normal procedures, I had to state in the papers permitting travel that I would not know until I arrived in which hotel I would be staying.

Looking over these points, set down with hindsight, you might wonder why I went ahead with the trip. It was an example of typical Chinese negotiating: keep on edging the demands slightly upwards, and the offer slightly downwards, so that each adjustment didn't seem like a deal-breaker. It was also, more simply, an example of how Joe exerted control: on any matter that might be controversial, give no prior information, just announce it when it is too late to do anything different. My organisation valued the connection; it was my duty to give Joe the benefit of the doubt. I did, nonetheless, feel like a lamb to slaughter as I went to Heathrow to board a flight at 4pm on Friday 29th June.

That landed in Doha at 12.45am on Saturday. At 2.30am I took off for Guangzhou, landing at 3.35pm local time. Joe was there to meet me. He drove me himself to a hotel; I don't think he told me which one it was, and I can't read Chinese characters – there was not a word of English outside or in – but I am pretty sure it was the Zhujiang. It was a tower block of fancy design, with embellished corners; much later I looked at pictures on websites which supported that view. Joe came in and managed the incomprehensible check-in process, then escorted me up to my room which was somewhere in the clouds. He said he would meet me at 7am for breakfast.

I asked about eating, and he told me starkly that there was no evening food service here, and there were no eating places in the vicinity. I reacted, and he said he would arrange for some fruit to be sent in. Then I noticed there was no bottled water. 'You can boil the tap water', he said, at which I reacted more forcibly, saying that was not good enough. With bad grace he replied that bottled water would come with the fruit.

Then he went away, leaving me to nurse my anger, on my own behalf and on behalf of my organisation, of which I was a senior representative.

A long time later, probably about an hour, there was a knock on the door, and Joe's long-suffering assistant handed me a plastic bag, paused a moment to check that I wasn't going to add to her woes, then made her escape. Inside the bag was a welcome bottle of water, an orange which I couldn't touch, a rock-hard kiwi fruit and some other unpleasantries. The water in the bathroom was stone cold; only the next morning did I discover that if it was left running for about 45 minutes, it came through hot.

I said earlier that I can't read Chinese characters: I should clarify also that I cannot tell apart the different Chinese languages, either in spoken or written form. Given the location, probably what I saw and heard was mainly Cantonese, but in this chapter it is easier to call it all Chinese.

On Sunday morning, I met Joe in the foyer at the appointed hour and he took me in to breakfast. I soon discovered why. He wasn't attempting to be sociable; there was no buffet and the itemised menu was in Chinese only. In my stay at the hotel I never saw another Westerner. The menu was long. Joe scanned it and listed his selections to the waiter, without a word of explanation or consultation, not a gesture towards normal polite hosting. While we waited for the food, he told me the hotel was run by the People's Liberation Army (PLA). A selection of dim sum and other bits and pieces arrived. Some items were pleasant, nothing was repulsive, and the quantity quite well judged: neither mean nor generous. Overall it was an interesting experience which I could not have had on my own.

Joe instructed me to pack my bags and checked me out of the hotel. I wasn't sure why. He drove me to the university and led me to the conference suite on the 21st floor. This was familiar territory and I started to feel as if I was standing on slightly firmer ground. There were the 25 school principals who were participating on the course, there were the university officials and academics, and interpreters, who were students: their interpreting skills were variable.

Although the first event was a formal opening ceremony lasting an hour and a half, the programme had in fact started the previous day: local faculty members had been teaching the group. One of the sessions had been on 'the key aspects of British basic education': I wondered about the content, accuracy and quality of that, but there had been no information about it, let alone consultation. Other sessions would have included the local faculty giving their version of the aims and purpose of the course: again, without any liaison with me. The local faculty either didn't understand, or didn't care about, pedagogic coherence: the merit of everyone working towards a shared set of learning outcomes.

The opening ceremony included speeches by several individuals projecting their senior status in the hierarchy. The interpreter wasn't brilliant at the role and didn't realise the extent to which my hearing impairment had developed, so I only picked up fragments of what was going on. At one point I thought it had finished, and started making my own introduction to the programme, and people looked horrified; someone explained that there were some other important people who needed to make comments before anything could happen. When it was all over, there was the pleasant relief of a tea break. There is always plenty of tea in China, even if it isn't necessarily the variety I would choose. In this conference suite, it was available for self-service in corners of the corridor, and, as I remembered from my previous visit, it was possible to find discreetly placed supplies of Lipton's Yellow Label tea. I would survive.

After tea, I lectured. Then there was lunch, pleasantly Cantonese, and then I lectured some more. Another tea break, another lecture. At 5pm, everyone, myself included, was herded down to the ground floor, carrying suitcases, out and into a waiting coach, its engine throbbing impatiently. What was going on? Joe told me to take the front passenger seat, and put one of the interpreters next to me: a lively, pretty young woman, keen to practise her English. At last a shaft of sunlight poured down between the dark clouds.

I had managed to grab hold of the course programme, which was brief, sketchy and partly in Chinese. I saw the words '17.00 leave for Zhongshan', so that explained what we were doing, as my delightfully pleasant companion confirmed. The interpreters were in competition with each other, because those considered the most competent would be allowed to come to London in September. While my companion's conversation was relaxing, with another part of my mind I was resenting the lack of communication on such a vital matter. No-one knew where I was: if anything happened to me, the trail would run cold at Guangzhou airport. Also, I hated not being able to visualise my movements on a map; I had no knowledge of Zhongshan, the journey seemed very long and its direction a mystery. As in so much of China, the view from the window while daylight lasted was of motorway and concrete tower blocks: everything massive, characterless, functional and unattractive.

Strangeness and anxiety made the journey seem longer. It felt a bit like when, on my regular drive up the A1 at night between London and Yorkshire, my eye on the clock and anticipating when I would arrive, I would sometimes come unexpectedly to a road closure and diversion. These always seemed to be set up so as to take me off in the wrong direction, down unfamiliar, unlit, minor country roads. Each yellow 'diversion' sign appearing in the headlights seems to point to a narrower lane: when will this end? Will I get lost, break down, run out of petrol? Annoyance because my planned arrival time will be significantly delayed. Then, with great relief, rejoining the known route, and later seeing on a map that it was not as bad as it had seemed at the time. My coach ride to Zhongshan triggered the same reactions. One of my first acts when I got home was to look at a map, and to learn that Zhongshan is a city 75 kilometres south of Guangzhou.

The coach drew into the forecourt of a large, well-lit hotel and we disembarked. It was a long time since I had arrived at a hotel as part of a coach party: it would have been during the package-holiday period of my late teens and early 20s. To my relief the Yihe Junli Hotel was a considerable improvement on the one run by the PLA. It made a passable attempt at achieving international standards, with some English signage and information, and good Wi-Fi connection, so I could e-mail home to report my location. Dinner was pleasant, served in the Cantonese style: round tables, with a rotating central servery. I asked for a knife and fork, which made it easier to grab some of the better bits before they whizzed past.

Some of the school principals from the 2010 course turned up to join the dinner party. Whatever my own reservations about the programme, they seemed happy enough, and their presence gave the occasion a pleasant, celebratory character. The meal was washed down with Macallan: an improvement on the local spirit I had been required to drink in fair quantities on my previous visit.

The pillows were hard and bouncy, shaped like humbugs: I kept waking in the night with a headache and cricked neck. In the morning after breakfast we were herded back into the coach and taken to the Zhongshan Overseas Chinese Middle School. The weather was heavily humid, with warm downpours and very bright, hot sunshine in between. The same interpreter I was with the previous day explained to me that this city was noted for being cleaner than others: you could see blue sky, rather than the haze hanging over most of the other Chinese cities I had visited. The school was enormous and modern; the principal was one of the group from the 2010 class who had joined us for dinner the previous evening. He led a brief, sketchy guided tour, then took the party into a lecture theatre to tell them a bit about the school. The tour and the talk were, of course, in Chinese, without much interpretation.

After a tea break, it was my turn to resume the teaching of the course, but I was dismayed with the lecture theatre as a venue. It was, by the standards of any Western school, a glorious facility: large and luxurious, with tiered seating arranged in an oval, a built-in sound system with microphones in front of each seat, and screens and podium at the front. All very impressive, but it was totally inflexible as a teaching space. Back at the faculty suite in Guangzhou we had been able to adapt the large room easily, to switch from lecture format to group discussions, to use break-out rooms for tasks, and generally to punctuate the day with a sense of activity and change. Moreover, I was the sole course presenter here, so not even a change of voice would relieve the monotony.

So this was Joe's understanding of fieldwork visits to schools: to travel to one and use it as a teaching venue. He was not alone in that. In the course of my international work I had encountered many groups of people who, despite being in senior positions and well qualified, interpreted 'fieldwork' as very basic tourism.

Lunch was in the teachers' canteen. I knew that it would be, because the programme said 'lunch in the teachers' canteen', which conjured up quite a range of possibilities, none of which matched the reality. The factor I had not taken into account was the size of this institution. We went downstairs to a sort of basement, into a dining hall which was larger, busier and noisier than a typical students' canteen in an English secondary school – and this was just the staff! I guessed there were 400 to 500 of them. We joined a queue which led to a pretty basic central servery of canteen tables laid out in a square, in the middle of which servers efficiently ladled out food from hot containers.

I like food, I was hungry; it smelled reassuringly Cantonese. Of course I didn't know the drill, and couldn't explain myself, but none of that was necessary: the servers offered food to all comers. When there were just a few people ahead of me, I saw that each plate received a selection of different things, including prawns cooked in their shells, with slight variations between plates. I was mildly disappointed to see that the plate passed to me did not include any prawns. I took it to a table where some of the interpreters and group members were sitting, and gladly shovelled in its warm, comforting contents, all the while feeling discriminated against in the matter of prawns.

That was it! Perhaps the variations between plates were because, amid the din, some people said things like, 'none of that, please'. I remembered now that the server dolloping things on to what was going to be my plate paused and glanced at me during the process. He probably assumed that a Westerner would not want to crunch up prawns in their shells, and omitted them as a kindness. His assumption was wrong, certainly at that time when my teeth were stronger.

Throughout my adult life, my home has been occupied by a lot of cats. Individuals have changed over the years, of course, but somehow the total number remains eccentrically high. A regular early morning task has been to set out an array of plates and to fill them with different foods to match each cat's fussy tastes. Quite often, and not in any disrespectful way, during that task I find myself remembering the Chinese teachers' canteen.

After lunch, we were taken by coach to another school. A senior manager there told us that it had 7000 students, the majority of whom boarded. The view from his office window was filled with residential tower blocks as extensive as a council estate: they were all part of the campus. Only recently, checking through old papers and researching a bit, did it dawn on me that this was not in fact another school, but actually another campus of Zhongshan Overseas Chinese Middle School. I had been puzzled by the word 'overseas' in the name, because my previous experience of 'overseas' schools was that they served expatriate communities. Putting the name together with the boarding element, I am guessing now that the school was primarily for students whose parents were working abroad.

Although I was a bit vague about that bigger picture, the discussion session did give me a lot of information useful to my professional interests: I learnt how teachers got involved with research, and how they moved up within the profession. It was also interesting to hear that all the teaching work of the school was monitored by video cameras, which management could access at will. We had a tour, during which I reflected on the universality of education: language apart, the pottery and fabric-printing lessons could have been in London.

Tuesday was broadly similar to Monday, but without a trip out to break the monotony of a whole day's teaching in the lecture theatre. The course having been shrunk to three days, this was the finish, so in the afternoon I conducted the exercises in reflection and personal action planning that I would normally use, but there was an element of going through the motions without any great enthusiasm on either side.

The others had dinner in the hotel, but I had a dinner-date with Lyn of the British Council. This was my first and only contact with the British Council during this trip. On our previous visit, Gordon and I had been pleasantly and reassuringly fussed over by quite a numerous team: all of them young Chinese women. Lyn met me at the hotel and we walked to the restaurant she had chosen, which was nearby. I had never felt any concern walking in Chinese cities. We were directed to a table for two, where we sat side by side on a settee, and our slightly awkward encounter unfolded.

For a start, Lyn was even more shy than me. Previously, Emma had been in charge: she was a self-confident natural organiser of social entertainment. Offering dishes, she had said that with the British it was necessary to offer four times: the first three offers would be met with 'No thank you, I'm fine, thanks', and the fourth with 'Yes please'. With Lyn, there was the issue that this was just the two of us, and I felt that she was reluctant to take the lead in that situation, even though she was the host. In the end, I more or less took over the process of deciding what sort of dishes I wanted to eat, and we settled down into a reasonable business conversation.

I remember a long night-time drive with Joe. I think he must have driven me back to Guangzhou, to the hotel run by the People's Liberation Army; probably the coach had left earlier with the main party. I remember the drive because I had no sense of place or direction, uncomfortably aware of my complete dependence, and because Joe was uncommunicative. The car was a high-grade, spacious, big-engined Toyota. I said it was a nice car. 'It goes with my job, it is a gas-guzzler', Joe retorted dismissively. For something to say, I declared that I was still a bit nervous about driving, having had a nasty accident some months previously, but added that I hadn't injured anyone else. 'If you had, you'd be in prison!', he retorted, confident in his knowledge of English law.

The following day, Wednesday, I was to give a lecture to two different audiences. I had offered a lecture as a free extra, separate from the course; the double delivery was Joe's decision. Since my flight wasn't until after midnight, I had no objection: I don't know how I would have filled the time otherwise. Joe hadn't told me much about the audiences. I had asked whether simultaneous translation would be available. 'I will translate', Joe said. I knew from experience that line-by-line translation takes longer: it almost halves the ground one can cover in a given time. 'I will keep pace with you, it will be OK', Joe had attempted to reassure me.

To overcome the language barrier at the hotel, Joe had booked me a room-service breakfast. I checked out and he drove me to the first venue, which was a steeply banked lecture theatre at the Liwan Education Bureau. That was all I knew; later I found out that Liwan is an administrative district of Guangzhou, and the Education Bureau runs the schools in the district.

The theatre was packed. My lecture was supported by a PowerPoint presentation in the normal way. I got going; Joe talked alongside, giving his Chinese interpretation. As he had his own views on everything, I was pretty sure he was adapting, adding and omitting as he saw fit. We soldiered on somewhat clunkily. A very ample two hours had been allowed, but with the extra time for translation I didn't use all my material. It was difficult to gauge how far the audience found it interesting or relevant to their work.

The afternoon lecture, in the university, seemed less thoroughly organised. The venue was smaller: a seminar room with an open end. It was two-thirds empty when I arrived; some more small groups shuffled in, I sensed slightly reluctantly, at the last minute. Most of the audience were young, and I fancied I recognised the situation from previous experiences in organisations where I had worked. A visiting speaker has been booked, and that information has been sent around, but people are busy doing other things, leading to a last-minute rush to scrape together a respectable audience. As a last resort, groups of students are sent in, regardless of the relevance of the subject matter to their studies. I didn't know if that was the case, and Joe wasn't going to say, but that is how it seemed.

The time allocated for this session was 90 minutes, in which, with Joe's translation, I used half of my material. I wasn't bothered, because I knew that the majority of the audience just wanted it to end so that they could escape.

I was to join Joe and some of his colleagues for dinner, and in the meantime to base myself in the visitors' lounge in Joe's suite of offices, where I had spent much time with Gordon on our previous visit. Joe presented me with a corporate gift, which had probably cost the university quite a bit. He explained that there are certain vintage years for tea, and that the older vintages are highly prized. He presented me with one; I remember it dated from before I was born. It may have been 1947. My first, somewhat ungrateful, thought was dismay at the enormous bulk of the fancy box it came in, worried about how I could cope with it in my luggage.

We went to dinner. This was not like the high-level official banquet of our previous visit: just a practical, workaday gathering around a rectangular wooden table. The main course was a large bowl of a kind of casserole with an assortment of different things in a pungent liquid. One of the ingredients was pink, with a rubbery texture, and tasted very strongly of how a pig-farm smells on a hot day: intense, concentrated essence of pig-farm filled my mouth and throat in a way I found distinctly unpleasant.

Interrupting Joe, who was talking to someone whose company he clearly valued more than mine, I asked what it was. Either accidentally or deliberately, he took it that I was pointing to a different ingredient, with a texture halfway between crêpe paper and corrugated cardboard. 'It is made from bean curd', he said, turning back to his conversation. I persisted: 'No, not that, this', and he reluctantly re-engaged. 'That is pig's stomach', he explained, with what I interpreted as almost a note of pleasure.

When I learnt that I was going to be in the university for many hours, I asked Joe whether there was a Western-style toilet I could use. 'What do you mean?', he asked, with an odd feigning of ignorance for someone who had spent months in London. 'One that is not a squat.' 'No.'

Picture the scene: a washroom, the ambience and smell of which took me back to schooldays. One tap, no soap, no towels; the only toilet paper the supply I carried in my pocket. A row of three or four shoddy cubicles, offering scant privacy, with massive gaps under the doors and partitions. In each cubicle, a wet floor and a squat hole, and the white porcelain slabs on either side of it where your feet are supposed to go. These had a knobbly texture presumably intended to improve grip, but in fact worsening it for anyone wearing shoes. No handrails of any kind, no hook for clothes. Now, coming into that scene, picture me: a middle-aged man, slightly overweight, with stiff joints, an explosively loose bowel, and wearing a business suit. Only in desperation would I attempt the awkward and undignified manoeuvre: trying to hitch my jacket up around me, trying to get my trousers into a position where I would not accidentally soil them, having no option but to put my hands on the wet floor to steady myself. Why am I doing this? Are there not easier ways to earn a living?

I found it hard to believe Joe's dismissive assertion that the university had no Western-style toilet I could have used. I wondered about the culture. There was money sloshing around – expensive chrome-and-leather chairs, sophisticated electronics, high-end staff cars – and yet they regarded this disgusting latrine as satisfactory? Even if it was actually intended for the use of students and junior staff it was still a disgrace.

So it was with a sense of relief, of escape, that I got into the taxi to go to the airport. Once I was within its safe and orderly environment, my first act was to minimise the wrappings around the vintage tea. Into a bin went the wooden box with ruched satin lining, an explanatory booklet in Chinese, and a thin cushion. The tea itself, in practical wrapping, was a rock-hard round block the size of a soup bowl, with a central hole, which I was able to tuck into my suitcase.

I had over four hours to wait, as my flight did not leave until 12.55am on Thursday. It landed in Doha at 4.20am, where my connecting flight left at 6.40am and arrived at Heathrow's Terminal 4 at noon on 5th July. During the flight, I reflected that Joe's management of the trip, despite the many indignities inflicted on me, had at least given me a more authentic Chinese experience than if I had been cushioned tenderly by the British Council.

When I got home, among the letters waiting for me was one from a publisher, confirming acceptance of my book proposal for *Education in the Balance* and enclosing the contract. It was a joyful event; later I thought the vintage tea might be a celebratory refreshment. It required force and tools to chip some of it off the block; the fragments had the texture of long-dried birch twigs, refusing to brew and just floating on the boiling water giving off a faintly stale smell. A waste of money, space and effort, not resulting in a satisfying outcome: a truly apt memento of my Guangdong project.

Chapter Thirteen

Insights in Santiago and Valparaíso

Change was in the air that July, as the end of the educational year approached. Two beneficial developments took place in my work situation. The first massively motivating factor was that I had been able to appoint a person at a senior professional level to help me. For a while I had found my workload and professional loneliness burdensome, but hadn't expected any solution. It had come as a surprise when, some weeks previously, I was told the post had been created: I have always assumed that someone at the top of the organisation must have taken an executive decision. Joyce, the successful candidate, was due to start towards the end of July and I was looking forward to working with her.

The second new thing at work was that I was asked by another department to help manage a project supporting developments in India. It had been going for three years and had another year or so to run, but from the outset there had been a difficult client interface, with arguments about an apparent major mismatch between the original contract and how the client chose to operate. The work was funded by the European Union and the client was a globally significant charity, so if those disagreements led to a serious breakdown there would be major and lasting reputational damage to our organisation. The project concerned research rather than consultancy: the team included several senior academics and a group of research assistants and administrators, so it was quite a big operation. All of which was attractive to me: early meetings had been auspicious and I welcomed the chance to help to keep the project on the rails.

I had been energised by the publisher's contract and looked forward to getting the book written. In my naivety I believed that people would read the book, see it was good, and that would enhance my reputation, whereas now I know that with academic writing the relationship is the other way round: the author's pre-existing status and reputation determines book sales.

On the home front, in the week following my return from Guangdong we stayed in Durham and went to Barnard Castle for viewings at Spring Grove, which made me determined to buy the property. I made offers, which were accepted, for the house, the freehold of the rest of the site, and the lease of the ground-floor flat. By 'determined' I mean that I was prepared to throw my last penny into the transaction if that is what it took to achieve the objective.

Those offers were conditional on my selling both what was then our current home and an investment property. The latter was unproblematical: it was an asset, managed by an agent, that I visited rarely. Our home was a different matter. We had lived there for 28 years. We bought it from good friends who entertained us often and generously, so when we took possession it was like moving from one home to another. Since then we had filled it with astonishing amounts of clutter and allowed it to become dilapidated. I took the view that you can sell anything, even in a really bad market, if you make it cheap enough. I also started a campaign of crack-covering, decorating and skip-filling.

The house contents would have filled a place twice the size, which was one of my motivations for moving to a larger property. On top of a natural tendency to hoard and clutter, add the effect of my six years of freelancing: the contents of a busy office. On top of that, there was a period when my partner was teaching children history, and to help with that we gathered artefacts, trawling junk shops and coming back from every holiday with a car-load. The domestic appliances of bygone days – mangle, dolly tub, tin baths, a million gadgets, utensils and storage containers – flooded in, and I added shelves and hooks to every metre of wall-space.

Some years previously, in my leisure reading, I had become interested in Henry James; books by and about the author would fill at least one entire packing box. The biographies described James's home in Rye, Lamb House, and its importance to him as a place for writing. I visited Lamb House with my daughter in July 2008 to get a better sense of the writer's setting, and to feel what connection there might be between where he was and what he wrote. Actually it was disappointing how little of the house was open to public view.

In July 2012 my own writing aspirations were still developing. Yet I did make a conscious, if fanciful, parallel between James's immediate feeling for and gradual acquisition (from rental to ownership) of, Lamb House and my fondness at first sight for Spring Grove. I say 'fanciful' not only because of James's eminence but because Lamb House represents a level of real estate many leagues higher than anything to which I could aspire. I am sure, nonetheless, that my entertaining the idea of buying a house suitable for a writer nurtured my desire to become one. Before the viewing, my aim had been to increase my academic and professional writing output, although I was also starting to develop some different ideas. After the viewing, I was clear that living in such a setting I would start writing in other genres as well.

So the background music to normal working life was quite interesting as I set off for my final foreign trip of the educational year.

To my delight, I was going to Chile: another South American country; another imaginary badge for the walking stick. The assignment was pleasing, too. The Chilean Ministry of Education was launching a scheme to develop a cadre of excellent headteachers who would lead an ambitious programme of school improvement. I was one of two international experts invited to speak at the ministerial launch of the scheme – the other was Jim, from Alberta, who I hadn't previously met. Modesty requires me to explain that it was my organisation, rather than me personally, which enjoyed such a monumental global reputation: I was just a handy, willing body to despatch as its representative.

The formal invitation came from Violeta in the ministry, but most of the pre-event liaison was led by Lenka on her behalf. Lenka knew and liked our organisation, and had had some previous connection with it. She was the one who had got us invited; she 'owned' our involvement.

As part of the event, Lenka was managing an exhibition where organisations like ours could give information about their development programmes. It was agreed that we would send materials and that Chileans would staff the stall. The programme we chose to showcase was a Masters degree in education leadership taught by open-distance learning, which was extremely popular internationally (Taymur and Joe had completed it). It was managed by my colleague Liz, with whom I had worked in Mexico. Although our organisation accredited its own degrees, this particular one was accredited by another organisation within our federal group, which owned the online learning platform it used. This seemingly technical detail became relevant later. Liz despatched course leaflets in English and Spanish.

On Tuesday 24th July I set off just before lunch for Heathrow's Terminal 5, to board a 4.05pm flight to Madrid. I was wearing my newly acquired hearing aids, which gave me added confidence: I felt like a spy, because I could hear other people's conversations in public places. The main flight left Madrid at 11.55pm, and landed in Santiago at 7.40am on Wednesday: with local time being six hours behind Spain, the actual flight time was just under 14 hours. Long haul indeed, which added to my sense of having travelled to the other side of the world. There was a cool tang in the air in Santiago: I had started the journey in mid-summer, and ended it in mid-winter. I was met by a ministry official, and taken to the Atton El Bosque Hotel, where my capacious room looked out over a forest of skyscrapers of interestingly different designs.

I met up with Jim, and as the day unfolded it became clear that we would be much in each other's company for the next few days. That was fine, because it would have been hard to imagine a more amiable companion. Jim was a few years older than me, and would be retiring in August. His work achievements had been built up solidly over many years in the same place, and were interesting and impressive. What I learnt from Jim about his professional context made me wistfully nostalgic. In Alberta, a culture of mutual respect and partnership had endured. Government at its various levels, university faculties, school leaders and teachers all wanted pretty much the same things and collaborated to achieve them, with each partner acknowledging and valuing the responsibilities and expertise of the others. That was such a contrast to England, where for decades, governments had rubbished and undermined both the teaching profession and the academic study of education, preferring either to shape the system through the market forces of parental preferences or through direct political interference in professional practice.

Jim's manner seemed to reflect his context: he didn't come over as competitive, arrogant or superior, as so many global experts can be. He shared experiences while showing interest in listening to and learning from others: a thoroughly nice guy. There were social interludes when topics other than education needed to be found. Jim was keen on various sports, including a minority one: I think it might have been hand-ball, which he followed seriously. My experiences at school put me off all that for life, so to join in I talked up my enjoyment of clay-pigeon shooting. I explained how when I spent weekends at our Yorkshire house, I would usually take guns and visit the shooting ground nearby, where I would do my best to destroy bitumen frisbees.

The event venue was a bit further up the Andes than the hotel, and distinctly cold. There was a marquee, and a partially open courtyard area where the exhibition stalls had been set up, and some covered spaces. Jim and I looked around the exhibition and admired each other's stalls, which were set up and staffed as effectively as if we had sent our own personnel. Most of the other exhibitors were South American organisations. Later, we had a working session in the ministry, with Violeta, Paula, Maria and Lenka. The session started with a major kiss-fest, which Violeta explained apologetically was an essential part of their culture. There was nothing apologetic about the gusto with which the women set about these proceedings. They thought I was reluctant and shy, perhaps even a little offended, which was a compliment to my acting skills.

We settled down to work, which for me was a sales pitch. The programme of change on which the Chileans had embarked was something that I felt I and my organisation would be very well placed to support. A small input of our accumulated experience, offered in a spirit of unobtrusive partnership, would help to steer them around the pitfalls and maximise the benefits. It was interesting and I wanted a slice of the action: I did my best to charm them and sketched out an inexpensive model of support which would mesh well with their approach. I got a lot of positive, encouraging signals, and felt optimistic. Jim wasn't in competition: he didn't do that sort of work, and he was about to retire.

Lunch was served in the office, and I regretted an earlier mistake. Usually I do not declare any food intolerances, because the special dishes produced in response are often worse. It is better to eat around things, to make my own judgements about what consequences to risk in the pursuit of gastronomic pleasure. For some reason I had broken my own rule during the preparations for this trip, and told them some things, including that I avoid citrus fruit. Officials making arrangements sometimes confuse intolerances with allergies and work to the latter. So, some seconds after the arrival of appetising plates piled with plump prawns, the one in front of me was whipped away and replaced with a pile of leathery shellfish. This would be far harsher on my digestion than the sprinkle of lemon juice on the prawns would have been.

In the afternoon Jim and I learnt that the programmes offered by both of our organisations had been selected by the minister for official sponsorship: various of the 'Headteachers of Excellence' would be steered towards them and have their fees substantially subsidised by the ministry. That sounded like good news, but later it emerged that certain decisions had been made and announced unilaterally by the Chilean government regarding who was to be enrolled on the courses and at what stages the official funding would be made available. I began to feel uneasy. I pointed out that the course leaflets we had provided specified a level of English-language proficiency as a pre-condition for registration: had that been taken into account when selecting participants for sponsorship? No, it hadn't, the ministry team advised, becoming uneasy themselves, looking at each other shiftily.

Thursday was the main event, in the big cold marquee, made slightly warmer by the packed bodies of hot-blooded, enthusiastic senior educators. After several layers of welcoming remarks, the minister, Harald, gave an opening address which lasted a good 20 minutes: he was passionate and knowledgeable, clearly in charge and knew what he was doing. Violeta followed with a longer, more detailed professional exposition of the project. After a coffee break, Jim spoke, then I spoke, various closing remarks were made and were followed by celebratory glasses of wine.

A period of general mingling was built into the schedule, and during this I was approached very formally and respectfully by a representative of the Regional Ministry of Education of the Lakes Region of Chile. After introducing himself, he handed me an official invitation, in Spanish and English, the Spanish version signed and stamped, asking me to repeat my presentation to the school directors of the region. 'Our region is to the south', he explained. 'If you could come after this, all expenses paid, we would be most honoured...' It grieved me to have to turn down such an attractive invitation, so nicely presented: I would have loved to see a different part of Chile. I was thrown by the complete absence of notice, and a bit surprised that they hadn't foreseen that would be a problem. My return flight had been booked and paid for by the ministry, I had a string of engagements in London immediately after my return, and there were procedures within my organisation that would have to be worked through to extend my stay in South America. All of which seemed too much, too hard to unscramble, and my apologies were heartfelt.

During our meetings on Friday, Violeta returned to the subject of the decisions announced by the minister regarding the sponsorship of headteachers to enrol on our course. She explained that once such statements had been made, they could not be changed or retracted: the governmental system did not allow for that. I understood and empathised, sharing my experience of working in Parliament, where there was no mechanism for or possibility of amending anything published in a written answer to a parliamentary question. If it was likely to pose a high-profile problem, then reality had to change in order to make the statement accurate. I assured Violeta we would work through any problems, but the issue cast a stain on our warm talk of a partnership project to support the ministry's initiative. The talk continued, but I felt that the possibility of it leading to something real had receded.

More immediately and positively, we learnt that we were dining in a restaurant that evening with the four ministry women, and that the following day, Saturday, a car and guide had been arranged to take us to Valparaíso. Taking afternoon tea with Jim, I shared my slight frustration at the elusiveness of the kind of partnership project I would have liked to establish. He didn't share it: his sentiments about the trip were entirely positive, coming as it did so close to his retirement. 'I see it as the pinnacle of my career, to be able to come here and present alongside you', he said, somewhat generously in relation to the latter point.

I could never have found the restaurant had we not been taken there: in the dark, we climbed on to a sort of platform that seemed to be in the middle of the road, then down a staircase, of the kind that in London might have led to a public lavatory, except that it didn't smell. We had a large table in a quiet wing of the restaurant, and the occasion was entirely pleasant, except that once again the nicest dishes were whipped away from me and replaced with rubbery shellfish. Conversation flowed amicably; Jim was relaxed with his brandy, smiling and enjoying the end-of-trip celebration. His earlier comment had set me thinking, questioning my stance and pondering the somewhat truncated pinnacles of my own career.

On Saturday we checked out early: the car collected us at 7.30am. We put our luggage in it because we would be going straight to the airport at the end of our sightseeing tour. Our guide was Hubert, who was typical of his profession: plump, amiable, talkative, full of knowledge, and an efficient, punctual courier.

The drive to Valparaíso would take two hours or so. I hadn't brought a camera with me on this trip, because I had expected to spend all the time inside a conference venue, and because I did not think it enhanced my professional persona to be fishing out a camera and taking snaps in the presence of clients. Now, I wished I had prepared for the unexpected, and tried to burn images into my memory. Nor did I have a map, but that was less of a problem given the distinctive geography of Chile, where any westbound journey involved descending from the Andes to the coastal plain.

Hubert kept up a patter of information. My impression of Santiago – this was to be another day of Neuman's 'travelling without seeing' – was of an attractive city, with a European feel, modern and old. That contradiction depended on where you were standing. From my hotel window, the dominant flavour was of modern high-rise buildings in attractive, individual styles. Now, at ground level, the old predominated: grand, ornate, 19th-century frontages. I looked up and there was the answer: in many cases, a modern tower block arose behind an old façade, or out of the middle of a gutted shell. Hubert explained that city planning regulations required this: he made it sound a nuisance, a bureaucratic imposition, but after I had got used to the initial weirdness, I thought it was a good thing that the old frontages had been preserved. I wondered what difference it might have made to the English urban scene if we had had such a requirement, but then remembered a key point of contrast: South American cities had not been blitzed.

Hubert mentioned that various edifices in the city were said to have been designed by Eiffel, the French engineer famous for his tower, who might have spent some time in Chile. There was also a German influence, German immigration having been strongly encouraged in the 19th century. Perhaps that had diluted the overall Iberian characteristics of the European immigrant population. Hubert said, 'Chileans are calmer than the people of other South American countries: we don't have to be shouting all the time'. We came out of the city into the countryside, the gradient always downhill, and the scenery still hilly. Passing scattered settlements, Hubert referred to the frequency of earthquakes in the area: 'All these houses have been rebuilt on rubber foundations'. As we moved into wine-producing country, the fields of vines looked the same as in any other wine-growing region, but Hubert said that the area had not had rainfall for over two years: the vines got their moisture from heavy morning dew. In *Chile: Travels in a Thin Country* Sara Wheeler describes visiting the Fray Jorge National Park on the coast some way to the north of Santiago, where a rainforest habitat was sustained almost entirely by the moisture from daily sea mist. Being a former geography teacher, inevitably my mind was set whirring with thoughts of diurnal temperature changes and atmospheric lapse rates. We crossed the course of a major river, but it was as parched as a wadi.

Valparaíso is a major coastal city, seaport and resort: vibrant with commerce, history, culture and politics. From that great tapestry Hubert selected some vignettes to fit into the time available. I remember walking across a great windswept square, and a man approaching Hubert with some request or proposition, and being sent packing. I enquired. 'He said "If I fix them up for an hour with a beautiful woman, is there a drink for me in that?"'.

We came to a seaside promenade, not far from some docks, and a row of sheltered seating areas with traditional decorative ironwork. Jim commented on the amount of litter and seemed slightly shocked by it. His home area must have been pristine: I hadn't noticed anything unusual. Hubert showed us some other things, then drove us to a different, less industrial, section of the seafront, where we were to enjoy a lunch that had been booked by our kind hosts.

Enjoying the view from that section of the seafront was one of the high-point moments in my travel experiences, both in what I could see and the sentiments those sights awoke. Endless blue sea stretched to the far horizon, under a mainly blue sky. The waves, quite turbulent, as if driven by strong currents, crashed on to rugged brown rocks that poked out into promontories and up into tor-like peaks. The rocks were covered with barking sea lions and squawking pelicans, both species I had previously seen only in zoos and parks. 'It is a nature reserve; they are protected', Hubert explained.

For me, at last being able to stand on the shore of the Pacific Ocean was in itself a significant achievement. It induced a kind of pleasant tiredness, an awareness of how far I had travelled. Not just in terms of distance, from my normal haunts in England, but in terms also of how far I had travelled from the circumstances of my early life, with its struggles and mediocre aspirations. I could have leant on the railings drinking in the scene, and those reflections, for a long time, but our table was ready, and Hubert guided us across the road.

The restaurant was of good quality, specialising in fish. We were taken to the first floor, to a light and pleasant room looking out to sea, at the view we had just been enjoying. The napery was pristine, and the restaurant nearly empty. Hubert spoke to the staff and showed us to a reserved table. 'Enjoy your meal', he said. 'I will be at the car when you are ready to leave.' This surprised me, so long had it been since I had spent time in the company of couriers. 'Are you not joining us? You have lunch arrangements?', I asked. 'The staff here will give me lunch', he explained. 'Out the back, similar food but differently presented. Drivers and guides do not eat in the restaurant.'

Jim and I settled to our treat, which was excellent fresh white fish with an interesting sauce. We talked. I said that back home, people had been watching the opening ceremony of the London Olympics, and I hoped to be able to see a recorded version of it. Jim said that in early October he would be coming to London as part of a holiday, during which he would also be visiting Ireland to attend the world championships of his favourite sport. We arranged that he would drop into my office for a brief social call: he would no longer be concerned with work matters then.

I was still pondering his comment of the previous day. Dear honest Jim, whose actual achievements were more solid than my own, could take and enjoy this trip for what it was. Whereas for me, each new border-crossing was potentially into a land of opportunity, where I might achieve success and recognition. It was a pity that a place as attractive as Chile was looking unlikely to offer such a prospect. I think I was starting to realise then that in my line of work, at my age, one's standing was set pretty much as firmly as one's physical height.

Unbeknown to him, Jim made me realise that worrying too much about where all this travelling might be leading professionally detracted from the pleasure of the travelling itself. And if the answer to that worrying question was going to be 'nowhere', then all the more reason to value the experience of travelling as an achievement in its own right. Which it was, undoubtedly: I never lost the sense of surprise and gratitude for having found, by accident, a role at the end of my career that enabled me to visit distant places. So that was my 'pinnacle': not any single trip, but the globetrotting phase.

After lunch, Hubert drove us up and along a steep cliff, where small, brightly painted wooden houses clung where they could at odd angles, almost as if they had started off higher up and had tumbled into their current positions in a landslide. I was now straining to remember everything, beset by an urge to do something constructive with these experiences of travel. I had no conception of what form that might take, but I couldn't bear the thought of it all wasting away into a few muddled memories. The flavours, aromas, fabrics and colours of South Asia; the human warmth of South America; vistas of stunning ancient mosques and mighty mountains: all needed to be captured and shared.

Into a more urban district, we passed a house which Hubert pointed out as a source of local amusement. Its three-storey frontage was covered with an elaborate display of bric-a-brac. I had not seen anything like that on the front of a house, but it did remind me of the interior and rear garden of my own.

At the airport, I was pleasantly surprised to find that the four women from the ministry had come to say goodbye. They formed a line, and the ceremony involved a lot of noisy kissing. I tried to put on an expression of restrained formality while actually, of course, thoroughly enjoying the experience. Lenka had put a lot into arranging the trip, and I felt the genuine emotion in her parting. But even while clasping pleasant shoulders, having close-up views of sparkling eyes, and kissing soft fragrant cheeks, part of my mind was back at the coast of the Pacific Ocean, with the sea lions and pelicans, with blue waves crashing on brown rocks: rhythmic bursts of foam beating the message, 'remember this'.

References

Bayley, R. (2010) *The Mango Orchard: The Extraordinary True Story of a Family Lost and Found*, London: Arrow Books.

Duffett, P. (2017) *Shanghai Stirfry*, Amazon self-publishing.

Feiling, T. (2012) *Short Walks from Bogotá: Journeys in the New Colombia*, London: Allen Lane.

Gardner, F. (2009) *Far Horizons*, London: Bantam Press.

Gardner, F. (2016) *Crisis*, London: Bantam Press.

Greene, G. (1939) *The Lawless Roads*, London: Heinemann.

Hart, A. (2018) *Departures: A guide to letting go, one adventure at a time*, London: Sphere.

Klein, D. (2013) *Travels with Epicurus: Meditations from a Greek Island on the Pleasures of Old Age*, London: Oneworld.

Laing, O. (2011) *To The River: A Journey Beneath the Surface*, Edinburgh: Canongate.

Neuman, A. (2016) (translated edition) *How to Travel without Seeing: Dispatches from the New Latin America*, New York: Restless Books.

Wheeler, S. (1994) *Chile: Travels in a Thin Country*, London: Little, Brown and Company.

Wilkins, R. (2011) *Research Engagement for School Development*, London: Institute of Education.

Wilkins, R. (2014) *Education in the Balance: Mapping the global dynamics of school leadership*, London: Bloomsbury.

Wilkins, R. (2016) *Accidental Traveller*, Guildford: Grosvenor House.